ARCHITECTURAL LIGHTING DESIGN

ARCHITECTURAL LIGHTING DESIGN

Gary R. Steffy, IES, IALD

 VAN NOSTRAND REINHOLD COMPANY
————————————————— New York

Library of Congress Catalog Card Number 90–34541

ISBN 0–442–20761–1

Manufactured in the United States of America

Published by Van Nostrand Reinhold
115 Fifth Avenue
New York, New York 10003

Chapman and Hall
2–6 Boundary Row
London, SE 1 8HN

Thomas Nelson Australia
102 Dodds Street
South Melbourne 3205
Victoria, Australia

Nelson Canada
1120 Birchmount Road
Scarborough, Ontario M1K 5G4, Canada

16 15 14 13 12 11 10 9 8 7 6 5 4 3 2 1

Library of Congress Cataloging-in-Publication Data
Steffy, Gary R.
    Architectural lighting design / Gary R. Steffy.
        p. cm.
    ISBN 0–442–20761–1
    1. Lighting, Architectural and decorative. I. Title.
TH7703.S78   1990
621.32—dc20   90–34541
                                                       CIP

CONTENTS

PREFACE

The idea for a lighting *design* textbook came to me nearly ten years ago when I was teaching lighting design to interior designers at Wayne State University. Obviously, the idea was not unique. What was unique was that I, a practicing lighting designer, saw no existing text that not only could be used to teach architectural students, interior design students, and architectural engineering students about lighting design, but also could serve as a reference for practicing architects, interior designers, and electrical engineers. Besides, many of the available textbooks stressed to the nth degree the mathematics, not the design aspects, of lighting. It might be nice for an architect to be able to perform some quick lighting estimating calculations, but there is no need for everyone who practices lighting design to understand flux transfer and Fourier series.

Indeed, it is very easy to calculate, or to get someone to make calculations for you, or to find a computer to do it. The challenge is to know which questions to ask a client and other designers in order to get to the heart of lighting design—*designing* lighting. Why use fluorescent indirect lighting? Why highlight the artwork? Why introduce glitter? Why are brightnesses so much more important than light levels? Questions of this kind should be raised, and are being asked, by designers; but they are not being answered collectively by any other text.

This is not a collection of disjointed notes on lighting, nor is it a compendium of manufacturers' literature—although, for purposes of real-world illustration, some actual manufacturers' datasheets are introduced in Chapter 4. In fact, the point of this reference text is that all of it relates to real-world lighting design challenges. It all has been tested. It all works. There are no discussions about laboratory experiments in black rooms, and no long dissertations about how lighting design has to mean custom luminaires. A section of four-color illustrations shows real-world settings, and is arranged as a series of project case studies. These four-color figures' numbers are prefixed by a "C."

Lighting is much more than just another building system. Without good lighting, there would be no reason to install such niceties as an expensive granite elevator-lobby wall. Without good lighting we would waste billions of dollars a year on salaries and benefits and ultimately on energy—spinning our wheels. Good lighting does not mean expensive, but its cost must be put into perspective with a building's other initial and operating costs. This book addresses the programming issues in lighting design, the need to conceptualize or visualize lighted space, the various lamps and luminaires and techniques available to help the designer achieve lighting concepts, some basic calculation tools available to the designer for estimation purposes, and the specification of lighting equipment to assure that concepts and performance indeed are met.

This has not been an easy undertaking. I needed new, original artwork to illustrate concepts and details. Photographs had to be purchased and/or made to illustrate lighting design—both good and bad. Grants of assistance from the Van Nostrand Reinhold Company, Peerless Lighting, and Gary Steffy Lighting Design Inc. were necessary, and I greatly appreciate them. Photo support from General Electric, Steelcase, Peerless Lighting, and Gary Steffy Lighting Design Inc. permitted me to use many black-and-white and color photographs to demonstrate good lighting design. Edison Price, Kurt Versen, Columbia, and Peerless Lighting contributed original artwork for Chapter 4 so that I could present real-world datasheets and photometric information here for the uninitiated. This approach is much better than using generic luminaire data to instill an understanding of lighting equipment.

The new artwork was developed from scratch by graphic artist Gloria Paul, whom I thank for her fine ideas, an excellent layout, and her patience while I made countless corrections and additions. My wife, Laura, and daughter, Heather, not only had to put up without me for many weekends while I created this book; Laura also provided essential typing of the manuscript. My love and thanks to these two troopers! Thanks to Noah Rockey for proofreading. Finally, special thanks go to Ev Smethurst, my editor, without whose enthusiasm from the outset this book would not have been possible. Without Ev's patience and perseverance, the project might well have been canceled! I deeply appreciate Ev's encouragement at all stages of the endeavor.

This book certainly is not the last word on lighting design, but I hope that it will help you along a path not only of design inspiration but also of logical and rational decision making. This guide should help both you and your clients to spend your lighting-design time and money most effectively.

Gary R. Steffy, IES, IALD
Ann Arbor, Michigan

CHAPTER ONE

LIGHTING:
A BACKGROUND

INTRODUCTION

Throughout this text, references will be made to what the author sees as good practice. Traditionally many shortcuts have been taken in lighting, so that legislators have found it necessary to intercede for energy considerations and now on behalf of workers in electronic offices to require good practice. This book will help the designer to maximize lighting successes and minimize failures. There will be "soft" issues discussed along with the "hard" ones. Although the soft issues are those with less experimental support, the application of soft-issue techniques will help to ensure that handling of the more quantifiable hard issues will indeed meet client expectations.

Lighting should not and cannot be simply an application of engineering principles. Lighting is both a physiological and a psychological inducer. Lighting involves space, volume, form, texture, color, impressions, and people—most of all people. Without light and/or the use of our eyes we have neither visual architecture nor interior design. Light is more than just footcandles (illuminance). The least important element of lighting design is illuminance, but unfortunately it happens to be the easiest lighting metric to calculate and measure. That is all the more reason why it should be the least of the designer's lighting design worries.

DEFINING THE PROBLEM

It makes little sense to attempt resolution of a problem, unless the problem is well defined and understood. In many cases, the problem of lighting is thoroughly hidden in a project's history. It often is convenient to regard lighting as an engineering problem; at times, it is considered a decoration problem; but seldom is it recognized as what it really is: a *biology* problem. Lighting design should not be done just to satisfy some (far away) engineering society's or state legislature's guidelines, or just to satisfy a client's budget. Lighting should be done first and foremost for the people who will occupy the spaces or areas being designed. The lighting problem is a people problem, a biology problem.

A BIOLOGY PROBLEM

Lighting is not straightforward. Contrary to popular belief, lighting design cannot and should not be a simple calculation problem. The human eye does not respond to illuminances (quantities of light falling on surfaces); rather, the eye sees chromatic (color) and luminance (brightness) contrasts. The eye responds to differences in specific reflected and transmitted electromagnetic energy. Figure 1–1 indicates the range of electromagnetic energy to which the eye responds. Both light source characteristics (lamps) and surface reflectance characteristics interact in an architectural environment to create specific wavelengths of visible energy for its occupants to behold.

THE PHYSIOLOGY OF THE PROBLEM

The eye, diagrammatically represented in Figure 1–2, can be critically analyzed for its response/reaction to light. The cornea is a protective sheathing over the eye. Constant exposure to ultraviolet radiation can lead to yellowing of the cornea. Such yellowing results in reduced color discrimination and contrasts; violets and·blues are grayed, greens tend to yellow, and reds are relatively intensified.

The iris is a membrane covering that dilates (opens) to allow more light to enter the eye during darkened conditions and constricts (closes) somewhat to minimize light entry during brightened conditions. This process of adjustment is known as adaptation. As the eye views from light areas to darker areas, and vice versa, adaptation occurs; so when one is designing interior space adjacencies or exterior site lighting, this adaptation should be considered. For example, the act of walking from a bright outdoor environment into a subdued theater can result in relatively long adaptation periods, readily leading to tripping or disorientation. This effect, from light to dark,

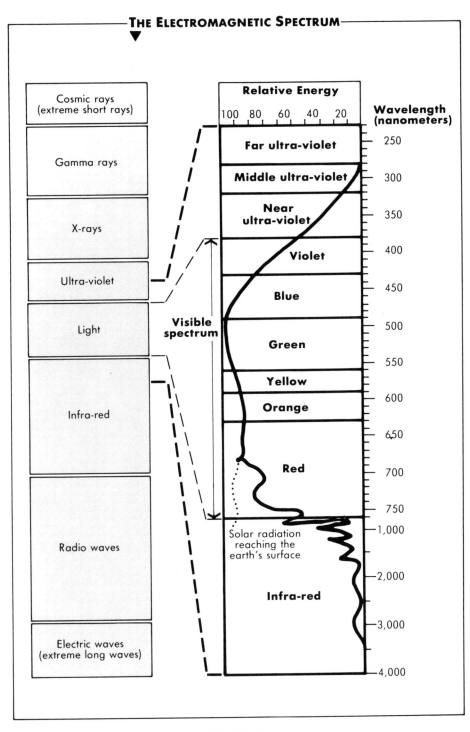

FIGURE 1–1

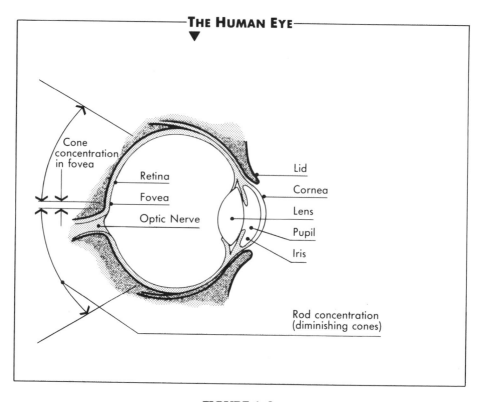

THE HUMAN EYE

FIGURE 1–2

is known as dark adaptation. Complete dark adaptation can take half an hour or more. Because of this lag, and because of the momentary sense of "blindness" experienced when one first enters a darkened space, dark adaptation can be dangerous. This adaptation can be minimized by designing a space or series of spaces that act as a transition between extreme bright and extreme dark conditions.

A person looking from a brightly lighted parking deck into nearby shrubbed surroundings can experience some inability to adapt, which could help muggers to hide from view. This effect is known as transient adaptation because the individual's position is stationary, but his or her view is changing.

Consider for a moment the effect of moonlight on a rural setting. Although the level of light is low, it is quite consistent, thus allowing the eye to adapt and remain adapted throughout its survey of the country scene.

Generally, only a few minutes are required for the eye to adapt from a darkened condition to a brighter condition. This process is known as light adaptation. Note, however, that some pain may be caused in extreme cases of changing from dark to light conditions.

The lens of the eye is elastic and transparent, and it focuses one's view onto the fovea in a process called accommodation. A structural defect in the lens can cause objects or scenes to appear out of focus. If the lens is a bit too round, then the focal length is too short, and objects actually are focused in front to the retina. This phenomenon is called myopia, or near-sightedness, as only nearer objects can be seen clearly. If the lens is a bit too flat, then the focal length is too long, and objects are focused behind the retina, in a condition called hypermetropia or farsightedness.

Another structural difficulty, usually associated with aging, is presbyopia, in which the lens becomes less elastic, reducing accommodation. Bifocal corrective lenses usually are required for this condition because the lens cannot focus well on either near or distant objects. This is especially problematic for video display terminal (VDT) users.

The retina contains the receptors responsible for transmitting an "image" to the brain for analysis. There are two basic categories of receptors, rods and cones. Cones are heavily concentrated in the fovea, providing sharp, distinct detail vision. Cones perceive color. Rods respond to very low light levels and occur over the entire retina except in the area of the fovea. Rods do not provide distinct, detailed vision, nor do they provide color stimulus to the brain. Peripheral vision is supplied by the rods.

Lighting that must satisfy the needs of the human eye is indeed a biology problem.

THE PSYCHOLOGY OF THE PROBLEM

The light falling on the retina initiates a photochemical response, sending signals to the brain. The brain then interprets these signals, in large measure, according to its experience. An individual's response, however, is not strictly analytical. For whatever reason, different light patterns and colors help to elicit various "feelings" or subjective responses; light not only helps us to perform seeing tasks, but also impacts how we feel in a given environment. Now, because lighting is a factor over which we have some control, and because it appears to influence task performance *and* our comfort and sense of well-being, is it not reasonable that we should attempt to get the most out of lighting? By understanding ideas set forth in this text and practicing lighting design on every project in which people are involved, we can maximize the built environment's potential.

Several subjective or psychological aspects of lighting were identified by John Flynn in the mid-1970s. These factors have since come under considerable scrutiny, and this research is ongoing in an effort to clearly define these factors. We can say, in any case, that some lighting conditions seem to elicit certain similar responses from people. Four of these factors, or responses, have been identified: impressions of visual clarity, impressions of spaciousness, impressions of relaxation, and impressions of privacy. These factors can have a profound influence on the acceptability of a space; thus they are addressed in some detail in Chapter 2.

THE DESIGN TEAM

It is clear that lighting is a human issue first. Once the human concerns of lighting are dealt with, then the technical and personal-design ego issues can be addressed. The design team is responsible for addressing these three main types of issues: human, technical, and ego. An assembled team of experts from several disciplines should address the issues together. This team should consist of an owner (or owner's representative), an occupant (or occupant's representative), an architect, an interior designer, a lighting designer, an electrical engineer, a mechanical (HVAC) engineer, a fire protection consultant, an acoustician, a landscape architect, a structural engineer, and a construction manager. Clearly, there are a lot of players involved. Ignoring representatives of certain disciplines or attempting to work without their input will only frustrate the owner and lead to unsatisfactory results.

The team approach—if the team members are willing to contribute and to receive constructive criticism—can lead to state-of-the-art results that work. The team must meet regularly and work together as a group to identify the problems, select appropriate criteria, and find solutions. Many projects are executed with one "team" member telling the other members what to do and how to do it. This is reminiscent of the old concept of car production where laborers *only* did what they were told to do, even if they saw ways to improve productivity and quality. A building contains too many components and too much technology for any individual ever to be expected to know all the parts and pieces and appropriate ways to assimilate them.

Team leaders are increasingly predominant in today's successful design projects. These leaders understand the total design approach and know that particular expertise is required for each part of the approach. In most cases the leader is an architect, an interior architect, or a construction manager. These leaders are somewhat like orchestra conductors: they know how the entire piece should sound, but they cannot play all the individual instruments as needed.

Each team member is in a position to contribute most positively if he or she understands something of the other disciplines. Therefore, it is reasonable for all architects, interior architects, electrical engineers, construction managers, and so on, to have some knowledge of lighting—not knowledge of hardware or even applications, but knowledge of basic design issues, of physiological and psychological aspects of lighting. This will help them expand their views on the total design, and it may lead to improved techniques of systems integration, as they all will understand *why* such integration is important to the total design. Lighting designers, on the other hand, must know about basic design issues in architecture, interior design, electrical and mechanical engineering, fire protection, acoustics, and landscape architecture. This cross-education helps team members to better communicate, to better understand other experts' opinions, and ultimately to better design built environments.

LIGHTING EDUCATION

There is no comprehensive lighting design program available at any American university. Some schools have excellent engineering programs, whereas others have less technical, more design-oriented programs. No program combines the two aspects, art and science, culminating in a recognized degree in lighting design. Several programs have been initiated that over the next decade could prove to be centers of lighting education, in particular those at the University of Kansas, University of Colorado, Pennsylvania State University, Rensselaer Polytechnic Institute, Cooper Union, Parsons School of Design, and Bartlett School of Architecture/University College London. Some money does exist to start or continue segments of programs at these schools although it appears that more money is needed to establish complete, bona fide, degree-granting lighting design programs.

Because there is no formal education path yet, most lighting designers have taken related but somewhat circuitous education and career paths to lighting. Theater, electrical engineering, architecture, interior design, and architectural engineering are some typical degrees and/or careers leading to lighting design. Various universities have excellent lighting courses within the human ecology, architecture, fine art, home economics, or engineering schools. Usually, one or two lighting courses are the extent of a student's exposure to lighting design. These courses will help people in the respective fields to understand lighting, giving them the potential to contribute significantly to the design team.

Perhaps the best way to learn about lighting is to observe. Observation is such an obvious tool, yet so seldom used. Every waking hour of every day we see built environments. Many are poorly lighted, and many people even comment about the poor state of the lighting; yet we continue to design dreadful solutions. We should be more observant, identifying what works or does not work in the lighted environment. A working journal is an appropriate means of recording observations. As Figure 1–3 indicates, a black-and-white sketch, which sometimes can be completed in less than 60 minutes, not only is good for the record but helps one to understand how light "renders" surfaces and spaces and can lead to better visualization of proposed

FIGURE 1–3.
Making a quick and rather simple light sketch is a good educational technique. It enables the renderer to improve his or her sketching skills and, perhaps more important, to gain "observation" experience.

designs. Included with the sketch should be a short description of the environment, the tasks, the technical aspects of the lighting equipment, whether or not the lighting is appropriate, and how it might be improved.

Continuing education in lighting can be found in week-long university seminars and in lamp, luminaire, and software manufacturers' courses, as well as in technical and professional society functions. The University of Wisconsin–Extension runs a week-long seminar nearly every year on lighting. (Contact Department of Engineering Professional Development, University of Wisconsin–Madison, 432 North Lake Street, Madison, Wisconsin 53706, 608–262–1299.) Similarly, Sylvania, Philips, and General Electric have various lighting seminars year-round at their respective lighting education centers, in Danvers, Massachusetts; Somerset, New Jersey; and Cleveland, Ohio. Contact a local representative of these lamp manufacturers for schedules, topics, and costs. The Illuminating Engineering Society of North America (IES; also IESNA) also holds both national and local programs on continuing education (Contact the IES at 345 East 47th Street, New York,

New York 10017, 212–705–7915.) The IES and the International Association of Lighting Designers typically sponsor an annual exhibition and seminar program known as LIGHTFAIR.

PUBLICATIONS

Staying current with technology and design fashion takes more than a week-long refresher course every couple of years. Within the past several years, a number of magazines have established broad appeal by addressing lighting design. *Architectural Lighting, Lighting Dimensions*, and *Lighting Design and Application* are periodicals on lighting. Also, such magazines as *Interiors, Interior Design, Progressive Architecture, Architectural Record*, and *Architecture* provide some observations on the lighted environment. The best of these magazines will list lighting design credits and manufacturers of the equipment used in each installation.

LIGHTING ORGANIZATIONS

There are several organizations in the lighting industry, from technical to professional to trade associations. The IES is the primary lighting technical society in North America, and has developed application guidelines for interior and exterior design, standards for the testing of lamps and luminaires, and calculation procedures for determining appropriate quantities and locations of luminaires. Several American National Standards Institute (ANSI) standards have been developed or codeveloped by the IES, including the Office Lighting Standard and the ANSI/ASHRAE/IES Energy Standards. Note that there has been controversy surrounding the energy standards, however. The American Society of Heating, Refrigerating and Air-Conditioning Engineers (ASHRAE) has been the primary sponsoring organization for these standards, and thus has determined membership of the committees responsible for writing the standards. Consequently, there has been considerable concern that the committees have not always been properly balanced with appropriate lighting design experts. The committees generally have had IES representation, but it is important to know that the majority of IES members are not lighting designers, but rather engineers, manufacturers' representatives and manufacturers of lamps, ballasts, luminaires, reflectors, and lenses, and utilities representatives. The intent of these energy standards is noble, but a considerable amount of engineering expertise without corresponding human-use rationale appears to have served as a foundation for the standards.

The International Commission on Illumination (CIE) is the international counterpart of the IES. Because many of the individual members are the same, there is considerable exchange of information between the two groups, resulting in similar guidelines. A list of CIE publications is available from the IESNA (see address given above).

The Chartered Institution of Building Services Engineers (CIBSE) is the United Kingdom organization corresponding to the IES. CIBSE produces documents and guidelines on lighting for a variety of applications. The organization has an annual awards program and an annual conference on lighting. Information from CIBSE allows the designer to remain current on lighting trends and guidelines in Europe. The organization's address is: Delta House, 222 Balham High Road, London, United Kingdom SW129BS.

The single professional society in the architectural lighting business is the International Association of Lighting Designers (IALD). Corporate and Senior Associate Members may not sell lighting equipment or represent lighting equipment manufacturers, and this stipulation assures the client that the member is an independent lighting designer. The IALD has continued to expand its membership base to cover Western Europe, the Far East, and North America. Its existence has helped to formalize the practice of lighting design and has elevated the practice to a profession. The IALD is located at 18 East 16th Street, Suite 208, New York, New York 10003.

Manufacturers' trade associations also exist in the lighting industry. The National Electrical Manufacturers Association (NEMA) has a rather active lighting division. Certified Ballast Manufacturers (CBM) have established criteria for fluorescent ballasts' operating characteristics.

THE INDUSTRY

Lighting is at least a 6-billion-dollar-a-year business in the United States alone. In the not-too-distant past nearly anyone with a tin bending press and some basement or garage space could and did manufacture luminaires, but as material and labor costs rose, it became increasingly necessary to mass-produce them. Finally, today, as the industry feels the pressure of foreign competition, and as many commodity products are nonproprietary, it has become necessary for the industry to consolidate into a few giants. GE, Philips, and Sylvania are the dominant lamp manufacturers. Genlyte, Jacobsen, Cooper Industries, National Service Industries, and Thomas dominate the U.S. luminaire market. This situation may be good for bottom-line economics, but it may not be best for the end user. Just like the auto industry of the 1970s, some of these manufacturers are selling what is good for their bottom line; but as foreign competition increases in this area, as the service sector/office segment of the workforce expands, and as concern grows over the work environment's appropriateness and safety, it is likely that lighting equipment will have to begin to respond to human user needs. The biggest-selling fluorescent lamp today is one of the worst color lamps available:

cool white. The biggest-selling line of fluorescent luminaires is the standard lensed unit (predominantly 2' × 4') of the three- and four-lamp type. These luminaires contribute to significant direct glare to the eyes and to reflected glare from VDT screens. What is responsible for this unfortunate situation? Of course, it is a catch-22. The cheapest fluorescent lamp is cool white, and the cheapest luminaire is the 2' × 4' lensed unit. People thus buy more of them, making them even more "mass-producible," resulting in even lower prices—so that the situation feeds on itself.

Perhaps the best way to combat such a situation is to educate the users although this clearly would be a massive undertaking. However, nearly everything that people do is influenced by vision and light; so everyone should be educated on the topic. Unfortunately, most professionals in the building industry have very little understanding of lighting and thus are not well prepared to educate clients on the subject. That is why this text has been written: to help educate students, building design professionals, and building owners.

CHAPTER TWO

CONCEPT DEVELOPMENT

PROGRAMMING

The basis for most lighting inadequacies in new and retrofit construction is programming, or, specifically, the lack of programming. In an effort to reduce both design time and fee expenditures, proper programming often is neglected; but no problem can be solved unless it first is clearly defined. Before anyone can make decisions on how much light and what color of light to use, whether sconces are better than downlights or wall washers, and so on, a good bit of information must be known about the persons who will be working or living in the new environment, what their collective likes and dislikes are, what sorts of tasks they will be required or will wish to perform, and so on.

It no longer is acceptable to develop design solutions according to an illuminance level for a given space type. A designer would be seriously abrogating his or her responsibility by deciding that an "office"—no matter how large or how small, in any type of facility, and for any type of occupant—should have a standard pattern of lighting equipment to meet such a simple and overrated criterion as light level. Programming a project does not necessarily take much time although larger, more unique projects generally will require a substantial amount of programming time. However, programming does take a concerned designer, who is interested in the kinds of criteria that make a space successful and deals sincerely with the occupants of the new space. If the design is for speculative construction, then its prospective occupants may not be available; but generally in today's leasing market it is reasonable to assume occupants' characteristics, existing working conditions, potential tasks, and so forth. The programming phase consists of two distinct steps: inventorying given conditions and establishing design goals.

INVENTORYING GIVEN CONDITIONS

Taking inventory of the "givens" on any project is a critical step in assessing vision, perception, and subsequently lighting needs. No intelligent lighting design can occur without knowledge of a variety of characteristics of the architecture and the client. The process of getting to know the architecture and the client will prepare the designer for making rational, appropriate decisions. A checklist, shown in Table 2–1, can be used as a guide for taking inventory on a project.

Table 2–1.
Inventory of given conditions.

_____ Space dimensions
_____ Space activities
   • Primary
   • Secondary
_____ Visual tasks
   • Prioritized by importance
   • Prioritized by time spent performing
_____ Occupants' ages
_____ Furnishings (layout)
_____ Surface finishes
_____ Spatial form
   • Rectilinear
   • Curvilinear
   • Long/narrow
   • Short/wide
_____ Users' existing conditions
   • Illuminances
   • Luminances
   • Luminaire type, layout, distribution, shielding
   • Daylight/exterior view
_____ Client expectations
   • Image
   • Environmental quality
   • Budget
_____ Designers' expectations

SPACE DIMENSIONS

The size of a space will impact a variety of its lighting criteria. Subjective aspects such as spaciousness and quantifiable aspects such as glare and illuminance are affected by space size.

SPACE ACTIVITIES

The definition of basic space functions will influence the type of subjective criteria to be considered, as well as impact illuminance, power budgets, and controls. For example, in a retirement center, the community room may be used for knitting, card playing, and shuffleboard by day, but may turn into a ballroom dance studio in the evening. Not only will its daytime lighting setting need to provide more illuminance to task areas, but its "activity level" atmosphere should be much different from its nighttime ambience.

VISUAL TASKS

The kinds of visual tasks that are anticipated are crucial to the development of appropriate lighting. If possible, the designer should walk through the occupants' current spaces and note the visual tasks that occur. One should consider establishing a list of tasks that occur most frequently and a list of the tasks that are most important. This task analysis can be used later to develop appropriate illuminance criteria, as well as to determine the need for relatively distant views. Opportunities for visually distant focuses are important where a lot of close visual inspection occurs for great lengths of time. Reading books and papers or VDT screens for long periods of time causes the eye muscles to "tense" in a specific position, and focusing on visually distant views (e.g., artwork or window views) helps one to rest these muscles.

OCCUPANTS' AGES

Generally, the older the eye is, the greater the amount of light required to perform tasks. As the eye ages, the lens tends to yellow. Also, the adaptation process slows, so that moving from relatively bright areas to relatively dark areas can be problematic. Glare sensitivity increases with age; so older persons probably should be exposed to less harsh light sources than might be acceptable for younger populations. This problem can be of particular concern in exterior lighting where, for the sake of efficiency, it has become acceptable to place high-wattage light sources on high poles at relatively great spacings. Such solutions contribute significantly to disability glare.

FURNISHINGS

Whether for interior or exterior use, it is important to understand where furnishings will be placed, their finishes, and their intended function. Lighting can and should be used to help define function areas and, of course, can enhance the intended use of a given area.

SURFACE FINISHES

Lighting can be used to accentuate the sheen of silk wall fabrics or highlight the grain and warmth of wood (see Figure C14). Many times, however, such expensive finishes are improperly lighted, as are many stone and brick wall surfaces. Generally, and unfortunately, it appears that the architecture of a structure has been designed by an entirely different team from the one that designed the lighting. The designer should take note of proposed wall finishes, and consider enhancing the texture, grain, sheen, or contour of the walls. One must remember that the colors and tones of surfaces influence the brightness appearance of a space. The designer ought to know surface colors when selecting the lamp color.

SPATIAL FORM

A spatial configuration can be enhanced with lighting. For example, the skylight well accentuated with neon shown in Figure C28 identifies the reception station. Long, narrow spaces can be made to feel less confining by locating light in perimeter zones, as illustrated in Figure 5–2. Curvilinear surfaces may be enhanced with light, as shown in Figure C23.

USERS' EXISTING CONDITIONS

Humans are indeed creatures of habit. Regardless of their merit, people become accustomed to certain rituals, events, foods, and places. A living or working environment may be quite inappropriate and ill-equipped to meet a user's needs, yet because it has been "home" or "the office" for a period of time, the user has adapted to it. To avoid negative reactions and complaints when users move into new environments, designers must either "account" or "educate."

By accounting for the features exhibited by the user's old environment, the designer may be able to avoid creating a distinctly different and thus less desirable (to the occupant) environment, and in that way probably can prevent complaints that the new environment has various deficiencies compared to the old one. In a classic example, users move from an office lighted with glary, lensed luminaires to one lighted with low-brightness parabolic luminaires. Although the parabolic lighting system is generally less harsh, users may complain that there is "less light" in the new space. The eyes respond to surface brightness; so the fact that the luminaires are less bright misleads the users into believing that less light has been designed into the new environment. The designer should carefully analyze the users' old environment and account for the glary brightness of the lensed luminaires by using higher-reflectance surface finishes, by introducing some uplighting onto the ceiling, or by lighting walls to increase the perception of brightness.

Educating users, though a noble goal, generally is a difficult process, as the designer usually cannot get an audience with all the users of a new environment. If one-on-one discussion is possible, or if educational literature (printed pamphlets or videotapes) can be developed, then user education may be an effective means of presenting new concepts, thereby avoiding or minimizing complaints or comparisons of old and new environments.

CLIENT EXPECTATIONS

Most clients may not be users. In any event, the designer should take stock of what the client expects the environment to do. Issues of environmental quality and budget should be addressed early in the programming phase to avoid later surprises and disasters, in both the planning and the financing of a project. Clients' ego issues must be aired. What sort of image is the new environment(s) expected to evoke for workers and visitors? Be sure to define budget matters rigorously. Let the client know the costs/benefits or lack of benefits of various approaches. For example, a client initially may indicate that the environment is to be "no frills," which probably means no decorative lighting to the client. Yet, decorative lighting is responsible for the human-scale aspects of an environment, providing a more homey, pleasing atmosphere. It also is responsble for establishing an image and alleviates the blandness of using just general overhead lighting.

DESIGNERS' EXPECTATIONS

Again, to avoid surprises and difficulties in the design goals and design concept phases, the designer(s) should clearly state any personal expectations.

Ego considerations are an inherent part of the design process and should be openly discussed with the client. Some designers have "signatures" or statements that are exhibited in nearly all of their projects, which may be responsible for the client's selection of the designer for a given project; and lighting can play an important role in expressing the designer's statement. For example, in recent years it has become increasingly desirable to use rich surfaces (e.g., marble, granite, wood) in speculative-building lobbies. Such an upgrade in materials could play a profound role in developers' abilities to sign and retain lessees, but often these surfaces are lighted by traditional inexpensive, unattractive lighting that does nothing to enhance the architectural finishes, and in a way expresses a lack of commitment and concern for quality, detail, and comfort—the very signatures for which designers hope to be recognized, and the very characteristics that landlords wish to promote. Therefore, the designer is encouraged to address his or her own expectations early and to follow through with lighting details that promote those expectations.

This given-conditions list is by no means exhaustive. A variety of other matters may surface that should be inventoried before one proceeds with the design goals phase. The point is that rather than simply to recite quantifiable criteria, it is imperative for the designer to fully understand client needs and wants. Then a comprehensive and firm list of subjective and objective design goals can be established toward a common end—satisfying users and clients.

ESTABLISHING DESIGN GOALS

Seldom are design goals conveniently straightforward and easily stated. Perhaps this is why many designers today elect simply to place a uniform array of downlights or fluorescent luminaires on a reflected ceiling plan in order to generate "enough light." This approach permits the designer to meet the legal requirements of a project without expending fees. In fact, it is ironic that as design has become more and more demanding, as the service sector of the economy has increased—requiring more attention to the human-scale aspects of design—designers have been discounting fees, thereby eliminating the time and money available to properly review the lighting and other systems needed for appropriate function and behavior. Providing only "enough light" may in fact create occupant complaints and dissatisfaction, and ultimaely lead to a reduction in performance, less time spent in the offensive environment, and an overall morale problem. A comprehensive list of lighting design goals is shown in Table 2–2, and discussed in this section. Some goals are straightforward (e.g., codes), but others may require considerable research and thought prior to their resolution (e.g., daylight-

Table 2–2.
Lighting design goals.

_____ Spatial factors
  • Visual environment pleasantness
  • Spatial definition
  • Spatial order (2-D vs. 3-D planning)
  • Visual hierarchy
  • Circulation
  • Focal centers
  • Flexibility
  • Controls
  • Acoustics
  • HVAC
  • Ceiling systems
    —Drywall
    —Exposed "t" lay-in
    —Concealed spline
    —Structural
  • Code requirements
    —Egress
    —Thermal protection
    —Power limits
_____ Psychological and physiological factors
  • Sensory responses
  • Desired impressions
  • Expectations
  • Subjective impressions
    —Visual clarity
    —Spaciousness
    —Relaxation
    —Privacy
  • Daylighting
_____ Task factors
  • Visual tasks
  • Luminances
  • Surface reflectances
  • Surface transmittances
  • Illuminances

ing). This list should be used as a guide to enlarge the designer's perspective on appropriate vision and lighting-related aspects.

SPATIAL FACTORS

Spatial factor goals relate to architecture and how lighting is used to enhance it. In fact, questions of lighting and architecture are inseparable when one must establish design goals concerning spatial factors. The designer must address physical issues of architectural surfaces and integration. What surfaces should be lighted, and how does this lighting enhance the architectural philosophy? How can lighting be integrated with the architecture and architectural systems to best meet the client's space planning needs? These are the kinds of questions that must be analyzed.

VISUAL ENVIRONMENT PLEASANTNESS

This is a design objective that few designers and clients seem willing to address. However, it is likely that the lighting system will be in place for fifteen years or so prior to any move or renovation, and the environment is built to support people—a very expensive asset; so it is quite appropriate to consider how pleasant the environment will or should be. Pleasantness results in improved morale, self-esteem, communication, and ultimately productivity. Visual environment pleasantness should be seen as insurance on an investment—investment in employees. With clerical staff salaries and benefits alone running to $150 per square foot per year in an office, and an entire facility's cost (including salaries) approximating $275 per square foot per year, an expenditure of $1.00 or $2.00 per square foot per year for lighting can be money well spent.

Visual environment pleasantness means an appropriate marriage of light and architecture toward a common goal of pleasantness—a very subjective yet attainable end. It is almost always easiest to identify what is *not* pleasant. For example, the monotony of color tones and brightness shown in Figure 5–13 makes for an unpleasant environment. Also, the low-brightness luminaires used in Figure 2–1 may be low in glare, but they produce a very "dark" feeling throughout the entire space. To make that space a more pleasant work environment, a cove and a valance were designed into it, as shown energized in Figure 2–2.

SPATIAL DEFINITION

Walls and ceilings are used to define space physically. Lighting key surfaces or parts of surfaces can enhance the spatial definition established by the architecture. Figure C9 shows a showroom private-office setting. The glass wall allows a significant view into the space, yet etched patterns on the glass pick up a motif used throughout the showroom. Lighting these etched patterns adds a visual cue to the spatial limits, as well as introducing a sconce-like element. Figure 2–3 shows the influence of having at least two

FIGURE 2–1.
The low-brightness, small-cell, parabolic louver luminaires in this installation produce very controlled downlighting. This leads to rather dark-appearing ceiling and walls, resulting in a sense of confinement.

walls that are dark. In spite of the dark finish, lighting one or both walls or lighting objects on the walls would significantly enhance the spatial definition.

SPATIAL ORDER

People tend to like order, and architecture usually is designed to make or promote order. Lighting can enhance this sense of order. Figure 2–4 illustrates lighting that competes with the order of the architecture. Unfortunately, most lighting in the past has been nothing more than two-dimensional layouts of luminaires. In plan view, a particular lighting layout may look appropriate, but in three-dimensional space, the lighting may not appropriately add to the architectural order of the space. An appropriate design goal is to design for three-dimensional order and use light to this end.

FIGURE 2–2.
By adding a wall valance that provides up/downlighting on the right wall, and just uplighting in the remainder of the space, a sense of spaciousness and brightness is introduced. The subjective impression of the space lighted in this way is entirely different from that of the same space lighted exclusively with parabolic lighting (see Figure 2–1).

VISUAL HIERARCHY

Visual hierarchies are quite appropriate to signify importance of various areas, surfaces, or objects. The wall around the core shown in Figure C12 is lighted for psychological reasons, but another design goal is to feature the artwork. In the visual hierarchy then, the artwork requires significant highlighting.

CIRCULATION

Lighting can be used to help move people from one zone to another. By establishing a bright and/or colorful focus, the designer can enhance circulation. Rather than providing a regular array of downlights over the entire ceiling for the food servery shown in Figure 2–5, the designer introduced a

FIGURE 2–3.
Dark wall finishes that are left unlighted result in a "black hole" effect. Spatial definition would be better enhanced with more lighted wall surfaces.

light slot along the tray rail to enhance circulation along this path. Obviously, this solution has other practical benefits—it lights the food and the signage. The entire servery is lighted primarily by the fluorescent slot around the perimeter of the space.

FOCAL CENTERS

Establishing or enhancing focal centers with light can contribute to several design goals already discussed: spatial order, visual hierarchy, and circulation. There are times, however, when a focal center is developed for visual interest, visual identity, and/or eye-muscle relaxation. As a design goal, one should identify those focal centers that are important and necessary to add interest or identity to an area. The three-dimensional aspects of space and light, however, also must be addressed. Otherwise, the result could be less than satisfactory, as shown in Figure 2–6 where art accents highlight the wall, not the art, because of misplacement of the accents in the reflected ceiling.

FIGURE 2–4.
Spatial order is destroyed with a lighting pattern that gives visual miscues. This is usually the result of using only two-dimensional planning, rather than exploring the three-dimensional results of various lighting solutions.

FLEXIBILITY

Flexibility means many things to many people; hence the design team must come to some agreement on what kind of flexibility is necessary for a given project. For example, flexibility may mean that:

- All luminaires (or many luminaires) are easily moved.
- No matter how furniture gets moved around, the lighting quantities and qualities are to remain the same.
- As tasks change or as furniture moves, lighting quantities are to be changed without physically moving the lighting equipment.

A particular client may even have other definitions of flexibility.

The need for all or many luminaires to be easily moved generally pushes the design toward lay-in ceilings of convenient modules, and usually means that luminaires are either wired with six feet of cable or are wired with

FIGURE 2–5.
Lighting is used to enhance the circulation path as well as to highlight the task—
the food. A simple fluorescent slot detail is used (see Figure 4–1) above the food
servery tray rail.

modular, quick-connect wiring systems. The quick-connect systems are
somewhat like a cord-and-plug arrangement. This enables facility maintenance people to unplug the luminaires, relocate them as desired, and plug
them back into the wiring system.

The need for lighting quantities and qualities to remain the same usually
pushes the design toward that of a rather uniform, diffuse lighting system.
This can be energy intensive and visually inappropriate.

The need to change light quantities without moving luminaires, removing luminaires, or changing lamps generally leads to control systems that
allow the dimming of individual luminaires or zones of luminaires.

CONTROLS

Controls, as a design goal, depend on flexibility of space and space use. Task
factors (discussed later in this chapter) can significantly influence the need
for controls. Also, there will always be some sort of lighting control (both

FIGURE 2–6.
Identifying focal centers is important during the programming phase, but the execution of the concept is critical if the project is to be successful. Here, art accents are placed in just the wrong location so as not to light the art, but to provide a distinct highlight to the upper wall.

electric and daylighting) in built environments. Controls make sense in terms of economics, global environment protection, and occupant protection and satisfaction. For electric lighting, controls may include: switches; dimming; time-of-day control; occupancy sensors; and energy management.

Switches need to be addressed in terms of type (toggle, slide, electronic pushbutton, or rocker), location (wall, door jamb, phone, or remote control), and quantity.

Dimming can be used to increase space flexibility, as discussed earlier, or to change the mood or image elicited by an environment.

Time-of-day controls typically are part of a comprehensive energy management system. These controls generally cover large zones and control a portion of the lighting in order to reduce energy consumption (e.g., half-level lighting during lunch).

Occupancy sensors, used to shut lights off when spaces are unoccupied, usually replace switches. Two types of devices are available: motion sensors (which sense motion) and infrared sensors (which sense infrared heat emitted by the human body).

Energy management systems generally offer a great potential for visual comfort and energy effectiveness. This is especially so if daylighting contributes to illuminances and luminances significantly.

ACOUSTICS

Lighting can negatively impact acoustics. For this reason, acoustics must be considered as a lighting design goal. The responsibility for acoustics, however, lies with an acoustician, not the lighting designer. The lighting designer needs to be in a position, however, to meet the goals established by the acoustician; so it is incumbent on the acoustician to relay these goals to the designer as early as possible.

Luminaire ballasts and transformers can introduce noise into spaces. Chokes are available to minimize this noise, or the remote location of ballasts and transformers will reduce noise. For most fluorescent lamps, quiet ballasts are available.

Perhaps even more problematic acoustically are the types and sizes of luminaires used in open-plan offices. Lensed luminaires, wide flat-bottomed indirect luminaires, and small-cell parabolic luminaires are all good sound reflectors. In an open office, these luminaires can negate the influence of a nice soft acoustic celing by reflecting sound from workstation to workstation.

HVAC

Heating, ventilating, and air conditioning can be influenced by lighting—both lighting loads (how many watts of lighting) and lighting equipment (air handling or static). The responsibility for HVAC lies with the mechanical engineer, not the lighting designer, but, as with acoustics, the lighting designer needs to be in a position to meet the goals established by the mechanical engineer. It is incumbent on the mechanical engineer to convey these goals as early in a project as possible.

Lighting power budgets are particularly important to the mechanical engineer in establishing cooling loads and in sizing heating equipment.

Some recessed luminaires have the capability to extract air from the environment (return air) and/or to supply conditioned air into the environment. Although this feature may be convenient for the mechanical engineer, it should never be the sole or primary criterion for selecting particular lighting equipment.

CEILING SYSTEMS

The architect will establish the ceiling system or systems to be used in a particular project, and these systems establish yet another design goal(s) for the lighting designer. The type of recessed luminaire and/or the method(s) of suspending luminaires usually will be influenced by the type of ceiling. This particular design goal does not play a major role in determining lighting equipment, but it will have some impact on the exact mounting hardware required in the specification.

CODE REQUIREMENTS

Codes, of course, are law. The registered professional (e.g., architect or engineer) on any project must assure that all codes are met prior to completing a project. If not acting in the capacity of one of these registered professionals, it is imperative that the lighting designer work with the appropriate registered professional team member in determining all applicable codes. Some of the more typical code requirements include egress lighting, luminaire thermal protection requirements, and power limits.

Egress lighting relates to providing a lighted path of egress during emergency conditions. Lighting requirements usually range from 1 to 3 footcandles/10 to 30 lux on the path, as well as exit signs of appropriate size, luminance, and color located over paths and egress ways indicating the direction of exit and the actual exit location. One must remember that such standards now are considered inappropriate for leading people through heavy smoke. As smoke rises, it tends to obscure ceiling-mounted exit signs and either reduces or eliminates the apparent brightness of the egress lighting. Additionally, any alarms that sound are of little use for the hearing-impaired. Ongoing research may set the tone for future codes, with flashing signs and or signal lights mounted near or at floor level (below the smoke layer and more readily visible to persons crawling to avoid smoke inhalation). The designer should check with local code authorities in the municipality in which the project is to be built or renovated. For large corporations, internal requirements may encompass the code, with other qualifications added to meet insurance or legal requirements.

Thermal protection devices now should be commonplace in all luminaires, both residential and commercial types, intended for recessed mounting in ceilings. These are essentially circuit-breaker type devices. If the luminaire overheats because the wrong wattage or wrong type of lamp has been installed or because the luminaire is surrounded by inappropriately positioned insulation that does not allow for proper heat dissipation, then the thermal protectors trip and shut off the luminaire, allowing it to cool down.

In nearly all residential construction, the luminaires are likely to come in contact with or to be surrounded by insulation, so most municipalities require that residential lighting be suitably thermally protected to withstand the effects of the insulation. However, such luminaires often have several deficiencies: the quality of their overall construction and appearance is not as good as that of commercial grade luminaires; their overall height must be less than 8 inches to permit their use in retrofit construction (between 2 × 8 joists), thereby increasing glare potential (with the lamp bottom close to the ceiling plane); and the breadth of finish, style, and lamping choices is limited (for economic reasons—to maximize profit—and/or for thermal reasons, most luminaire manufacturers limit production variations). To overcome any of these deficiencies it generally is necessary to specify commercial grade luminaires, which are not rated for surrounding-insulation thermal protection. Therefore, to satisfy code requirements, the designer must meet with the local electrical inspector, and, if it is agreeable to the inspector, consider using special gypsum board housings or chicken wire cages in the plenum around the commercial luminaires. This step eliminates the possibility of insulation coming in contact with the luminaires, but installation costs increase significantly with the additional construction of such "thermal breaks" around the luminaires.

Power-limit codes, a direct result of the oil embargoes of 1973 and 1979, were intended to reduce energy consumption by limiting the amount of power used to light a given environment. Unfortunately, these power codes were implemented in a state of crisis and *only* respond to reducing connected load. Connected load is measured in watts and is a simple indication of the electric power required to operate a device or a bank of devices; but power, or connected load, does not provide a true indication of energy use.

Energy is power times time (the amount of power needed for a period of time), usually measured in terms of watt-hours, or kilowatt-hours. Because we can control lighting through normal (switches) or automatic (computer time clock, motion sensors) means, we can significantly reduce energy use without necessarily reducing power requirements.

For example, a power code in a given state may require the designer to use lower-wattage lamps and/or fewer lamps. Obviously, this may mean less appropriate luminance patterns (perhaps less bright, more gloomy-appearing space) and less appropriate illuminances (perhaps 30 footcandles/300 lux instead of 50 footcandles/500 lux). Such lighting changes can lead to reduced worker satisfaction and reduced task performance, ultimately requiring more energy to complete the task.

Most power codes of the 1970s and 1980s were established by well-intentioned individuals and organizations, but nearly all of them were uninformed on lighting, and some, in fact, had special interests that were significantly different from lighting considerations.

The key to wise energy use for today's designer is to better program the design requirements of a project. It is important to work with other team members to maximize the effect of lighting. For example, if a wall wash technique is used to enhance the sense of spaciousness, selecting lighter-toned wall finishes to enhance the effect will allow for the use of lower-wattage lighting—ultimately providing a more energy-effective installation. There is a real need for designers to work with latest-technology lamps and ballasts in order to meet the power codes and still provide a comfortable, productive environment. It is tempting to fall into the power (watts per square foot) vs. illuminance (footcandles/lux) trap. Most assuredly, if we select lighting equipment only to maximize footcandles/lux while minimizing watts per square foot, an unsatisfactory environment will result. All one needs to do is to take a look around. Energy is *not* the issue; lighting is the issue!

It is every designer's responsibility to be familiar with applicable codes and to meet them. One must have a copy of the most recent National Electric Code and a copy of the code enforced by the jurisdictions in which one's projects are built. Only some of the more critical (and sometimes misguided) code requirements have been addressed here.

PSYCHOLOGICAL AND PHYSIOLOGICAL FACTORS

The way in which an environment is presented to its users is at least partly responsible for the way they perceive and react to it; thus lighting can play a significant role in people's psychological and physiological responses to an environment. The distribution of luminances in a space can influence perceptions of the space's intended function, level of comfort, and apparent size. Luminance levels and ratios are responsible for visual comfort.

SENSORY RESPONSES

Light and color not only seem to influence vision, but may also influence hearing and thermal sensations. Although work in this area is not conclusive, the designer should recognize that a sensory cross-feed may exist and that collaboration with the other team members is important for the development of a totally integrated, goal-oriented environment.

DESIRED IMPRESSIONS

Designers' egos generally are substantial. Team members ought to address this concern early in the design process by soliciting each other's desired impressions. Designers may have a particular "look" or "feel" in mind, which they should state for the team. This may be achieved with mood shots, verbal descriptions, or visits to other sites.

EXPECTATIONS

This may be the opportunity most often disregarded by the design team during design programming, the chance to learn what the occupants expect from a new or renovated space. One way of establishing some sense of expectations is to visit the occupants' existing facility (or facilities). What sorts of work do the people perform? What size area does each worker have? What are the room surface colors? What are the illuminances and the luminances? Is the lighting produced indirectly or directly? Uniformly or nonuniformly? Is the lighting warm- or cool-toned? Although the new or renovated space need not—indeed, probably should not—be designed identically to the existing space, observations about the existing environment and people's work habits can help the designer to form appropriate resolutions of the lighting design problem. For example, a new or renovated space is scheduled to be VDT-intensive. The existing space is lighted with 2 feet by 4 feet, 4-lamp lensed luminaires that are quite glary and produce significant illuminances on the desks. It is likely that the occupants have become accustomed to lots of light from glary luminaires. Introducing very low-brightness lighting at half the illuminance level in the new space may result in complaints that the new space is too dim and underlit. The designer should take cues from the existing environment: the ceiling has brightness; worksurfaces have brightness. The new lighting system should be designed to provide some brightness on the ceiling and worksurface, which may mean including some indirect lighting or using semi-specular parabolic louvered luminaires instead of specular parabolic louvered luminaires (see Chapter 4). It may mean suggesting that desks not be a dark wood tone, but a lighter laminate.

SUBJECTIVE IMPRESSIONS

Luminance patterns can influence how people perceive a given space. The late Professor John Flynn, of The Pennsylvania State University, found five specific impression factors that are influenced by luminance patterns: visual clarity, spaciousness, relaxation, privacy, and pleasantness. The designer thus has some clear ways to determine design goals with respect to subjective impressions. These impressions can be used to establish design directions that ultimately will result in more occupant-sensitive spaces. Subjective impressions should be considered a primary concern for any space where people are expected to live and/or work.

Visual Clarity

This factor is not to be confused with visibility or "how well a task can be seen." Visual clarity refers to the overall visual impression of a given environment. An environment can be considered hazy, clear, or something in between. "Hazy" is generally an impression elicited when architectural features and facial features are not crisp and distinct. Flat, shadow-free, low-to-moderate level lighting has a tendency to produce a hazy impression. Both low-to-moderate level, uniform, totally indirect lighting alone with no visible light sources and low-to-moderate level, low-brightness (low glare) direct lighting alone tend to create somewhat visually hazy environments. An overcast condition outdoors produces sufficient light for seeing, but causes many objects to appear flat and shadowless. Clear outdoor conditions, however, produce very distinct shadow patterns, resulting in clearer, more crisp images—hence the descriptor "clear" for interior environments. Visual clarity primarily is a concern in mostly work spaces where occupants will be present for relatively long periods of time. Indeed, it seems appropriate that the work setting should present a crisp, distinct impression, as a hazy setting can be associated with blandness and disinterest. Figure 2–7 graphically illustrates relative luminance patterning to promote a sense of clarity.

Spaciousness

This particular subjective impression, although recognized as some sort of factor influenced by lighting, has been greatly debated in recent years. The matter appears to be an issue of semantics rather than of cause and effect. An impression of being confined generally is elicited when vertical surfaces (full-height and partial-height walls) and/or ceiling surfaces are quite dark compared to the lower horizontal plane (e.g., worksurface and/or floor). An impression of spaciousness usually is elicited when vertical surfaces and/or ceiling surfaces are relatively bright (e.g., the surfaces are lighted). Figures 2–1 and 2–2 illustrate a space with and without wall lighting. In Figure 2–1, the room has dark and consequently "enclosing" room surfaces (walls and ceiling), whereas Figure 2–2 shows the same space with lighted vertical surfaces and a lighted ceiling, which give a more visually open or spacious appearance than that of Figure 2–1.

An impression of spaciousness appears particularly important for circulation and assembly spaces where large numbers of people are likely to congre-

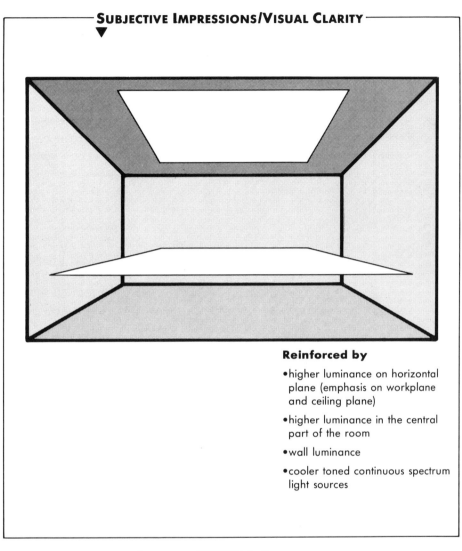

FIGURE 2–7

gate or pass, and/or where the space is inherently small. Nevertheless, this subjective factor also seems an appropriate concern for office areas where small workstations or private offices exist.

Figure 2–8 is a graphic representation of luminance patterning that promotes a sense of spaciousness.

Relaxation

A sense of relaxation is especially important for casual spaces such as waiting rooms, lounges, restaurants, conference rooms, and living areas. A sense

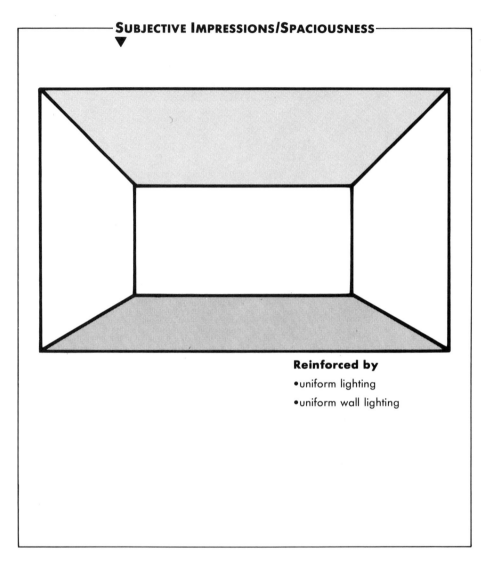

FIGURE 2–8

of relaxation reflects a comfortable pace of activities; so this impression should not be disregarded in work settings. By combining relaxation with visual clarity we can create a comfortable yet highly productive environment.

The impression of relaxation is especially influenced by nonuniform wall lighting and by the use of warm-toned light sources. Figure 2–9 illustrates conceptual luminance patterning necessary to promote the sense of relaxation.

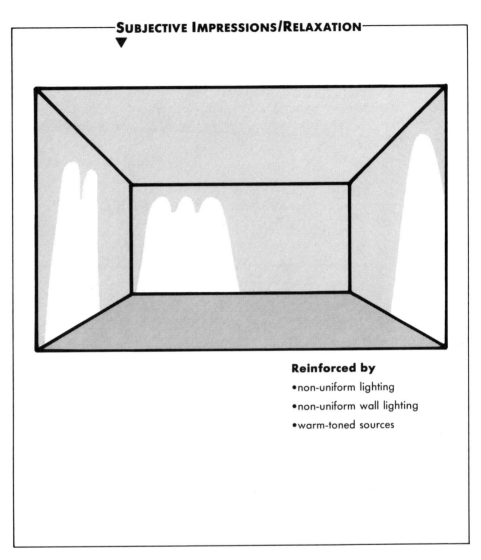

FIGURE 2–9

Privacy

This subjective impression is particularly important in the more intimate casual spaces, a category that includes primarily residential spaces as well as lounges and some restaurants. Creating a privacy setting is the opposite of designing for being "on stage" for public view. The lighting emphasis should be located away from the occupant area, drawing attention and subsequent visual inspection to the surround. Specifically, the use of nonuniform lighting away from the occupant zone is appropriate in achieving a sense of privacy. Figure 2–10 indicates possible luminance patterns that can be used to achieve privacy.

Like the other subjective impressions, privacy can be used in conjunction with other impression factors.

Once the designer has programmed appropriate impression factors into a project, it is a relatively straightforward matter to design for the quantitative aspects.

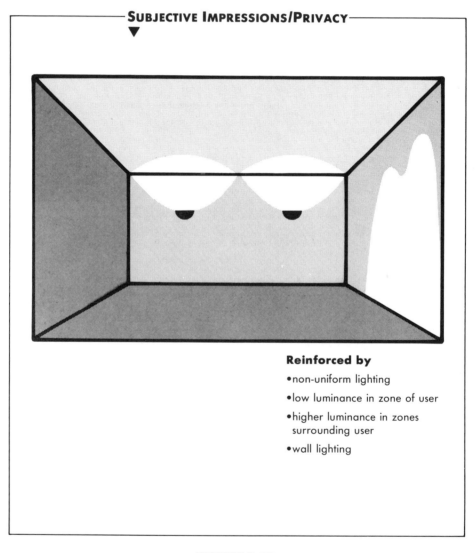

SUBJECTIVE IMPRESSIONS/PRIVACY

Reinforced by

•non-uniform lighting

•low luminance in zone of user

•higher luminance in zones surrounding user

•wall lighting

FIGURE 2–10

DAYLIGHTING

Daylighting is both a qualitative and a quantitative matter. Its quantitative aspects are discussed in Chapter 3, under "Daylight Sources." Daylighting has a significant influence on how people feel in a space. Having a real-time connection to the outside world and having a distant view for eye-muscle relaxation are favorable, if not essential, aspects of daylighting; these are the view aspects. Psychologically, the view aspects of daylighting are quite important. They are the reasons why vertical glazing and skylights should be specified on buildings. The fact that some illuminance and luminance can be had in the process, if properly controlled and managed with electric lighting, may be an additional benefit of daylighting.

TASK FACTORS

Task factors relate specifically to the quantitative aspects of lighting, which, because they are quantifiable, are relatively easy to satisfy. Calculations and/or realistic mockups are performed until appropriate quantities are achieved. Because task factors are so quantifiable, or "hard," most designers only address these "known" issues. This is unfortunate. Designing just for task factors usually results in visually uninteresting, less people-oriented solutions. Task factors, as discussed here, are intended to be only one part of the programming of a project—to be included with spatial factors and psychological factors.

Programming appropriately for task factors involves a review of visual tasks, luminances, and illuminances. Making a full analysis of the kinds of visual tasks that are likely to occur is the best means of preparing the designer to solve unique lighting challenges. A complete review of tasks is likely to lead to a comprehensive lighting solution that will meet occupants' requirements for most or all tasks most or all of the time.

VISUAL TASKS

While visiting occupants' existing facility or facilities to establish a reference base of their expectations (see above discussion of expectations), the designer should make a task survey. Of particular interest are the kinds of visual tasks performed, the occupants' general range of ages, the percent of time spent on various tasks, and the apparent importance of those tasks.

For this exercise to be useful, the designer must be quite specific in analyzing the visual task. For example, it is not sufficient to observe an accounting function and simply jot down that the task is accounting. Is/are the occupant(s) reading/writing hardcopy? If so, what is the medium(s) (black pen on white paper, hard pencil on green ledger, etc.)? Is the occupant reading/writing with a computer? If so, what are the screen characteristics? Is the screen internally illuminated, or is room light needed for viewing the screen?

Tasks such as facial recognition tend to be overlooked or ignored by many designers, but recognizing such tasks usually means that the designer must provide sufficient vertical illuminance. This is particularly important for corridor, sidewalk, and street lighting.

Occupants' ages tend to indicate the general level of operating characteristics for the visual system. Typically, older eyes require more light to see as well as do younger eyes under lower light. Further, by age forty, the eyes change enough in many instances to require some sort of corrective lenses. Harsh downlighting can be problematic for eyeglass wearers, creating shadowing and glare due to frames and glass lens refraction.

Establishing the amount of time that occupants spend on given visual tasks may help the designer to determine the ambient lighting requirements for a space. For example, if VDT tasks are performed for less than an hour a day, and if handwritten paper tasks are performed most of the day, then it may not be reasonable to design an ambient lighting system for the VDT task operation. Generally, the tasks that people perform most of the time are the tasks that should be accommodated by the lighting. An exception to this rule occurs when a critically important task is performed only for a short period of time. Then it is reasonable to design the lighting to accommodate the very important task(s).

Obviously, such task analyses cannot take place in a vacuum. The designer should work with other team members and *must* work with the client to understand the kind and scope of visual tasks that may occur.

LUMINANCES

Luminance and chromatic ratios are responsible for our sight. Luminances play a significant role in how we see, react, and produce. Although maximum luminances should be limited to 250 fL/860 candelas/square meter or less for typical VDT-filled environments, luminance ratios generally are much more important than maximum luminances.

From paper documents to the immediate surround (desk), luminance ratios should be 3:1; that is, the bright paper should be no more than three times as bright as the desk surface or ink blotter. This precludes use of dark ink blotters and dark desk tops. Typically medium-value to lighter-value laminates are appropriate for desk tops, as are lighter woods (e.g., light oak).

A general guideline is to maintain worksurfaces at no less than 20 percent reflectance and no more than 40 percent reflectance. If the desk becomes too light, it actually may contribute glare and distract the occupant's concentration from the paper document.

For distant background surfaces, luminance ratios generally should not exceed 10:1; that is, the brightest area should be no more than ten times as bright as the darkest area. Therefore, a distant window (usually the brightest area) should not be more than ten times the brightness of the paper. The bottom line is that the window will need some sort of shading treatment to reduce its luminance to acceptable levels. On the other hand, if a wood paneled wall is in the background (the darkest area), the paper task (brightest area) should not be more than ten times the brightness of the wood paneled wall. This usually requires that the wood paneled wall be specifically lighted.

For VDT tasks, luminance ratios are especially critical. In addition to the 3:1 and 10:1 guidelines, maximum surface luminances and surface-to-surface luminance ratio guidelines should be observed. Maximum surface luminances should be 250 fL/860 candelas/square meter or less; hence, windows, skylights, and luminaires must be well controlled. Further, luminance ratios of light room surfaces to dark room surfaces should be near 4:1. The uniformity of brightnesses in a VDT-intensive space has a significant impact on the visibility of the VDT screens. Generally, the more uniform the brightnesses, the less problematic is VDT screen imaging and reflected glare. The *IES Recommended Practice for Lighting Offices Containing Computer Visual Display Terminals* includes a more thorough discussion and a complete listing of criteria guidelines for VDT-intensive spaces. Figure C6a shows an installation where ceiling and window luminances meet the previously discussed maximum luminance and luminance ratio design goals.

SURFACE REFLECTANCES

Luminances often are the result of illuminances (light quantities) and surface reflectances interacting, resulting in reflected light (luminance). Therefore, surface reflectances should be a conscious design goal.

Lighter-surface finishes reflect more light, which can result in glare in settings where the lighting is not appropriately planned. If surface reflectances and illuminances are considered together, the result can be reduced energy consumption.

Generally, matte surface finishes are better for work environments than specular surface finishes. This eliminates the harsh, glary reflections com-

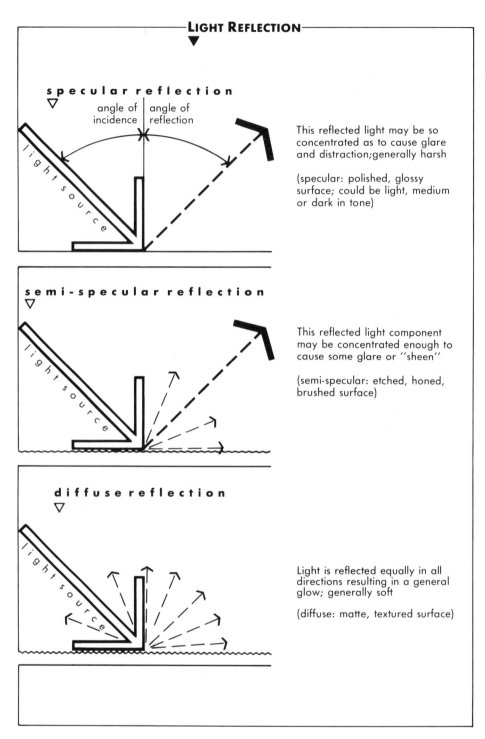

LIGHT REFLECTION

specular reflection

angle of incidence | angle of reflection

light source

This reflected light may be so concentrated as to cause glare and distraction; generally harsh

(specular: polished, glossy surface; could be light, medium or dark in tone)

semi-specular reflection

light source

This reflected light component may be concentrated enough to cause some glare or "sheen"

(semi-specular: etched, honed, brushed surface)

diffuse reflection

light source

Light is reflected equally in all directions resulting in a general glow; generally soft

(diffuse: matte, textured surface)

FIGURE 2–11

mon when electric light or daylight reflects from specular surfaces at a particular angle. Figure 2–11 illustrates graphically how light reflects from various surface finishes.

For most office furniture, 20 percent reflectance should be a minimum and 40 percent, or so, a maximum. This can be achieved with some light woods and most medium-to-light laminates. Table 2–3 outlines guidelines for typical surface reflectances in work environments. These guidelines are based on realistically attainable reflectances, not theoretical maximums.

There is a common misbelief that changing a given color surface from matte to specular will increase total reflectance. In some cases, for example, a kitchen countertop has been specified as black, honed granite, but when reminded that this countertop would appear dark, the designer has changed the honed granite to polished (specular) granite and proceeded to inform the client that such a surface will reflect more light. This statement, of course, is absurd—the total visible reflectance is unchanged from honed to polished. Instead, what does happen, as shown in Figure 2–11, is that the light that is reflected from the polished surface is directed in a very specific direction. If

Table 2–3.
Surface reflectance guidelines for work environments.

Surface	Suggested reflectance (matte finish)	Complying material
Worksurfaces	20 to 40%	• Light woods • Medium and light laminates • Medium and light ink blotters
Window treatment[1]	30 to 50%	• Medium to light fabrics • Medium to light blinds • Frit pattern glass
Floors	10 to 20%	• Medium to light carpet • Medium to light wood • Medium tile
Ceilings	70% or greater	• White fabric/cloth ceiling • Pure white mineral ceiling • Off-white to white drywall
Walls	30 to 50%	• Light fabric • Medium to light vinyl wall paper • Medium to light paint
Open office partitions	20 to 50%	• Medium to light fabrics • Medium to light laminates[2]

[1] Preferably image-preserving to permit view.
[2] Generally not appropriate acoustically.

the viewer's eyes happen to be located in the same direction, they will see a relatively large amount of light in a small area (glare). If the viewer's eyes are not located in this direction, they will see no reflected light (dark). The point is this: the designer should not specify dark honed or polished worksurfaces; in both cases the worksurface will appear dark, and in one case (polished) the potential exists for reflected glare.

Typical surface reflectances are listed in Table 2–4.

Table 2–4.
Light reflectances.

Typical specular materials	Reflectance (%)
Luminaire reflector materials	
Silver	90–92
Chromium	63–66
Aluminum	
Polished	60–70
Alzak polished	75–85
Stainless steel	50–60
Building materials	
Clear glass or plastic	8–10
Stainless steel	50–60

Typical diffusing materials	Reflectance (%)
Luminaire reflector materials	
White paint	70–90
White porcelain enamel	60–83
Masonry and structural materials	
White plaster	90–92
White terra-cotta	65–80
White porcelain enamel	60–83
Limestone	35–60
Sandstone	20–40
Marble	30–70
Gray cement	20–30
Granite	20–25
Brick	
Red	10–20
Light buff	40–45
Dark buff	35–40
Wood	
Light birch	35–50
Light oak	25–35
Dark oak	10–15
Mahogany	6–12
Walnut	5–10
Paint	
New white paint	75–90
Old white paint	50–70

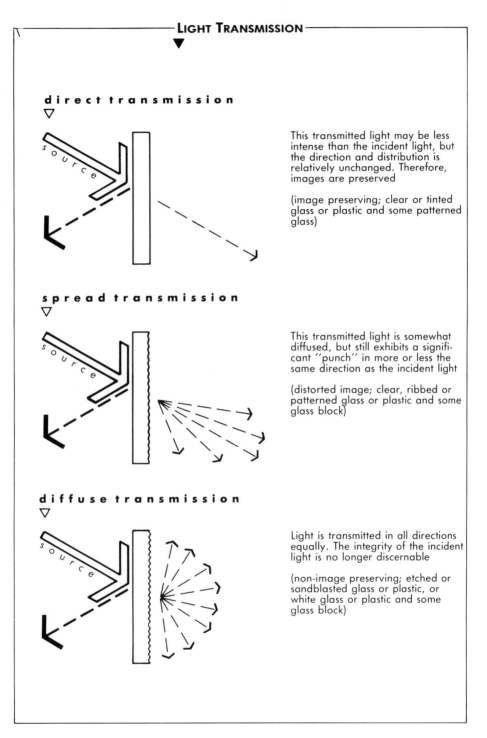

LIGHT TRANSMISSION

d i r e c t   t r a n s m i s s i o n

This transmitted light may be less intense than the incident light, but the direction and distribution is relatively unchanged. Therefore, images are preserved

(image preserving; clear or tinted glass or plastic and some patterned glass)

s p r e a d   t r a n s m i s s i o n

This transmitted light is somewhat diffused, but still exhibits a significant "punch" in more or less the same direction as the incident light

(distorted image; clear, ribbed or patterned glass or plastic and some glass block)

d i f f u s e   t r a n s m i s s i o n

Light is transmitted in all directions equally. The integrity of the incident light is no longer discernable

(non-image preserving; etched or sandblasted glass or plastic, or white glass or plastic and some glass block)

FIGURE 2–12

SURFACE TRANSMITTANCES

Although luminances can be a result of light being reflected from surfaces, they also can result from light being transmitted through surfaces. Figure 2–12 illustrates graphically how light is transmitted through various surface types. Surface transmittances as a design goal will depend on the luminance and luminance ratio goals established. Surfaces with high transmission are likely to be outside the 10:1 luminance ratios for typical paper tasks and the 4:1 light-area-to-dark-area ratios for VDT environments. Hence, some sort of transmission reduction is necessary (tint, perforated filters, mesh screen, etc.). If an image-preserving transmitting surface has a high transmission, then changing the surface to a non-image-preserving surface *will not necessarily decrease luminance.* In fact, luminance may increase, on average, across the entire transmitting surface. This action also negates the view benefit of window surfaces.

ILLUMINANCES

Illuminances are partially responsible for luminances. As a design goal, then, illuminances are important. By establishing illuminance design goals, the designer assures appropriate task contrast. The Illuminating Engineering Society has established an elaborate method for determining illuminance design goals. This system is quite flexible, responding to almost any visual task, speed and accuracy requirements, and occupants' ages, but it is

Table 2–5.
Basic interior illuminance classifications.

Classification	Illuminance target[1,2]	Task
Low	10 to 20 footcandles/ 100 to 200 lux	• Circulation • Facial recognition • Casual reading • Storage • Reading VDT • Dining
Medium	30 to 50 footcandles/ 300 to 500 lux	• Reading/writing paper documents of high contrast • Conference participation
High	50 to 100 footcandles/ 500 to 1000 lux	• Reading/writing paper documents of small print or low contrast • Some drafting

[1] Target value is to be achieved on the plane of the task.
[2] Values are to be maintained over time.

necessarily somewhat cumbersome. Because the IES Illuminance Selection Procedure can be quite time-consuming, many designers believe it is the only criterion necessary for lighting design (these designers equate time expended figuring out criteria to the importance of the criteria). As this text has already shown, many other design goals are as important as illuminance, or are even more important than it is.

For purposes of this presentation, there are basically three task classifications: low, medium, and high illuminance. Table 2–5 indicates the illuminance ranges that can be considered appropriate for each classification. Obviously, many other classifications occur. The designer should refer to the latest *IES Handbook Application Volume* for complete illuminance classifications and target selection procedures.

CHAPTER THREE

DESIGN DEVELOPMENT: LIGHT SOURCES

INTRODUCTION

The concept development phase should not be burdened with preconceived notions of what the lighting hardware should or could be for a given area or space. The design development phase includes research, searching, innovation, and collection of definitive equipment and details that may meet the needs, wants, and wishes established during concept development. Concept development, then, represents the "wishful thinking" stage and design development the "realization" stage of a project. This chapter discusses hardware that is generally available to meet a great variety of concepts developed by many designers. Obviously there is room here for modifying, customizing, or innovating. Such options sometimes are most effective and desirable, as they may satisfy more needs, desires, and wishes than can off-the-shelf equipment.

Lighting equipment, whether standard or custom, is the basis of the design development stage. Light sources (lamps), luminaires, room surfaces, and light distribution devices are all included as equipment that comprises the lighting system. This chapter provides a thorough review of the light sources that ought to be considered during design development. Chapter 4 provides a review of luminaires in which these light sources can be most effective. Design development is not complete until the designer has some idea of the appropriateness of the proposed equipment in meeting the concept development criteria; so design tools are introduced in Chapter 5 as still another step in the design development process and as a finalization step in the contract document process.

LIGHT GENERATION AND CONTROL TOOLS

A host of off-the-shelf lighting products is available to help the designer to achieve the design goals. Sometimes, however, it is necessary to modify products or develop custom products in order to meet all the design goals that one wishes to satisfy. This chapter will present the most readily available off-the-shelf products, and will discuss the attributes that should be considered when product modification or custom products are required.

This discussion is intended to act as a base of generic product knowledge so that the designer can make preliminary selections to meet design concepts. Specific manufacturers' products (lamps, luminaires, ballasts, controls) exist to serve specific needs. While learning about these products, the designer probably will find additional ways of achieving design concepts. Such knowledge can only be gained over time, as one assimilates collections of literature and products and makes field observations. Therefore, it is important to understand that one should always define the visual effect desired and then embark on a search for equipment that can help create that effect. It is inappropriate and poor design practice first to select equipment and then to attempt to justify that selection by working backward to see what effect can be achieved.

AVAILABLE LIGHT SOURCES

A variety of light sources are available to the designer. Some occur in nature, while others are man-made. The term artificial light, however, is a misnomer; all light, or visible electromagnetic energy, is natural. Visible electromagnetic energy is more consistent and reliable when generated by man-made devices, whereas natural sources of light produce visible energy in varying amounts and in varying mixes over time (hence the great differences in quality and quantity of daylight, for example). Temporal changes in light quantity and quality, though preferred by occupants and regarded as stimulating, can be detrimental to their sustained visual performance. Therefore, very careful analyses of both daylighting and electric lighting are necessary to achieve comfortable, satisfactory, and productive work environments.

DAYLIGHT SOURCES

The sun and the sky are the two daylight sources available to designers. Luminances introduced at a window from the sun and/or the sky can be so much higher than other surfaces' luminances within the room, that one or several of the following may occur:

- Distraction
- Direct glare
- Reflected glare
- Veiling reflections
- Transient adaptation

Of course, nearly all people "like daylight"; so how can the designer effectively provide daylight? First, define daylight. People who use windowed spaces generally do not care very much about the origination (generation) of illuminance; that is, most people do not really care how footcandles are generated in their environment. However, most people do want a view, and these same people use the terms view and daylight synonymously. Including lots of windows and subsequently providing diffuse, non-image-preserving shade devices will severely limit their view, resulting in dissatisfied occupants.

Second, simply providing large zones of raw uncontrolled daylight in a space is not effective daylight design. Managing daylight to provide at the least a view, and at the most a view *and* illuminance *and* environmental luminance, is the key to successful daylighting. Using daylight media (monitors, clerestories, skylights, windows) with appropriate orientation, shading control, and room surface finishes along with proper electric lighting is necessary to achieve cost- and occupant-effective daylighting.

Daylight media that might be used in workspaces are listed in Table 3–1 with a variety of respective design goals. Because many workspaces today involve reading and identifying electronic-based tasks (using VDTs, LED display gauges, electronic typewriters, and calculators), daylight quality and quantity requirements are different from those of the recent past. In general, a daylight design should provide for large areas of moderate-to-low uniform brightnesses. This means not only controlling the daylight media with appropriate glass and shading, but also controlling room surface finishes and electric lighting with great care. With our continuing concern for energy conservation, daylight media are bound to become more important in new and renovation design.

The orientation for daylight media depends on the geographic and topographic location. Generally, the more diffuse the daylight is, the less cumbersome the control technique and the more uniform the brightness of the daylight media. Brightness uniformity and brightness limits are critical if glare and VDT imaging problems are to be minimized. Nevertheless, diffuse north skylight luminances can still exceed 3,000 footlamberts, which is more than ten times the luminance limits set for indirect lighting by the Illuminating Engineering Society (IES) VDT Guidelines. Therefore, shade

Table 3–1.
Daylight media for workspaces.[1]

Media	Design Goals		Surface Finish Tones		More appropriate electric light options[2]
	Orientation in order of preference	Most appropriate control technique	Walls	Ceiling	
Monitors	North East West South	• Low-transmission glass (30–50%) • Architectural baffles • Architectural set-backs • Overhangs and light shelves	Medium to light (30–55%)	Light (70–80%)	• Indirect • Indirect/direct
Clerestories	North East West South	• Low-transmission glass (30–50%) • Architectural baffles • Architectural set-backs • Overhangs and light shelves	Medium to light (30–55%)	Light (70–80%)	• Indirect • Indirect/direct

Skylights (continuous, relatively large)	North East West South	Medium (35%)	Light (70–80%)	• Extremely low-transmission glass (around 2%) • Architectural baffles • Frit pattern glass • Blinds • Solar shades • Deep wells	• Indirect • Indirect/direct • Direct
Windows (continuous, relatively large)	North East West South	Light (55%)	Light (70–80%)	• Very low-transmission glass (around 10%) • Frit pattern glass • Solar shades • Blinds • Significant overhangs with lightly colored ground cover	• Indirect • Indirect/direct • Direct (wall washing necessary to balance window brightness)

[1] Less stringent requirements apply to more casual, transient-type spaces where glare is not a significant concern, or where the drama of the view or the sky is paramount.

[2] All are with photocell/zoned controls.

control techniques are advisable even for north-oriented daylight media. The control techniques range from simply using low-transmission glass, usually tinted gray or bronze, to overhangs, shelves, and solar shades. Low-transmission glass, while allowing an unobstructed view of the outdoors usually will alter the color of the view and of the incoming daylight. With gray-tinted glass, the exterior view appears grayed and dull, and it always seems that the sky is cloudy. The incoming daylight has a stark, cool appearance with gray glass. Bronze-tinted glass, while also skewing colors, seems more acceptable, as the exterior scene looks somewhat rosy, and incoming light has a warmer, more skin-flattering color. Newer, low-emissivity (Low-E) glass tends to provide an improved-color view of the exterior and improved-color incoming daylight.

Frit pattern glass has increased in popularity recently, as the technique has been perfected by PPG. Frit is a ceramic coating that actually is part of the glass and thus is permanent. The frit patterns can vary significantly, from dot patterns to horizontal lines reminiscent of venetian blinds, while still preserving the image beyond. When used in conjunction with low-transmision glass, frit pattern glass can reduce light transmission by as much as 98 percent and still provide an acceptable exterior view in large-scale applications.

Solar shades also provide a reasonable way to reduce daylight transmission and preserve the view. A better-known trade name is Mecho Shade. These shades generally are made of a woven fiberglass fabric that permits a view as well as varying degrees of light transmission. Solar shades generally are motor-driven and controlled by a photocell. It is necessary periodically to clean both the solar shades and the glass.

Low-transmission glass, frit pattern glass, and photocell-controlled solar shades are very appropriate daylight control techniques for large areas used by many people. On the other hand, more independently controlled, smaller-scale daylight control techniques such as horizontal or vertical blinds and drapes can be very problematic for large areas used by many individuals. A horizontal blind properly set for one person may cause severe VDT imaging problems for someone working nearby. Of particular concern are vertical blinds and drapes. A vertical blind set properly for one side of a room is inevitably set improperly for the other side, unless set in the closed position. Once a drape is opened just a slight bit, the potential exists for serious glare and VDT imaging problems. Hence, these two techiques should be reserved for single occupancy rooms.

Where daylight media are used extensively in workspaces, finishes of wall and ceiling surfaces should be matte in order to avoid harsh, glary reflections. The walls should have a minimum reflectance of 30 percent, and the ceilings should have a minimum reflectance of 70 percent. These reflectances allow the daylight to interreflect within the room, providing more efficient use of that light source. Also, these reflectances allow the designer to balance the brightness of the reflecting surfaces with the potentially high brightnesses of the daylight media plane (e.g., a window wall). Balanced brightnesses lead to better visual comfort and reduced VDT imaging.

The balancing of daylight media brightnesses with other room surface brightnesses is best achieved by uniformly lighting the ceiling and walls. Hence, indirect or indirect combined with direct ambient electric lighting can be quite appropriate.

Finally, use discretion and caution when designing for daylighting. There is no "free" light. To properly control incoming daylight and to properly balance room surface brightnesses, reasonable expenditures of capital will be required. The beaming of sunlight, although possible with mirrors and fiber optic techniques, is neither straightforward nor as yet cost-effective for workspaces. Also, the design fees can be substantial if one undertakes the design of extensive beaming techniques.

ELECTRIC LIGHT SOURCES

There are four general families of electric light sources: incandescent, cold cathode, fluorescent, and high intensity discharge (HID). These families of sources provide the palette from which most lighting designers choose lamps. Incandescent and cold cathode lamps serve primarily as decorative and accent sources for most commercial workplaces, and are used as general lighting, accent, and decorative sources in conference, hospitality, and residential settings. Fluorescent lamps are used primarily as general lighting sources for commercial workplaces, and as decorative sources in commercial workplace, conference, and hospitality settings. HID lamps are used almost exclusively for most commercial outdoor lighting applications, with some limited application in commercial workplaces as general or accent lighting.

Certainly, as manufacturers continue lamp development, and as designers become increasingly innovative in meeting a host of lighting criteria, we should see broader uses of all lamp types; that is, fluorescent lamp use is likely to increase in residential, conference, and hospitality applications, while HID lamps probably will gain in popularity in interior environments. Incandescent lamps are likely to be used only in areas requiring decorative sparkle or very low light-output sources. Table 3–2 outlines the four general lamp families (incandescent, cold cathode, fluorescent, and HID) and their respective operating characteristics.

INCANDESCENT LAMPS

Incandescence is light emission from a heated object. In a typical incandescent lamp, an electric current passes through a tungsten filament, heating

Table 3–2.
Four general lamp families and operating characteristics.

Characteristics	Incandescent family	Cold cathode family	Fluorescent family	HID family (mercury vapor and metal halide)[2]
Advantages	• Low initial cost • No auxiliary equipment[1] • Operable over wide range of ambient temps • Easily dimmed • Excellent control • Excellent color rendering • Instant on	• Small size • Formed to any shape • Many colors • Rather easily dimmed • Low glare potential • Long life	• High efficiency • Long life • Low heat output • Excellent color rendering available • Reduced glare potential • Large-area lighting • Instant on	• High efficiency • Moderate life • Good color rendering available • High lumen packages for large-area floodlighting or focusing
Disadvantages	• Low efficiency • High heat output • Short life • Failure due to physical shock • High operating cost • Significant glare potential	• Large noisy transformer • Relatively high initial cost • Inconsistent quality (local manufacturers) • High voltage cabling	• High initial cost • Auxiliary equipment required • Temperature-sensitive • Expensive to dim	• Inconsistent color lamp-to-lamp • Poor lumen maintenance • Bulkiness • Large noisy ballasts • High initial cost • Very difficult to dim • Significant glare potential • Warm-up time required • Flicker potential
Color rendering	• Excellent • 90–95 CRI • Familiar to people	• Fair	• Poor to excellent • Available in 75–90 CRI	• Poor to good • Available in 65–70 CRI • 3100K

Table 3–2.   (Continued)

Characteristics	Incandescent family	Cold cathode family	Fluorescent family	HID family (mercury vapor and metal halide)[2]
	• Renders skin tones well		• Tri-phosphors render skin tones very well	sources render skin tones well
Color temperature	• 2700 to 3100K	• 2800, 3500, 4500, 6500, 8500K	• 2700, 3100, 3500, 4100, 5000K	• 3100, 4200, 5300K

[1] Low voltage incandescent lamps require transformers.

[2] Standard high pressure sodium is not considered appropriate for most architectural applications. Philips' and GE's new high CRI HPS lamps may be appropriate, however, for such applications.

the filament to the point of producing visible radiation. Generally, in standard household incandescent lamps, only 10 to 12 percent of the radiation produced is visible, the remainder being thermal (heat). Incandescent lamps are much better heat sources than light sources, causing a cooling load concern in commercial buildings. Incandescent lamps have excellent color rendering, with CRI's of 90 to 95. A CRI of 100 is considered perfect. People compare all other lamps to incandescent lamps. Color temperatures of incandescent lamps range from 2700K to about 3100K. Color temperature is degree of whiteness, with zero K as black.

Incandescent lamps remain the most popular lamps in the United States. Their almost exclusive use in residences, along with the perception that these lamps look best and create the best environments, contributes to their high usage. Increasing pressure from state and federal agencies and the economy, however, will likely force a major change in incandescent lamp usage by the twenty-first century, unless lamp manufacturers implement new techniques to increase incandescent lamp efficiencies significantly.

There are four basic bulb types of the line voltage class of lamps and three basic bulb types of the low voltage class, which together make up the palette of incandescent lamps used in nearly all built environment applications. Note that the word "bulb" is used to describe the actual envelope shape of the lamp. The word "lamp" refers to the entire assembly of bulb, filament, and base. There are four incandescent lamp technologies, which can and are being applied to both classes of incandescent lamps. Table 3–3 indicates the relative efficiency, cost, life, and whiteness of the four technologies and lists the respective bulb types to which these technologies are applied. Table 3–4 outlines typical application characteristics for incandescent bulb types.

Table 3–3.
Incandescent lamp technologies.

Attributes	Tungsten filament	Quartz enclosure with tungsten filament and halogen cycle	Tungsten filament with halogen cycle	Infrared dichroic coating
Relative efficiency	1	2	3	4
Relative cost	1	3	2	4
Relative life	1	4	3	3
Degree of whiteness (color temperature)	1	3	3	4
Available bulb types	A, R, PAR, tubular, 12VPAR, miniature	PAR, tubular, miniature	TB,* PAR, 12VPAR	PAR, tubular

1 = lowest
4 = highest
*Shape resembles "A" but is modified; see Figure 3–2.

For most architectural lighting, the significant incandescent lamp technologies are, in order of efficiency (from least efficient to most efficient):
tungsten filament (tungsten), quartz-halogen (quartz), tungsten-halogen
(halogen), and infrared dichroic coating (IR). All of these incandescent lamp
technologies allow for convenient dimming. The dimming of incandescent
lamps will decrease the color temperature (the lamp appearance being more
yellow to yellow-orange when dimmed) and shift the lamp's spectral power
distribution characteristics. That is, the light emitted from the lamps has
more red and infrared components so that blues and greens under dimmed
incandescent lighting tend to appear less intense.

Incandescent lamp life generally is increased significantly with dimming.
Figure 3–1 shows the exponential relationship between lamp life and dimming (voltage reduction). Reducing voltage slightly (e.g., by 10%) results in
a significant increase in life (nearly 400% in this case). However, this increase is not achieved without sacrifice (the light output is reduced by 30%
in this case).

Quartz halogen and tungsten halogen lamps, while dimmable, do have
some limitations with respect to life and proper lamp function when
dimmed. The halogen cycle works to minimize the effect of the process
inherent in heated tungsten—vaporization of the tungsten. In standard tung-

Table 3–4.
Incandescent bulb types and application characteristics.

Application characteristics	A	R	PAR	Quartz tubular	Low voltage PAR	Low voltage MR	Low voltage miniature
Low general direct lighting	•	•			•		
Moderate general direct lighting	•	•	•	•			
High general direct lighting			•	•			
Low-to-moderate general indirect lighting				•			
Soft accent		•					
Decorative accent	•				•	•	•
Dramatic accent			•		•	•	
Dramatic accent with minimum glare					•		
Grazing wall washing (walls ≤ 9′)		2	4				
Frontal wall washing (walls ≤ 9′)	1	2	3	4			
Grazing wall washing (walls ≤ 15′)		1	3				
Frontal wall washing (walls ≤ 15′)			2	4			
Transformer required					•	•	•
Dimmable	•	•	•	•	•	•	•
Protective shields often required*				•		•	
Relative lamp cost (low, moderate, high)	Lo	Lo	Mo	Hi	Hi	Hi	Mo

1 = fair
2 = good
3 = better
4 = best
*Glass lens or mesh screen required; some MR lamps have a built-in glass shield.

sten lamps, the tungsten slowly evaporates from the filament and collects on the bulb wall. The result is bulb wall darkening and finally lamp failure—the filament eventually evaporates enough that it becomes structurally unstable, or it entirely evaporates. In halogen lamps, the halogen prevents the tungsten from depositing on the bulb wall, causing it to redeposit back onto the filament and thus giving lamp life ratings of 2,000 to 6,000 hours. This cycle only works under relatively high temperatures; so dimming to certain levels (say more than 10% below normal voltage) will keep the halogen cycle from operating sufficiently. However, an occasional increase of the voltage to full normal will reactivate the halogen cycle. The designer should consult with lamp manufacturers for the latest information on halogen dimming.

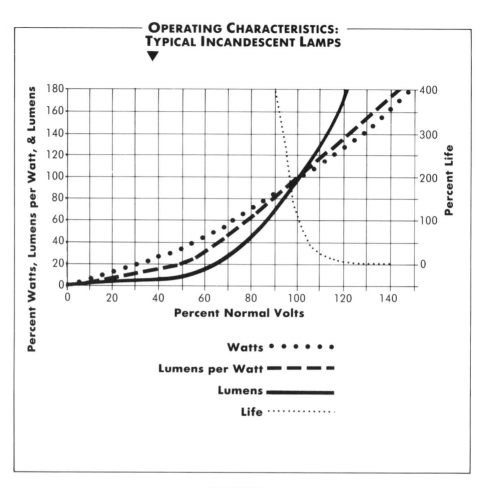

FIGURE 3–1

The low voltage class of lamps is so named because of the very low voltages required to power these lamps. Most of the architectural applications of low voltage lamps require 12 volts, with 5.5-volt and 24-volt lamps used to a lesser extent. The lower voltage permits very tiny filament designs that approach the theoretical "point" source of light. Point sources are the easiest source to control optically, permitting the development of pinpoint beams of light; hence they are used nearly exclusively as decorative and objet d'art accents. They are especially effective for highlighting glass or small merchandise, or for distinct areas or segments of artwork or merchandise. These lamps require transformers, which are available in either electromagnetic or electronic versions. Although bulkier and hotter, the electromagnetic transformers generally are quieter at full output, easier to dim, quieter when dimmed, and generally more reliable.

Low voltage lamps usually should not be used for general lighting. Two exceptions could be the 12-volt PAR 36 lamp and the 24-volt miniature lamp, discussed later in this section. These lamps usually are not cost-effective for large-area, general lighting or for large-area highlighting.

In an effort to improve incandescent lamp life or efficiency, some lamp manufacturers have used diodes, which are devices that convert alternating current (AC) to direct current (DC). Generally, such devices can be used to increase lamp life, and, in conjunction with other technologies, diodes also can be used to provide significant energy savings. Unfortunately, there are several significant drawbacks in using diode-type lamps. Lamps with diodes are continuously pulsed, on/off, very quickly. Some people see this pulsing as a flicker. This effect is particularly bothersome in static work environments without much daylight or with little other-than-diode electric lighting. The effect is especially noticeable with peripheral vision. New technologies are now available that allow manufacturers to achieve longer life and more efficient lamps without the use, and consequent disadvantages, of diodes.

The A Bulb Type

The A lamp is so designated because of its arbitrary shape (see Figure 3–2). Although the lamp technology has certainly changed, the bulb shape is quite similar to that of the first incandescent lamps of general use in the late nineteenth century. A lamps are available in clear bulb envelopes or as diffuse lamps. Depending on the country of manufacture, the diffuse lamps will have either a white coating or an etch frost on the inside of the bulb. A lamps are made of blown glass and cannot withstand direct exposure to rain and snow.

A lamps usually carry a numerical designation, such as A19. The number (e.g., 19) indicates the diameter of the bulb envelope in eighths of an inch (e.g., $1\frac{9}{8}$ inches or $2\frac{3}{8}$ inches). Dimensional characteristics that are important for many incandescent lamps are shown in Figure 3–3. This information is particularly useful in the proper specification of luminaires and corresponding lamps, and for the appropriate ongoing maintenance of an installation. A luminaire that has been designed around the physical characteristics of an A19 lamp is unlikely to perform as well optically with an A21 lamp. In fact, the A21 lamp may not physically fit the luminaire designed around an A19 lamp. Typical A lamps are A19 and A21.

Because they are used for general lighting in table, floor, wall sconce, or recessed luminaires, A lamps are considered "general service." They are used where low levels (20 footcandles/200 lux or less) of ambient light are desirable. These lamps are available in a variety of colors from pink to blue to white, with pink being especially popular where skin tone enhancement

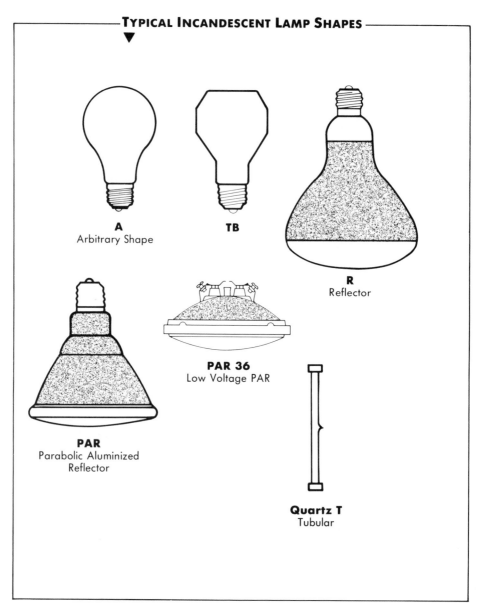

TYPICAL INCANDESCENT LAMP SHAPES

A
Arbitrary Shape

TB

R
Reflector

PAR
Parabolic Aluminized
Reflector

PAR 36
Low Voltage PAR

Quartz T
Tubular

FIGURE 3–2

and a casual atmosphere are desirable. The efficiency of A lamps is among the lowest of incandescents, at 9 to 19 lumens per watt. The A lamp is the least expensive lamp available today, but is also the shortest-lived. Typical A lamp life ratings are 750 to 1,000 hours. Although such poor life and efficiency may be acceptable to a homeowner who uses only a few lamps for a few hours a day, this lamp is generally shunned in commercial applications.

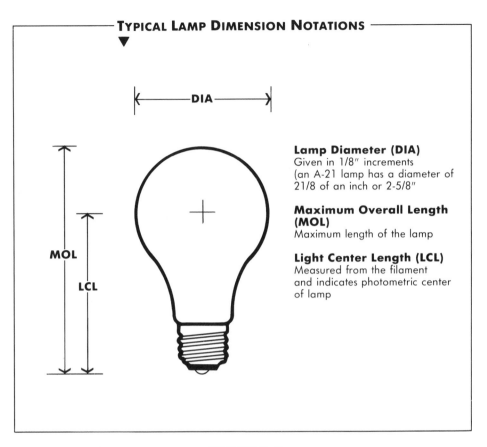

TYPICAL LAMP DIMENSION NOTATIONS

Lamp Diameter (DIA)
Given in 1/8″ increments
(an A-21 lamp has a diameter of
21/8 of an inch or 2-5/8″

Maximum Overall Length (MOL)
Maximum length of the lamp

Light Center Length (LCL)
Measured from the filament
and indicates photometric center
of lamp

FIGURE 3–3

The TB lamp, so designated because the bulb houses tungsten-halogen technology, is similar in shape and function to the A lamp, with an efficiency of nearly 20 lumens per watt and an averge life of 2,000 hours. This lamp is well suited for commercial applications where incandescent lighting is desirable without the life and efficiency characteristics of traditional A lamps.

For A and TB lamps to provide efficient controllable light, they must be used in luminaires containing reflector or refractor optics. Figure C16 illustrates a TB-lamp downlight application.

The R Bulb Type

R lamps have a bulb shape and an internal silver coating that make them somewhat more effective in directing light than A lamps. "R" stands for reflector lamp, the shape of which is shown in Figure 3–2. The bottom of the lamp (the large end) is either clear glass or etch-frost glass, depending on whether a spotlight (SP) or a floodlight (FL) beam distribution is desired. Like A lamps, R lamps are made of blown glass, are relatively fragile, and cannot withstand rain or snow (the glass bulb will shatter if the lamp is energized and exposed to water).

As in many lamp specificatons, the numerical designation with the R (e.g., R40) indicates the diameter of the largest portion of the bulb envelope in eighths of an inch (e.g., $^{40}/_8$ inches or 5 inches). Typical line voltage R lamps are R20, R30, and R40.

R lamps are appropriate for ambient lighting in spaces with 8- to 10-foot ceiling heights. They are used where low to moderate levels of light (30 footcandles/300 lux or less) are desirable. These lamps, particularly the spot versions, are also appropriate for soft-edged art highlighting and wall wash lighting. Figure 3–4 shows a rather typical architectural detail using R lamps for a grazing wall wash. This is particularly effective with specular surfaces (e.g., shiny writing surfaces, polished wood, and stone) under 9 feet in height. R lamps are available in a variety of colors.

Although efficiency ranges from about 7 to 13 lumens per watt, R lamps generally are more effective in lighting specific objects or surfaces than are A lamps because of their light distribution characteristics. Put another way, the A lamp may be more efficient overall in generating light, but that light is dispersed in all directions, while the light from an R lamp is concentrated effectively in a specific direction.

The average rated life for most R lamps is 2,000 hours, making them more attractive for selected applications in commercial installations.

PAR Bulb Type

PAR is an acronym for parabolic aluminized reflector, which describes the shape and type of the bulb (see Figure 3–2). Made of cast glass and a precisely formed parabolic internal reflector, PAR lamps generally can withstand direct contact with rain and snow; so they are popular, although unsightly, as household security floodlights. The bottom of the PAR lamp (large end) usually is clear, partially stippled, or fully stippled for a beam distribution of narrow spot (NSP), spot, or flood, respectively.

Like R and A lamps, PAR lamps have a numerical suffix designating the lamp diameter in eighths of an inch. Typical PAR lamps are PAR 20, PAR 30, and PAR 38. The use of PAR lamps is appropriate where moderate to high levels (20 to 60 footcandles/200 to 600 lux) of ambient lighting are desirable in spaces with 10- to 25-foot ceilings. The spot and narrow spot lamps are appropriate for dramatic accenting (see Figure C14). PAR lamps also are desirable for washing walls up to 15 feet in height, particularly when used in slots along the wall for grazing specular walls (e.g., granite,

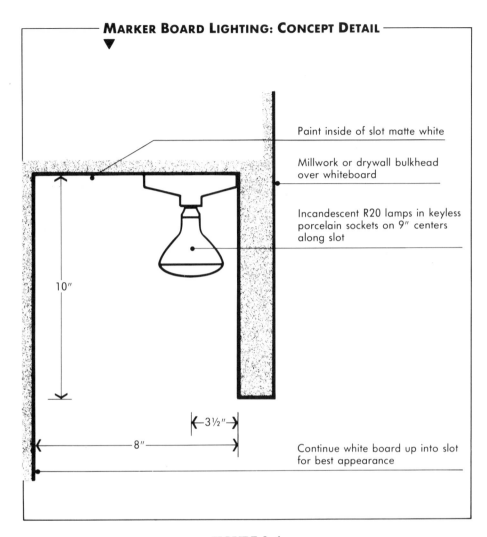

MARKER BOARD LIGHTING: CONCEPT DETAIL

Paint inside of slot matte white

Millwork or drywall bulkhead over whiteboard

Incandescent R20 lamps in keyless porcelain sockets on 9″ centers along slot

10″

←3½″→

8″

Continue white board up into slot for best appearance

FIGURE 3–4

marble; see Figure C16). Figure 3–5 illustrates a typical PAR-lamp incandescent wall slot architectural detail.

PAR lamps have efficiencies in the range of 10 to 14 lumens per watt, but this is a very misleading statistic. Precise beam control allows for significant efficiency in the distribution of the light to a specific surface or object, but this same control results in harsh, potentially glary light. For spaces where people will be mostly static, PAR-lamp general lighting can be unsatisfactory. The lamp life ranges from 2,000 hours for tungsten to 6,000 hours for quartz-halogen PAR lamps. GE is perfecting an infrared dichroic coating for tungsten filaments which promises to nearly double the efficiency of PAR lamps.

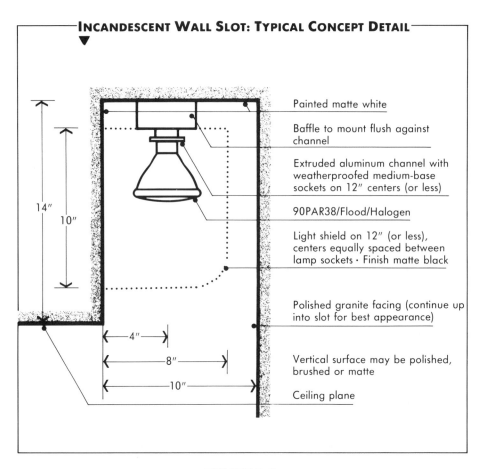

INCANDESCENT WALL SLOT: TYPICAL CONCEPT DETAIL

Painted matte white

Baffle to mount flush against channel

Extruded aluminum channel with weatherproofed medium-base sockets on 12″ centers (or less)

90PAR38/Flood/Halogen

Light shield on 12″ (or less), centers equally spaced between lamp sockets · Finish matte black

Polished granite facing (continue up into slot for best appearance)

Vertical surface may be polished, brushed or matte

Ceiling plane

14″
10″
4″
8″
10″

FIGURE 3–5

PAR lamps are available in a variety of colors, with either a standard colored-lens arrangement or a dichroic filter arrangement. The dichroic-filtered lamps generally provide a more saturated color of light than the colored-lens types.

Quartz T Bulb Type

The quartz-tubular bulb type is so named because the bulb is made of quartz and shaped like a tube (cylinder). These lamps operate on the halogen cycle. This feature combined with their tiny size (for precise light control by external reflectors) necessitates the use of the hard, high-temperature bulb material quartz. Quartz T lamps are available in either clear or frosted bulbs, depending on the degree of control, or feathering, required. These lamps are typically a few inches in overall length; and, numerically designated like other incandescent lamps, a T4 lamp is ⅛ (½) inch in diameter.

Quartz tubular lamps are appropriate where moderate to high levels (20 to 60 footcandles/200 to 600 lux) of ambient lighting are desirable in spaces with 10- to 25-foot ceilings. They are particulary effective in luminaires expressly designed for wall wash lighting, or wall or art area lighting (see Figure C3).

Because these lamps are so small and yet produce great amounts of light, they potentially are significantly more harsh and glary than A, R, and PAR lamps. They generally are used in downlights in large, high-ceiling spaces; or in torchieres providing indirect light; or in tightly controlled wall wash luminaires where direct view of the light is minimized; or in precisely focused theater-like accent lights.

The lamp efficiency is about 18 to 20 lumens per watt, with the average lamp life ranging from 750 to 2,000 hours.

Quartz lamps run at very high operating temperatures. At times, these lamps can fail rather violently, exploding hot quartz and filament fragments; so they should be used only in shielded or protected housings. This may require glass protective lenses or fine wire mesh screens over the luminaire aperture.

Other Line Voltage Bulb Types

There are many other bulb types of line voltage incandescent lamps, constituting a small part of the architectural lighting market compared to the A, R, PAR, and quartz T types. Although these other lamps are relatively quite expensive, they do have niche applications, as described in Table 3–5. Figure 3–6 illustrates the bulb shapes of these lamps.

The ER lamp is probably the most overrated and certainly the most improperly used incandescent lamp. A response to the energy crises of the 1970s, the ER lamp was intended only as a retrofit for then-existing deep, inefficient recessed downlights. Ellipsoidal reflectors are quite effective at collecting light and redirecting it into a dispersed pattern at some distance in front of the light source; so, in deep downlights, an ER lamp can be used to redirect light into a dispersing pattern below the ceiling plane. The result is a significant overall efficiency increase for the luminaire. Unfortunately, however, many purchasing agents and maintenance people think ER lamps will save energy in almost every incandescent lamp application, but this simply is not true. In fact, the misuse of these lamps usually results in lamps that actually extend below the ceiling from downlights, creating an unsightly appearance and increased glare.

Table 3–5.
Applications of niche incandescent bulb types.

Bulb types	Application benefits
G (globe)	• Pleasant appearance as bare bulb • Low brightness • General diffuse light provided in all directions • Popular as "Hollywood mirror light" • Decorative use
S (sign)	• Long life • Various colors • Small size • Low wattage • Decorative use
CA (candle)	• Tiny size • Low wattage • Decorative use
ER (ellipsoidal reflector)	• Improved control for deep downlights • Functional use
A/SB (silver bowl)	• Low glare • Pleasant appearance • "Indirect quality" of light provided • Decorative use

Low Voltage Miniature Bulb Type

Low voltage miniature lamps, long used as indicator lamps in various appliances and cars, now are being used in architectural applications where only tiny architectural details can be used to accommodate light. Small-scale coves and ceiling molding details can house the miniature lamps and sockets, which are generally no wider and no higher than ¾ inch, and come in almost any length up to a practical limit that varies with lamp wattage, voltage, spacing, and transformer capacity. While typically producing only 3 to 5 lumens per watt, these lamps have lives of from 5,000 to 50,000 hours. Figure 3–7 shows the low voltage miniature lamp in a typical cove application.

Low Voltage PAR 36 Bulb Type

For years, PAR 36 low voltage lamps were the mainstay of pinpoint architectural accent lighting. Twelve-volt lamps are available in narrow spot (NSP), flood (FL), and wide flood (WFL) versions. The 5.5-volt "bullet beam" lamp

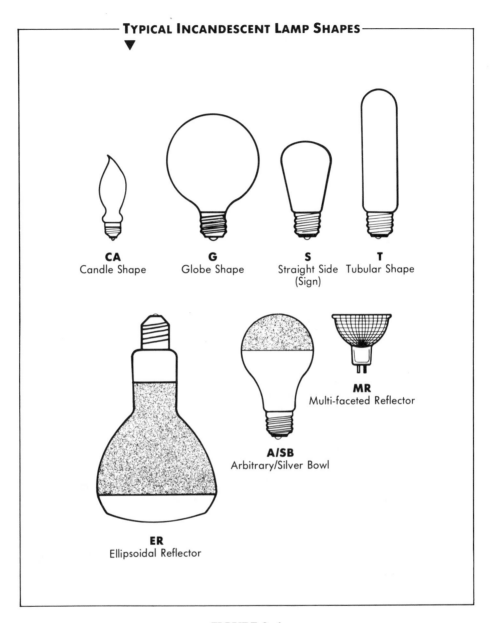

FIGURE 3–6

is available as a bullet beam—an extremely narrow spot lamp. Figure 3–8 illustrates the effect of the 5.5-volt bullet beam.

These lamps are similar in concept to their line voltage counterparts, the PAR 38 lamps. Yet because of the small filament, which is a result of the reduced voltage, these lamps have a flatter profile than the PAR 38 lamps. To eliminate potentially hazardous use in line voltage sockets, PAR 36

FIGURE 3–7.
The ceiling coves in the project are lighted with 5-watt, low voltage incandescent indicator lamps on 3-inch centers. These lamps allow for a very shallow cove design. Note also the use of MR-16 low voltage accents to highlight the architectural columns (see the MR bulb type discussion later in this chapter). Photo courtesy GE Company.

FIGURE 3–8.
Accenting of the tabernacle in the upper left and the altar in the foreground is accomplished with 5.5-volt, bullet beam lamps in adjustable accent luminaires. The bullet beam is both intense and very well controlled, highlighting only small areas with little or no direct lamp glare. Photo courtesy INAI Studio; photo credit: Hedrich Blessing.

lamps are not screw-in lamps, but rather have screw-terminals at their base, for direct wiring to the low voltage line.

The PAR bulb and the low voltage filament help produce good beam control, but it is necessary to put a cap over the lens side of the filament for precise optical beam control. This filament cap has the added benefit of not allowing a direct view of the filament, resulting in a very low-brightness light source from most viewing angles.

The color of light produced by most low voltage PAR 36 lamps has a somewhat yellow-white quality, similar to that of standard voltage tungsten lamps. The NSP lamp and the 5.5-volt bullet beam lamp produce a neutral white color of light, amplified by their inherent light intensity.

PAR 36 lamps provide a very effective means of producing dramatic lighting effects while expending a minimum of electric energy. Note that, because of their extreme beam control, PAR 36 lamps do not provide any spill or "ambient" light, only lighting surfaces toward which they are aimed.

Low Voltage MR Bulb Type

The MR type of lamp became quite popular within just a few years after being introduced. Traditionally, these lamps were used in slide projectors, and they still serve that purpose, among others. "MR" designates multifaceted reflector, as the highly polished reflectors in these lamps are arranged in discretized segments for superior control (see Figure 3–6). In order to produce a maximum amount of light in the smallest available area, these lamps use the quartz-halogen technology operating on 12 volts, and they have no filament cap. Thus they are inherently glary sources and must be used with great care.

Appropriate applications of MR lamps include lighting objets d'art and small artwork, as well as small area merchandise accenting. Their size (MR 16–2-inch diameter; MR 11–1⅜-inch diameter) makes them visually unobtrusive and allows the designer to hide them in architectural pockets and niches. Recessed downlights that use MR lamps are usually only 4 to 5 inches in diameter, with an aperture of only 2 inches or so (see Figure 3–9).

Because these lamps are composed of quartz and run at very high operating temperatures, a protective lens or screen at the luminaire aperture is necessary to protect room occupants from hot glass and filament, should the lamp violently fail. Some of them are now available with an integral glass shield on the front of the lamp.

A dichroic film on the mirror reflector helps to extract infrared radiation from the lamp. This results in some red light escaping as well, leading to a very crisp white, slightly blue-white color of light. This is generally beneficial for highlighting merchandise and attracting attention; but without a straw or light-amber filter, MR lamps may not render wood tones the way

FIGURE 3–9.
This detail of the MR-16 accent lighting illustrated in Figure 3–7 shows the small aperture available with MR-16 lamp luminaires, as well as the intensity and effect of an MR-16 lamp. Photo courtesy GE Company.

most people are accustomed to seeing them under typical standard voltage incandescent lamps.

The MR class of lamps has been greatly misused. It appears that this lamp is actually being used in many applications simply for fashion purposes—because it is trendy—rather than for appropriate optical and visual characteristics.

Low Voltage Transformers

Low voltage lamps typically require 5.5, 12, or 24 volts. To achieve this, transformers must be used at the lamp or remotely. Using a remote transformer eliminates hardware from the luminaire and usually allows the operation of more than one lamp. Note that, depending on the power requirements, the main power wire size, and the distance from the transformer to the lamps, the lamps actually may operate at reduced voltage, appearing dim (in a phenomenon known as voltage drop).

Transformers that are used adjacent to lamps and are intended to operate just a single lamp usually are available in either an electromagnetic version (the old-style iron core with a continuous coil of wire around it) or an electronic version (solid state components). Each type has its benefits. The electromagnetic transformer is bulky and relatively heavy, but is also relatively quiet and easily dimmed. The electronic transfomer now is small and lightweight, but it can be quite noisy and is not very conveniently and quietly dimmed.

Low voltage transformers consume some energy just in the transforming process; for example, a 50-watt low voltage lamp and its associated transformer may draw 55 watts of power or more. This is a particularly important consideration in determining electrical loads and cooling loads.

When large, remote transformers are used (which could be 8 inches by 8 inches by 12 inches or larger), it is necesary to provide convenient access to them for repair or replacement. Sound isolation is desirable, as the larger transformers are more likely to hum. Because of a potentially significant heat buildup associated with the large transformers, their locations should be well-ventilated.

COLD CATHODE LAMPS

Cold cathode lamps are so named because of the use of a filament-like device known as a cathode at each lamp end. These cathodes, installed in a tubular glass structure usually filled with some sort of mercury, argon, or neon gas mixture, act to strike an electric arc from one end of the tube to another. Unlike many standard commercial/residential fluorescent lamps, which always retain a bit of electricity to keep the cathodes "warm" and ready for instant starting, cold cathode lamps rely solely on a large voltage surge to start the lamp. Cathodes are not prewarmed or hot, but are cold. This is an important distinction because cold cathode lamps thus require relatively high voltage transformers that have the potential to be noisy and require careful wiring/connecting by the installer. The term cold cathode is, at times, used interchangeably with neon. Technically, neon is a type of cold cathode lamp—filled with neon gas and typically very small in diameter.

Cold cathode lighting, initially developed as signage lighting in the early twentieth century, was a precursor to today's fluorescent lighting. Cold cathode lamps typically are three times as efficient as incandescent lamps, with life ratings that can be as high as 25,000 hours or more.

Typically, cold cathode tubing diameters, traditionally expressed in millimeters (25.4 mm = 1 inch), are 12 to 25 mm. Diameters of 15 mm and 18 mm are quite common. Such small-diameter lamps can be neatly tucked into small architectural coves, shelves, and niches. One such detail is shown in Figure 3–10. Repetition of the detail shown in this figure results in a series of coves of crisp blue-white light, as shown in Figure C3. Cold cathode lamps have the added benefit of being continuous "lines" of light that can be bent to almost any shape. Because these lamps are hand-made to order from stock tubes, which usually are 4 feet in length, the tubes can be molded end-to-end to 8- or 12-foot runs. The installation techniques developed for cold cathode lamps allow the designer to custom-design large runs of any length and give the appearance of an unbroken line of light. Figure C3 illustrates the effect of an unbroken line of light in an indirect cove application, while Figure C23 and C24 illustrate the same unbroken-line-of-light effect in a direct-view-of-the-lamp situation.

Cold Cathode Transformers

Cold cathode lamps require transformers for starting and operation. Because these transformers are of relatively high voltage, they must be out of reach for the casual occupant. At the same time, these transformers need to be easily accessible for electrical connections, replacement, or repair.

These high-voltage transformers have a tendency to hum or buzz. For this reason, they should be located in a sound-isolated compartment or area. Operating at these high voltages can cause heat buildup, so well-ventilated locations are a necessity. Finally, to minimize magnetic interference, hum, and potential code difficulties, transformers should be located as close to the cold cathode lamps as possible.

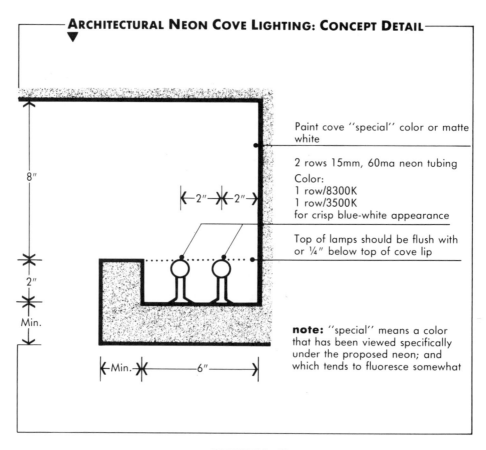

ARCHITECTURAL NEON COVE LIGHTING: CONCEPT DETAIL

Paint cove "special" color or matte white

2 rows 15mm, 60ma neon tubing
Color:
1 row/8300K
1 row/3500K
for crisp blue-white appearance

Top of lamps should be flush with or ¼" below top of cove lip

note: "special" means a color that has been viewed specifically under the proposed neon; and which tends to fluoresce somewhat

8"

2" 2"

2"
Min.

Min.   6"

FIGURE 3–10

Cold Cathode Light Output

The light output of cold cathode tubing depends on: (1) the glass tube color, if any; (2) the glass tube phosphor, if any; (3) the tube diameter; (4) the electric current, in milliamps (ma); and (5) the gas fill mixture in the tube. White light typically is produced with white phosphor-coated tubes filled with mercury or mercury and argon; clear tubes filled with mercury or mercury and argon typically produce blue-toned light; clear tubes filled with neon generally produce red-toned light; and white phosphor-coated tubes filled with neon tend to produce warm-toned white or pink-toned light.

Small-diameter tubes (12 and 15 mm) can be very bright, to the point of glare compared to larger-diameter tubes. The larger-diameter lamps, however, are more efficient generators of light. A low electric current, 30 ma, through the tubes results in a lower light output compared to 60 ma, and, for 25 mm tubing, 120 ma. A typical 4-foot segment of "white" (3500K) cold cathode tube 15 mm in diameter with 30 ma current will produce 520 lumens; and at 60 ma current, it will produce 920 lumens. Light output is also dependent on the ambient temperature of the environment in which cold cathode is to operate. Especially sensitive are tubes filled exclusively with mercury. At cold temperatures, below 50°F, the output of mercury-filled light sources is reduced. At freezing temperatures and lower, some mercury-filled cold cathode lamps may not start—they may not light up. Mixing argon with the mercury helps to minimize this effect. For outdoor applications in very cold environments, it is advisable to use only neon-filled tubing.

Cold cathode lamps are relatively easily dimmed.

Cold Cathode Color of Light

Cold cathode lamps not only offer the unique built-to-any-shape aspect, but these lamps can provide a rainbow—and then some—of colors for architectural lighting design. Yellow to green and blue and red are rather standard colors. Perhaps of more interest are recent experiments with various gas fills and phosphors and colored glass tubing. Peach, coral, lavender, pink, rose, and other more subtle shades of color are possible with cold cathode lamps. Innovations include recent applications of mixed-color tubing and multicolored "chips" or bits of glass and phosphor-coated glass inside the tubing.

Cold Cathode Fabrication

The key to the quality and reliability of any product lies in its manufacturing and installation. There are several nationally recognized manufacturers of architectural cold cathode (or neon); and there are many more local sign manufacturers, some of whom also provide architectural cold cathode. In either case, the supplier/manufacturer should be able to supply a resume of previous work, a sample product that can be illuminated, and references. Cold cathode tubes that are properly blown, vacuumed, sealed, and installed should operate in excess of 25,000 hours before requiring replacement. Transformers are likely to last 15,000 hours or so. When lamps do burn out, one should consider group-relamping the contiguous segment affected because a new lamp in the middle of a group of old lamps probably would look significantly different, in both output intensity and color, from the old lamps.

Cold Cathode Applications

Architectural cold cathode typically is used as either an image enhancement or a light source or both. Figure C23 shows an image enhancement use.

Bands of blue brick that serpentine along the building facade are redefined at night with blue cold cathode; using a clear tube presents a view of the blue brick during the day. In Figure C22, the exposed cold cathode is used as an image enhancer outlining the exterior walls of a room, while the architectural cathode tucked into coves inside the room acts as an ambient (general) light source. Figure C21 illustrates architectural cold cathode completely hidden from direct view by coves. In this case, not only is the light of sufficient quality and intensity to provide appropriate ambient light, but the cool-toned pale lavender color enhances the image of a very contemporary, architecturally dramatic space.

FLUORESCENT LAMPS

Fluorescence is light emission from an ultraviolet-radiated material (the phosphor coating—a white, powder-like substance). When phosphors are radiated or bombarded by ultraviolet light, they react by emitting visible light. Typically, 20 to 30 percent of the radiation produced is visible; the remainder is thermal. In a fluorescent lamp, the ultraviolet light is produced when gas in the tube is electrically charged. Like cold cathode lamps, fluorescent lamps have cathodes that strike an electric charge in the lamp. With fluorescent lamps, these cathodes require preliminary heating to ease the electric arc through the tube; thus fluorescent lamps generally are categorized as hot cathode lamps (the cathodes must be hot in order to strike the electric arc through the tube). Three types of hot cathode fluorescent lamps are now in use: (1) instant start, (2) preheat, and (3) rapid start. All fluorescent lamps require auxiliary electrical devices to provide the starting voltage and to limit the operating current. Sometimes all of these devices are mounted in a black box, or ballast, whereas at other times they consist of separate components—ballast and starter. The instant start lamps, while not requiring a starter device, need a significant voltage surge to start. For this reason these lamps traditionally require noisy ballasts and have a lower average life, compared to many of the preheat and rapid start lamps. Most lamps in use today are of the rapid start or preheat type.

Although fluorescent lamps are more than four times as efficient as incandescent lamps, they have not yet been generally accepted by homeowners. Nevertheless, the energy crisis, the lamps' commercial uses, new technologies affecting both color and efficiency, and their life and maintenance benefits have resulted in their growing use. This continually improving light source is becoming more and more appropriate for residential, commercial, and hospitality applications.

There are six basic types of preheat and rapid start fluorescent lamps: (1) standard T12; (2) improved efficiency T12; (3) improved efficiency T10; (4) improved efficiency T8; (5) high output; and (6) compact. These six lamp types will be referred to here as "fluorescent." Although other types of fluorescent lamps exist, these six types are the most appropriate and most widely considered for today's architectural lighting design. See Table 3–6 for general application characteristics of these fluorescent lamp types.

Fluorescent lamps generally are much longer-lived than incandescent lamps. Their typical average life ranges from 10,000 to 20,000 hours. A fluorescent lamp's life increases somewhat if on/off switching is kept to a minimum over the life. Increased switching causes cathodes to burn out prematurely. Fluorescent lamps generally operate considerably cooler than incandescent lamps. The lamps themselves are temperature-sensitive, with an optimum ambient temperature of 77°F around the lamp (bulb wall temperature of 100°F).

Fluorescent lamps generally can be operated in any orientation (vertical, horizontal, or in between) without any adverse effect on the color or the light output.

The 34-watt energy-saving fluorescent lamps are particulary sensitive to temperature. Using these lamps in air supply/return luminaires may lead to a reduced output and even a noticeable flicker.

In any environment below 60°F, fluorescent lamps are likely to operate at a reduced output. This condition occurs in buildings where nighttime

Table 3–6.
Fluorescent lamp types and typical application characteristics.

Application characteristics	Standard T12	Improved-efficiency T12	Improved-efficiency T10	Improved-efficiency T8	High output	Large compact	Small compact
Low general direct lighting							•
Moderate general direct lighting	•	•	•	•		•	
High general direct lighting	•	•	•	•	•	•	
Low-to-moderate general indirect lighting	•	•	•	•		•	
Moderate-to-high general indirect lighting	•	•	•	•	•	•	
Portable task lighting							•
Soft accent							•
Grazing wall washing (walls ≤ 10')		•	•	•	•	•	
Frontal wall washing (walls ≤ 10')						•	•
Ballast required	•	•	•	•	•	•	•
Easily dimmable	•	•		•			
Relative lamp cost (low, moderate, high)	Lo	Mo	Hi	Mo	Mo	Hi	Mo
Relative lamp/ballast/luminaire efficiency (low, moderate, high)	Lo	Mo	Mo	Hi	Lo	Hi	Mo

HVAC conditions drop the ambient temperature to near 60°F. When the lighting system is turned on early in the morning, the lamps may operate at a reduced output for 10 to 20 minutes while they warm up.

Standard T12 Type

The standard T12 fluorescent lamp is so designated for its tubular shape (see Figure 3–11). This bulb shape is identical to that of the very early fluorescent lamps. As in incandescent lamp designations, the "12" indicates the diameter of the tube in eighth of an inch increments ($^{12}/_8$ or $1^{1}/_2$ inches). Until recently, T12 lamps were the mainstay of the fluorescent lamp business. The T12 lamps produce more lumens per watt than incandescent lamps, but typically are less glary than the incandescent lamps as the light of T12 lamps is distributed over a much larger light source area. This means, however, that T12 fluorescent lamps pose a more difficult control and focus problem than do the incandescent point sources. T12 rapid start fluorescent lamps are widely used in direct and indirect lighting equipment. Typically, T12 lamps are used when moderate-to-high levels of rather uniform illuminance are desired. They also are appropriate for grazing wall lighting where walls are 10 feet in height or less. These lamps are available in a variety of colors and sizes, with 24-, 36-, and 48-inch linear lamps being common. U-bent lamps (see Figure 3–11) are best suited for 12-inch by 24-inch (1 × 2) and 24-inch by 24-inch (2 × 2) luminaires.

Standard T12 rapid start fluorescent lamps are the workhorse of commercial lighting. Unfortunately, most of these lamps are specified in the very bad color "lite white" or the only slightly better "cool white." Both lamp colors are near 4100K, and they have color rendering indices of 48 and 67, respectively. Neither lamp renders skin tones well; so both are disliked by many people. These two lamps have given the entire family of fluorescent lamps a bad name. Triphosphor coatings, introduced in the early 1980s on T12 lamps, have dramatically improved the color of light and color rendering produced by fluorescent lamps. At the same time, these new coatings provide more light output, given the same power input as standard T12 lamps. Hence, they are termed improved efficiency lamps. Table 3–7 identifies the typical fluorescent lamp colors used in architectural lighting design, and outlines some of their color, efficiency, life, and cost characteristics. A typical T12 rapid start fluorescent lamp designation is outlined in Figure 3–12.

Although a host of fluorescent lamp colors are available from no fewer than five lamp manufacturers, there exists a common specification standard for only five of the many lamps. The American National Standards Institute (ANSI) provides specification standards for lite white, cool white, warm white, cool white deluxe, and warm white deluxe. These standards assure

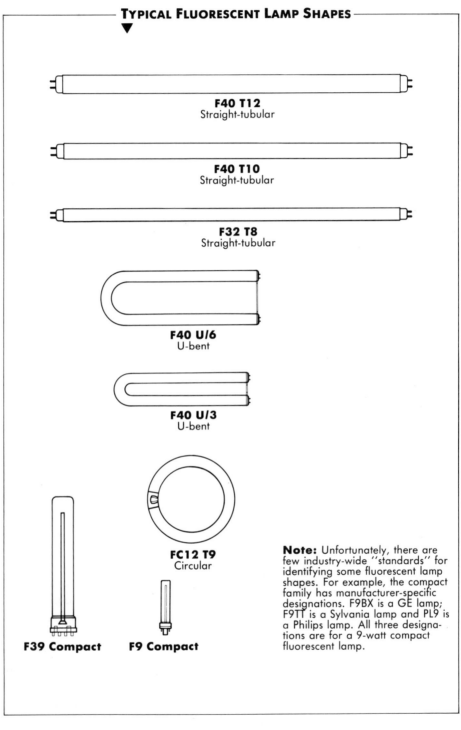

TYPICAL FLUORESCENT LAMP SHAPES

F40 T12
Straight-tubular

F40 T10
Straight-tubular

F32 T8
Straight-tubular

F40 U/6
U-bent

F40 U/3
U-bent

FC12 T9
Circular

F39 Compact   **F9 Compact**

Note: Unfortunately, there are few industry-wide "standards" for identifying some fluorescent lamp shapes. For example, the compact family has manufacturer-specific designations. F9BX is a GE lamp; F9TT is a Sylvania lamp and PL9 is a Philips lamp. All three designations are for a 9-watt compact fluorescent lamp.

FIGURE 3–11

Table 3–7.
Typical fluorescent lamp colors used in architectural lighting design.

Characteristics	Lite white	Cool white	Warm white	Triphosphor 3000K	Triphosphor 3500K	Triphosphor deluxe 3500K
Color impressions	Bad	Poor	Fair[a]	Good	Good	Excellent
CRI	48	62	52	70	70	82
Color temperature	4150K	4200K	3000K	3000K	3500K	3500K
Efficiency (LPW)[b]	86	79	80	81/84 92/90[c]	81/84 92/90[c]	82
Typical life[d] (hours)	12,000 to 20,000	12,000 to 20,000	12,000 to 20,000	12,000 to 20,000	12,000 to 20,000	10,000 to 20,000
Relative cost (low, moderate, high)	Mo	Lo	Lo	Mo–Hi	Mo–Hi	Hi
Available lamp class[e]	ST12 IET12 HO	ST12 IET12 HO	ST12 IET12 HO	ST12 IET12 IET10 IET8 HO	ST12 IET12 IET10 IET8 HO	ST12 IET12 C

[a] Fair because skin tones look good.
[b] Without ballast loss; for standard T12 unless otherwise noted.
[c] First value for standard T12, second value for improved efficiency T12, third value for improved efficiency T10, and fourth value for improved efficiency T8.
[d] Improved efficiency, high output, and compact fluorescent lamps generally have shorter life.
[e] Where: S = standard; IE = improved efficiency; HO = high output; C = compact.

the designer that each manufacturer's version of lite white, for example, will look the same and have the same operating characteristics as every other manufacturer's version. Standardizing lamp color appearances is a fine idea, but here it is not very useful because the five lamp colors covered are obsolete. Meanwhile, the newer, more appropriate, improved-efficiency triphosphor colors do not have established ANSI standards. Hence one manufacturer's 3500K triphosphor lamp may (and usually does) appear different from another manufacturer's. This inconsistency leads to obvious difficulties in relamping. Designers should continue to urge manufacturers to support the development of ANSI standards for the newer, more efficient, better-color fluorescent lamps. Standardization could only enhance their application potential.

The T12 lamp that probably is best-suited for residential lighting is Sylvania's Incandescent/Fluorescent fluorescent lamp. Its unique phosphor coating produces visible light from a fluorescent tube that very nearly matches the color and color rendering of standard incandescent A lamps.

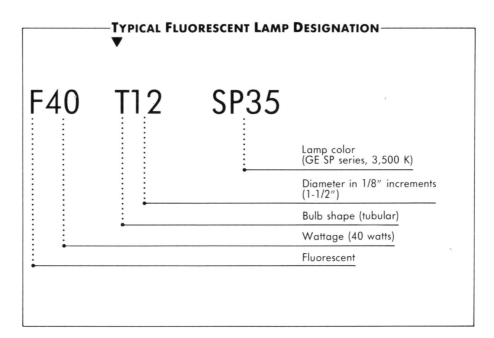

FIGURE 3–12

Although the Incandescent/Fluorescent lamp is twice as efficient as the best incandescent lamps, it is only half as efficient as the best fluorescent lamps. Hence the lamp is not nearly as bright as a standard fluorescent, and thus is not as glary *and* is not capable of providing as "commercial" a level and look of light as a standard fluorescent. For under-cabinet lighting in kitchens, for indirect cove or valance lighting, or for indirect lighting in bathrooms, the Incandescent/Fluorescent lamp can be very successful, with the added benefits of better efficiency, less heat, and much longer lamp life than the incandescent provides.

Improved-Efficiency T12 Type

The improved-efficiency T12 lamps use the triphosphor technology coupled with lamp cathode and ballast changes. This yields dramatically improved color rendering along with relatively high-efficiency light production.

"Triphosphor" indicates that the phosphor produces light peaks in three specific color regions—red, blue, and green, as shown in Figure 3–13. By producing light in these three regions, triphosphor lamps will illuminate most objects to full, bright color.

Improved-efficiency T12 fluorescent lamps have efficiencies of about 84 LPW. Although this is about 10 percent less than comparable-colored metal

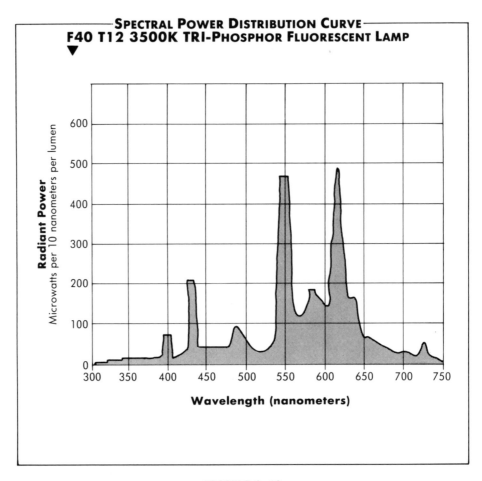

FIGURE 3–13

halide for interior applications, the metal halide lamp is accompanied by significant wattage loss in the ballast. Further, typical metal halide lamp lumen loss over life (shown in Figure 3–14) is significantly worse than that of a fluorescent lamp (shown in Figure 3–15). Therefore, after about a year's use in a typical office application, a fluorescent's maintained efficiency is actually better than that of a metal halide. Over the lamp's life, a fluorescent is generally a better interior-environment light source than a metal halide.

Experience seems to indicate that the triphosphor lamps also provide added brightness intensity to a space, compared to the standard T12 cool white, warm white, and lite white sources. This effect may be due to increased color brilliance from the light peaks in red, blue, and green.

Although the triphosphor technology has improved the T12 lamp immensely, these triphosphors actually provide even better efficiency in smaller-diameter lamps than the T12. At the same time, smaller-diameter lamps

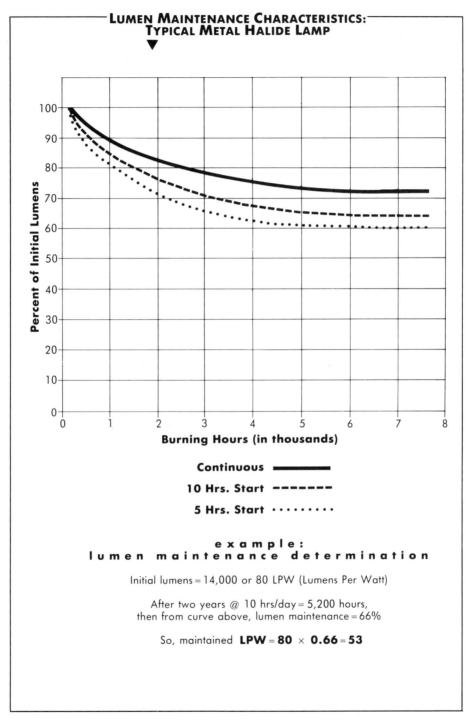

FIGURE 3–14

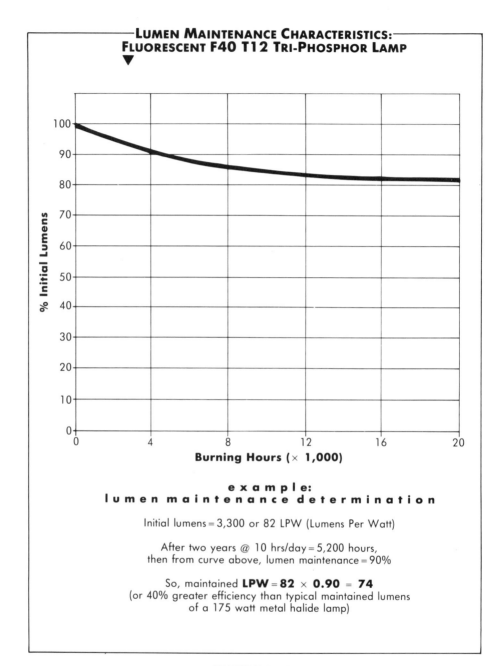

LUMEN MAINTENANCE CHARACTERISTICS:
FLUORESCENT F40 T12 TRI-PHOSPHOR LAMP

Burning Hours (× 1,000)

e x a m p l e :
l u m e n   m a i n t e n a n c e   d e t e r m i n a t i o n

Initial lumens = 3,300 or 82 LPW (Lumens Per Watt)

After two years @ 10 hrs/day = 5,200 hours,
then from curve above, lumen maintenance = 90%

So, maintained **LPW = 82 × 0.90 = 74**
(or 40% greater efficiency than typical maintained lumens
of a 175 watt metal halide lamp)

FIGURE 3–15

are easier to control optically. Therefore, improved-efficiency T10 and T8 rapid start lamps are recent welcome additions to the fluorescent family.

Improved-Efficiency T10 Type

This is a relatively new type of rapid start, triphosphor fluorescent lamp. All indications are that these lamps may have some of the highest efficiencies yet available from the fluorescent family. These efficiencies, 92 LPW, are virtually as good as those of any high intensity discarge (HID) lamps available today in size and wattage appropriate for commercial interior applications; but, of course, with the triphosphor coating, the T10 fluorescent type produces unparalleled color and color rendering compared to HID sources.

Because this lamp class is so new and because luminaire manufacturers have been working on designs for the more common improved-efficiency T12 and T8 fluorescent lamps, not much lighting equipment is yet on the market to accommodate this lamp. In fact, the recent revolution in fluorescent lamps—improved-efficiency triphosphors in T12 and T8—has overshadowed the improved-efficiency T10 lamp. Further, total lighting system efficiencies seem to be better with the T8 lamp. With an even smaller diameter than the T10, it allows reflector and lens designs to more efficiently focus the light. Hence, in linear tubular lamps the most widely available high-efficiency light source today for interior environments is the improved-efficiency T8 lamp.

Improved-Efficiency T8 Type

The T8 improved-efficiency lamps are part of a significant trend toward more compact and better-color light sources. The three major benefits of this lamp lie in its efficiency in producing light, efficiency in luminaire control, and luminaire aesthetics.

Efficiency in producing light is a direct result of the triphosphor coating used on a small-diameter bulb (T8 = $\frac{8}{8}$ inch, or 1 inch). These lamps have efficiencies of up to 90 LPW, and are available in 24-, 36-, 48-, and 60-inch lengths.

Efficiency in luminaire control results from use of a smaller-diameter bulb. The T8 lamp approaches a theoretical line or linear source. With appropriate reflectors, a linear source is very efficient. So the lamp efficiency coupled with the luminaire efficiency yields a potent, highly efficient lighting package.

Luminaire aesthetics have always been a bone of contention among architects, interior designers, lighting designers, and owners. The T8 lamps allow for extremely thin-profile luminaires. For indirect equipment, this means less bulky hardware intruding into the spatial design. For direct equipment, it can mean relatively shallow equipment that still has exceptional performance. For furniture- or millwork-mounted task or indirect lighting, the thin profile means significantly less obtrusive lighting equipment for better-integrated designs. Along with shallower-depth equipment, the T8 lamp permits the use of narrow-width equipment; so 6-, 8- and 12-inch-wide luminaires are efficient as well as aesthetically pleasing.

Improved-efficiency T8 rapid start fluorescent lamps are revolutionizing architectural lighting design. Combined with the possibilities offered by compact fluorescent lamps, T8 lamps allow the designer an energy-effective, comfortable, attractive, and human-scale approach to lighing.

High-Output Lamp Type

There are times when significant light output is required from fluorescent lamps. For example, high-detail, low-contrast tasks requiring high color rendering and occurring in large-volume spaces may be appropriately lighted with high-output fluorescent lamps. One must remember, however, that these lamps are not to be confused with high-efficiency lamps. In fact, the lumen output per power input for high-output lamps is relatively low for fluorescent lamps (about 72 LPW). By operating these lamps at higher current, both the light per lamp and the power consumed per lamp are increased. The higher-current requirement means that a different ballast is needed compared to that required for standard and improved-efficiency rapid start lamps, and the high-current ballasts generally are more noisy than standard ballasts. Therefore, high-output fluorescent lamps generally are used in environments where ballast noise will be masked by other environmental noises or where people are not particularly sensitive to noise (e.g., a transition space where people spend little time and do not require quiet; a space where HVAC and background masking sound systems mask the ballast noise; and so on).

The lamp life of high output (HO) fluorescent lamps is less attractive than that for standard and improved-efficiency lamps. HO lamps are available in a full range of colors; but because of ballast noise, lamp efficiency, and life limitations, the use of the HO class of lamps is declining.

Compact Lamp Type

Compact fluorescent lamps were first introduced by Philips under the PL brand designation; so some designers erroneously refer to the compact fluorescent lamp class as PL lamps. These compact fluorescent lamps are so named for their relatively miniature size. The 7- and 9-watt lamps are 7 inches in length. Compact fluorescent lamps are possible only because of the use of triphosphor coatings. Hence these lamps have excellent color temperature and color rendering abilities. Originally intended for residential retrofit projects, the lamps have become so popular with designers, engineers, and building owners that they are now available in many sizes and a variety of colors. Typical compact fluorescent lamp shapes are shown in Figure 3–11 (F9 and F39).

With the continued interest in and potential of compact fluorescent lamps, manufacturers have expanded the concept to somewhat larger lamps. Therefore this compact lamp type can be divided into small and large compact lamps.

The small lamps range from 7 to 18 watts and are preheat-type lamps requiring small starter and ballast components. These lamps typically are used in table and desktop task luminaires, floor luminaires, and ceiling recessed downlights. In terms of light output, a 13-watt compact fluorescent lamp has a lumen output similar to that of a 60-watt A19 incandescent lamp. For a desktop task luminaire, use of a 13-watt compact lamp means a significant reduction in local heat compared to a 60-watt incandescent lamp. Energy savings in electric energy for the light and in terms of cooling load requirements are significant. The large lamps are a recent addition to the compact class of lamps. Ranging from 18 to 40 watts, these larger lamps are rather potent light sources. Care generally must be taken in using these lamps in direct downlighting applications to avoid glare conditions. Their small size does permit the design of small-scale, well-controlled direct and indirect lighting equipment. These lamps are creating a revolution in luminaire design and in the application of fluorescent lighting.

The near-term future of lighting is in the triphosphor improved-efficiency T8 and compact fluorescent lamps. With efficiencies approaching those of high intensity discharge lamps but without the drawbacks of HID-associated lengthy startup times, color deficiencies, and drastic color shifts, improved-efficiency T8 and compact lamps may very well change residential and commercial lighting. GE has made the use of these lamps extremely convenient by introducing nearly all of its Fluorescent lamp types and wattages in 3000k, 3500k, and 4100k triphosphor colors. This allows for the design of a complete facility using fluorescent lamps of one color family—from task lights to downlights to general lights.

Other Fluorescent Types

There are other fluorescent lamp types, which are used for specialty or niche-market applications. Miniature fluorescent lamps are available, and typically are seen in speculative residential construction in under-cabinet lights. Unfortunately, these particular lamps do not enhance residential finishes. Also, their life is relatively short, and the starters and ballast typically hum. The triphosphor improved-efficiency T8 lamps and compact lamps are much more efficient, attractive, and quiet than these lamps.

Energy-Saving Fluorescent Lamps

The energy crises of 1973 and 1979 produced a knee-jerk reaction in the fluorescent lamp business. Before then, many buildings were designed with lighting systems that provided 150 to 200 footcandles even when 75 to 100 footcandles would have been sufficient for nearly all visual tasks—except, of course, VDTs (which were not widely used until the mid–1980s). To allow building owners and managers to reduce their buildings' electricity demands, lamp manufacturers introduced several lamps over a period of years. Chronologically, these lamps were: (1) the reduced wattage/reduced lumen lamp; (2) the reduced wattage/high-efficiency/poor-color lamp; (3) the improved-efficiency series of lamps previously discussed (see discussions, above, of the improved-efficiency T12, improved-efficiency T10, and improved efficiency T8); (4) compact fluorescent lamps (previously discussed); and (5) fluorescent R/PAR lamp incandescent substitutes.

The reduced wattage/reduced lumen lamps were clearly an interim means of providing quick energy savings by reducing wattage and subsequently light output. Environments lighted to 150 to 200 footcandles could no doubt be as satisfactory at 120 to 165 footcandles. The efficiency of these fluorescent lamps was no different from that of standard lamps. Now there is no reason whatsoever to use these lamps in new or renovation construction. Today there are more efficient, better-appearing fluorescent lamps (e.g., the improved-efficiency family).

The reduced wattage/high-efficiency/poor-color fluorescent lamps were the next generation in higher-efficiency fluorescent lamps. To improve efficiency, however, a significant sacrifice in color was necessary. These lamps were called lite white (discussed above under "Standard T12 Type"). But the attitude in the mid–1970s was color be damned; building owners and managers were looking for ways to keep lighting quantity adequate while cutting energy consumption. ("Never mind lighting quality—these lamps fit the bill!") Fortunately, today, the triphosphor, improved efficiency family of fluorescent lamps has rendered the lite-white lamps obsolete.

Fluorescent improved-efficiency T12, T10, and T8 lamps and compact lamps (all discussed above) are today's most efficient and most likable white light sources.

Fluorescent R and PAR lamp incandescent substitutes are generally inappropriate substitutes. Most R and PAR lamp applications require light either to be thrown or projected over a reasonable distance or to highlight specific surfaces or objects. Fluorescent R and PAR lamp incandescent substitutes generally do not have the candlepower distribution (the "punch") to perform such long distance projecting or highlighting. These lamps usually are sold to uninitiated facilities' managers, purchasing agents, or novice designers as energy saving and/or as less-maintenance-intensive than their incandescent counterparts. Unfortunately, the energy used to operate these substitutes cannot perform the required task of projecting or highlighting; so these substitutes actually waste energy.

"Full spectrum" fluorescent lamps have been promoted as a healthy alternative to almost all other "artificial" sources. Unfortunately, repetitive conclusive studies have not been forthcoming to substantiate the many claims made for these lamps. What can be said, however, is that these lamps typically are much less efficient than the improved-efficiency fluorescent lamps and more costly (both initially and over life). These "full spectrum" lamps seem to be quite deficient in the red portion of the spectrum, resulting in a gloomy appearance.

Here, as in all transactions, caveat emptor—let the buyer beware. A prospective user should ask for documentation, evidence, a mockup, and a host of common (not esoteric) references, not just manufacturers' promotional literature.

Fluorescent Ballasts

Fluorescent lamps require a voltage surge to energize the lamp and a constant current to assure continuous, stable operation. The devices that serve these two functions are known as ballasts, a ballast usually being a black box located in or near the luminaire.

Ballasts typically consume energy in order to start and control lamps. A standard electromagnetic fluorescent ballast operating two F40T12 lamps may itself require 8 watts (for a total system-connected load of 88 watts: two 40-watt lamps and an 8-watt ballast).

Electromagnetic ballasts are the present industry standard. These ballasts are relatively inexpensive and have a life of about 15 years in a typical office lighting application. When specifying an electromagnetic ballast, one should look for the following attributes: class P thermal protection; an A sound rating; CBM certification; UL listing; a two- or three-year warranty; and a power factor of 0.9 or greater (high power factor, or HPF).

The thermal protection helps minimize the risk of ballast overheating. An A sound rating assures the quietest possible operating ballast in the electromagnetic family, although even A-rated ballasts produce an audible hum in a quiet environment. Because A-rated ballasts are available only in rapid start, high-output lamps must operate on a C-rated ballast; and the hum potential of a C-rated ballast is significant. Putting any electromagnetic ballast in a metal luminaire in a room full of hard surfaces can lead to hum reverberation. CBM certification indicates that the ballast meets a variety of criteria established by the Certified Ballast Manufacturers. The UL listing indicates that the ballast meets the requirements of Underwriters' Laboratories. A two-year warranty is considered a minimum for electromagnetic ballasts. A power factor of 0.90 or more indicates that the ballast efficiently uses the incoming electricity to operate the lamps. A whole series of low power factor ballasts in a given building can seriously impact the electric power distribution system for the building. Compact fluorescent lamps, especially 7-, 9-, 13-, and 18-watt versions, generally are sold with low power factor (LPF) ballasts, but these LPF ballasts should be avoided if large quantities are to be used.

Electromagnetic dimming ballasts are available to allow for the dimming of fluorescent lamps. These ballasts generally do not provide continuous dimming; that is, the dimming range is usually from 30 or 40 percent output to 100 percent output. Below 30 percent, lamp flicker is quite noticeable and disturbing. Also, electromagnetic dimming ballasts typically hum when dimmed. Dimming fluorescent lamps may alter both color temperature and color rendering characterstics, especially with the improved-efficiency (tri-phosphor) lamps. When a series of fluorescent lamps must be dimmed, it is advisable that all the lamps be of identical size, wattage, and color. Otherwise, serious color shifts are likely from lamp to lamp. For example, if a cove is to be dimmed, and the cove is 15 feet in length, one must not use three 4-foot lamps and one 3-foot lamp because the 3-foot lamp is likely to dim at a different rate and color than the 4-foot lamps. Instead, one should consider using five 3-foot lamps.

Electronic ballasts have been available for some time and are highly touted as efficient, absolutely noise- and flicker-free, and lightweight. These are excellent attributes, but many of the early so-called electronic ballasts were quite unreliable. In the past few years, several electronic ballasts have appeared that are highly reliable. The cost of electronic ballasts has begun to fall to nearly acceptable levels. As costs continue to drop, these ballasts will replace electromagnetic ballasts as the industry standard.

Electronic ballasts have brought a dimming revolution to fluorescent lamps. With electronic ballasts, fluorescent lamps can be dimmed continuously, with no flicker or noise from 100 percent output down to zero output. Although relatively expensive, electronic dimming systems promise to be cost-effective energy controllers and function controllers in the near future.

HIGH INTENSITY DISCHARGE LAMPS

High intensity discharge (HID) lamps are so named for their ability to produce significant amounts of light by discharging electricity through a high-pressure vapor. There are three types of HID lamps: mercury vapor, metal halide, and high pressure sodium. Generally, these lamps are characterized by their warm-up time, restrike time, and color rendering. Most HID lamps are not instant-on, requiring upwards of five minutes for full light output.

If there is a power interruption while these lamps are on, they typically must cool down before they will restrike and warm back up to full light output. Therefore, where emergency lighting is required, auxiliary lighting systems are used to provide instant light during and immediately after power outages. This is usually achieved with a quartz restrike option—HID luminaires fitted with a quartz incandescent lamp that switches on instantly in the event of a power outage, and remains on until the HID lamps are back up to reasonable light output.

Until recently the color rendering of HID lamps had been fair at best and unacceptable at worst. Now great advances in color rendering have been made in metal halide and high pressure sodium lamps, which are discussed below under the respective lamp sections.

As in the designations of other lamp types, a letter indicates the bulb shape, followed by a number indicating the bulb diameter in eighths of an inch. HID lamps typically are available in four basic bulb shapes: B, BT, E, and T (see Figure 3–16). BT and E lamps are relatively bulky, while B and especially T lamps are rather small. T lamps are particulary easy to control photometrically because of their relatively small size. The designation T7 indicates an HID source that is tubular in shape and $\frac{7}{8}$ inch in diameter.

HID lamps are not especially efficient compared to the newer improved-efficiency fluoresent lamps, but are more appropriate for exterior lighting because they are less affected by temperature than fluorescent lamps. The rated life for HID lamps ranges from 5,000 to over 20,000 hours.

Like fluorescent lamps, HID lamps have seen a recent miniaturization. This has been most beneficial in producing more subdued interior and exterior lighting, resulting in more architecturally sensitive luminaires. In fact, until miniaturization, one of the faults of HID lamps was the size of the luminaires required to optically control the lamps, and to house the bulky lamps and the auxiliary starters and ballasts.

HID dimming has been attempted many times over the past ten to fifteen years, usually with little success. The starting and operating characteristics of HID lamps are such that changes in voltage seriously affect the lamps' operation, which in turn may affect lamp life and does affect color rendering and color temperature.

Ballasts for HID lamps usually are significant in size, especially compared to fluorescent ballasts. HID ballasts typically are not available in an A sound rating and so are likely to cause some hum. The smaller the lamp is in wattage, generally the less noticeable the ballast noise.

Mercury Lamps

Mercury lamps are the oldest HID lamp technology, and typically are the least efficient lamps of the HID family. However, their low efficiency is an asset where a long-life lamp with little or no glare is required.

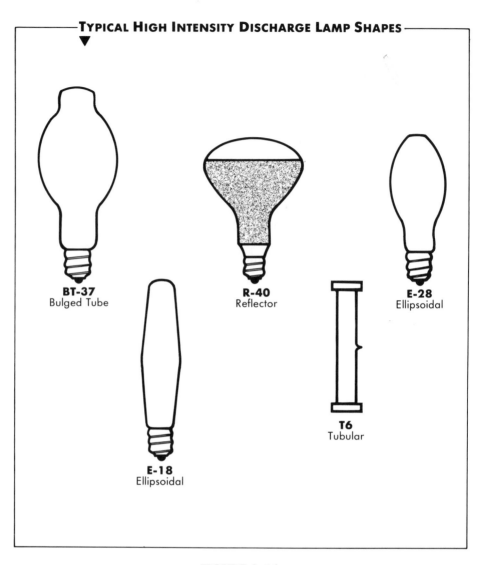

TYPICAL HIGH INTENSITY DISCHARGE LAMP SHAPES ▼

BT-37
Bulged Tube

R-40
Reflector

E-28
Ellipsoidal

E-18
Ellipsoidal

T6
Tubular

FIGURE 3–16

Early mercury vapor lamps were extremely blue in appearance and exhibited poor color rendering. Unfortunately, even as new, improved phosphors were being developed, most mercury vapor lamps specified were of the clear or the standard "deluxe white" color. Perhaps the best-color and best-color-rendering mercury lamp available is the Philips Styletone.

Mercury vapor lamps have efficiencies of up to 63 LPW. The color temperatures available range from 3000K to 6000K, and color rendering indices range from 22 (for clear lamps) to 52 and greater.

Typical appropriate applications include tree uplighting; exterior low-scale pedestrian lighting; interior low-to-moderate-level downlighting. The blue-green radiation obtained even from "color-corrected" mercury vapor lamps enhances green foliage. The Styletone lamps seem particularly appropriate for the lighting of skin tones and many architectural materials.

Mercury vapor lamps are particularly long-lived lamps. Unfortunately, they also are notoriously poor lumen-loss lamps; that is, as the lamp ages, it produces less and less light. So a twenty-year-old mercury lamp, while still operating, may produce only 10 or 20 percent of its initially rated light output. This is especially troublesome in exterior applications where the lighting system was originally designed to produce 1 footcandle/10 lux. If the mercury lamps are not group-relamped on a regular basis, it is likely that the lighting system may only generate 0.15 footcandle/1.5 lux after five or more years.

A phenomenon related to lumen loss is color loss over time. As mercury lamps age, the phosphor breaks down and no longer produces the same color of light as it did when the lamp was new. Therefore, replacing lamps as they burn out can result in a multicolored appearance from the mixture of older and newer lamps. Both the lumen loss and the color loss, along with beneficial economics, are compelling reasons for group-relamping mercury vapor lamps on a regular basis.

There was no real alternative to mercury twenty-five years ago, but today mercury vapor lamps are inappropriate for spotlighting and floodlighting. Metal halide lamps with significantly improved efficiency and color rendering over mercury are much more appropriate for major floodlighting or accenting where lamp life is a factor (e.g., signs, billboards, streets, parking lots, industrial plants, etc.).

Metal Halide Lamps

Of the HID family of lamps, metal halide lamps provide the best color temperature and best color rendering. In the recent past, much development activity has centered around metal halide technology, resulting in very compact lamps and, in at least one case, significant color consistency. Metal halide lamp efficiencies are approaching 95 LPW (no ballast loss included). Couple this with color rendering indices of 70 or more, and these lamps are finding growing application in those retail and office spaces where incandescent lamps once reigned, and where maintenance and energy are top priorities. (See Figure 3–17.)

Metal halide lamps are by no means a panacea in lamps. Lumen loss over their life is significant (see Figure 3–14) compared to the more stable fluorescent lamps (see Figure 3–15). The color consistency for many of the metal

FIGURE 3–17.
Low-wattage, compact metal halide lamps are used in wall wash luminaires to light this mural at a station stop on the Detroit People Mover. This lamp, combined with the right reflector, yields excellent wall lighting uniformity for a minimum connected load. Photo courtesy Gary Steffy Lighting Design Inc.; photo credit: Robert Eovaldi.

halide lamp types is still fair to poor. From lamp to lamp, even on new installations, it is possible, if not likely, that a noticeable shift in color will occur; and after several months of operation, this lamp-to-lamp color shift will be more pronounced. This is especially so with the newer, low-wattage, double-ended compact metal halide lamps (see T6 lamp shape in Figure 3–16). Ballasts are relatively large and relatively loud for metal halide lamps. Typically they consume 10 to 20 percent more watts than the wattage rating of the lamp. Clearly, for indoor applications where ambient temperatures are between 70°F and 80°F, fluorescent lamps are most appropriate for most applications.

Available color-temperatures of metal halide lamps are typically 3100K and 4200K, with 5500K lamps available in some sizes. The 3100K lamps generally have the best color rendering of the metal halide lamps and are most appropriate for human environments. These lamps tend to mix rather well with the improved-efficiency 3000K and 3500K fluorescent lamps and with most incandescent lamps. Typical interior applications of the low-wattage lamps (32, 70, 100 watts) are low-to-moderate-level downlighting and wall washing or art accenting. Lamp manufacturers' literature must be reviewed carefully, as many of these lamps have operating limitations (for example, as this book went to press, the 32-watt lamp could be operated only with the base in the up position, for use in downlights, and was available only for 277-volt operation and intended only for indoor application).

Interior applications of the higher-wattage lamps (150, 175, 250, 400 watts) are in green foliage lighting (for its survival) and in industrial plant lighting (for large-area/high-ceiling downlighting). These lamps can cause significant glare. The 70-watt and 150-watt double-ended lamps are also finding application in indirect lighting of interiors. The small size of these lamps allows for considerable control over light distribution.

Exterior applications of metal halide lamps include tree uplighting, facade highlighting, parking area lighting, and street lighting. The high-color-rendering white light produced by these lamps provides a stunning, pleasant, and efficient contrast to the gloomy blue of mercury and the drab yellow of high pressure sodium.

Several precautions usually are necessary with the use of metal halide lamps, as reported in manufacturers' literature. Of particular concern are the potential for violent failure and the potential for ultraviolet radiation. Most metal halide lamps can fail violently. To minimize, if not eliminate, the hazards of such failure, all metal halide luminaires should have lensing or clear shield media that will contain hot glass. The newer compact metal halide lamps also produce UV radiation; so to limit this radiation, UV protective glass lenses are required on all luminaires using these lamps.

The lamp life for metal halide lamps ranges from 6,000 hours for the 70-watt compact lamps to 20,000 hours for the larger, higher-wattage lamps. Because there are 250-watt quartz PAR lamps with 6,000 hours of life, it becomes clear that the use of these metal halide lamps is in its infancy. Some designers erroneously perceive that these compact metal halide lamps have a maintenance and an operating edge over the incandescent quartz PAR lamp. Certainly, where energy alone is a clear priority, the compact metal halide lamps should be favored over the quartz PAR alternative.

High Pressure Sodium Lamps

Until just a few years ago, high pressure sodium (HPS) lamps were the most overrated, oversold, inappropriate lamps available, with the possible exception of low pressure sodium lamps. (*Note:* Low pressure sodium lamps are not considered in this text to be appropriate for architectural lighting designs.) HPS lamps traditionally have been very poor color rendering sources with a color rendering index of about 20, with a poor appearance (color temperature of 2100K). Because these lamps happen to produce visible radiation at a peak of about 570 nm, however, and because the human eye's peak sensitivity under daylight conditions is 550 nm, a questionable marketing campaign was born: "HPS lamps will help people actually to see better." Two very basic principles of seeing apparently were overlooked. The human eye "sees" brightness contrasts and color contrasts, both of which are influenced by the color characteristics of light sources. Therefore, to make work environments more productive or streets safer, it is necessary to render tasks in the office and objects in the street more "contrasty." Increasing the contrast of a black-and-white task can be achieved by throwing more white light onto the surface or object of interest. Increasing the contrast of colored tasks can be achieved by increasing or broadening the light's spectral distribution characteristics, thereby clearly establishing visible colors of the surface or object. Until recently, HPS lighting did neither. These lamps produced yellow light, which reflected well from yellow objects and was absorbed by most other colored objects. The result is a very bland and drab visual scene that actually appears less bright and less colorful than white-light environments. Perhaps poor visual scenes are acceptable on freeways, where people are not walking, and where visual tasks are rather gross on a relative scale (not running into other large objects—e.g., cars—and staying in a particular lane of traffic are the visual tasks); but such poor visual scenes are not appropriate where people interact or work. In the name of energy conservation, HPS lamp usage has increased; but, unfortunately, the energy-mongers understand little about the visual system. As the American population ages, broader-spectrum, whiter sources will be necessary if people are to be expected to see, discern, and enjoy a colorful environment.

A high-color-rendering, white-source high pressure sodium lamp has long been promised. By 1987 Philips had a demonstration lamp available, and in 1990 GE and Philips introduced a production white-source, high-color-rendering HPS lamp. These lamps offer significant application potential and may indeed signal the future direction in HID lighting.

HID Ballasts

HID lamps traditionally require substantial ballasts and starters to provide the necessary starting voltage. Therefore, as noted earlier, HID ballasts are typically bulky and heavy, require an additional power consumption of 10 to 20 percent over lamp wattage, and are noisy. For these reasons, HID lamps have not gained wide acceptance in the quieter interior spaces.

Table 3–8.
Lamp troubleshooting.

Problem	Standard voltage incandescent	Low voltage incandescent	Fluorescent	HID (mercury and metal halide)
Flicker	• Diode lamp		• Too cold • Dimmed too low • Near burnout	• All lamps on same phase
Low output	• 130V lamp in 120V socket • Dimmed too low		• Too cold • Dimmed too low • Near burnout	• Wrong ballast • Overvoltage • Near burnout
Cycling on/off	• Thermal protection in luminaire is tripping		• Near burnout • Ballast failing	• Burnout condition
Constant burnouts	• Vibration shock • Overvoltage • Voltage surges	• Wrong transformer	• Poor socket/lamp contact • Wrong ballast	• Poor socket/lamp contact • Wrong ballast
Humming	• Dimmed too low • Wrong dimmer (for LV)	• Bad transformer • So-called electronic transformer • Wrong dimmer	• Bad ballast	• Normal • Bad ballast
Massive burnouts	• Overvoltage • Voltage surges • Lamp too high in wattage for socket design • Poor quality control	• Wrong transformer • Overvoltage • Voltage surges	• Poor socket/lamp contact • Wrong voltage • Wrong ballast • Wrong lamp (T8 in T12 socket) • Poor quality control	• Poor socket/lamp contact • Wrong voltage • Wrong ballast • Wrong lamp • Poor quality control

Lamp Family

ELECTRIC LIGHT SOURCE TROUBLESHOOTING

On some occasions, for reasons of poor manufacturing, poor installation, poor maintenance, or poor design and application, lamps do strange things. Some of the more common difficulties that may arise in lamp usage are outlined in Table 3–8, along with possible sources of the trouble.

CHAPTER FOUR

DESIGN DEVELOPMENT: LUMINAIRES

INTRODUCTION

It is no accident that much of this book thus far has been devoted to light sources. Lamps are responsible for: inherent system efficiency; color of light; appearance; maintenance (relamping); potential control (dimming); potential focus (intensity). Luminaires should be built around, and for, lamps. This chapter will discuss and give examples of some of the more important physical qualities and photometric aspects of luminaires, as well as the various families of luminaires available.

Luminaires are responsible for how light is distributed on room surfaces, worksurfaces, tasks, and people. Luminaires can be very noticeable, as a significant part of the overall look of a room may come from the actual hardware appearance of the luminaires (see Figure C18). On the other hand, luminaires can be quite subtle (see Figure C21). There are many off-the-shelf or standard luminaires available to meet many of today's lighting needs. The key, however, is to start the design by establishing *all* of the appropriate lighting needs for a project (see Chapter 2, section on "Programming") and then, based on these needs, to formulate concepts. Once the concepts are established, the designer is in a position to think about which lamps and luminaires can be used to achieve them.

Luminaires can be either off-the-shelf, or modifications of standard equipment, or totally custom. Many times, a unique way of using off-the-shelf equipment will lead to a successful project. The mirror detail exemplified in Figure C15 uses a simple strip light (which could be either incandescent Lumiline or fluorescent tubular lamps) behind an etched mirror. Light emanates to the face in a nonglary way, and the look is clean. Arriving at such a solution did not mean starting with the assumption that somehow, someway a strip light was going to be used. The interior architect's *program* of lighting needs led him to conclude that light needed to come from the mirror in a very clean, Mies-ian fashion.

Understanding lighting hardware is critical to knowing if and how light can be introduced into a given space or architectural setting. Light reflection (Figure 2–11) and light transmission (Figure 2–12) are both important concepts in developing lighting solutions. Understanding luminaire photometric qualities is also key to being able to resolve lighting design challenges.

LIGHTING HARDWARE

Clearly, lighting design is much more than just applying available equipment, more than tacking luminaires onto or into the architecture—hence the importance of programming and conceptualizing. There comes a time, however, when hardware must be selected if the designer is to maintain control over the quality of the project, in terms of both aesthetics and performance. Lighting hardware generally is judged on quality of construction, quality of appearance, and quality of photometry (light distribution characteristics); and the degree to which each of these factors contributes to luminaire selection depends on the use of the equipment. For example, the fluorescent wall wash lighting shown in Figures C12 and C19 typically is known as an architectural slot. A slot about 10 inches wide and 9 inches high is made from drywall. The lighting equipment is comprised of a T8-lamp fluorescent strip light and an extruded aluminum baffle as shown in the detail of Figure 4–1. The quality of appearance of the strip light is unimportant, but the baffle, which is a very visible, lighted element, must look good. In fact, because the baffle is used in long runs, its straightness is an important aspect. Also, because the baffle needs to be removable for lamp replacement, it should be rather rugged as well as easy to remove. An extruded aluminum baffle was selected for these reasons. A slot detail like that shown in Figure 4–1 will provide a relatively uniform wash of light down a wall, provided that the wall height is 10 feet or less.

There are instances, of course, where the luminaire hardware needs to meet all three attributes—quality of construction, appearance, and photometry. Figure 4–2 shows an architectural ceiling step with a luminaire used to provide cove lighting. The luminaire housing should be comprised of extruded aluminum for long, straight runs. Although seams will be necessary every so often, these are generally more acceptable than weld lines or weld

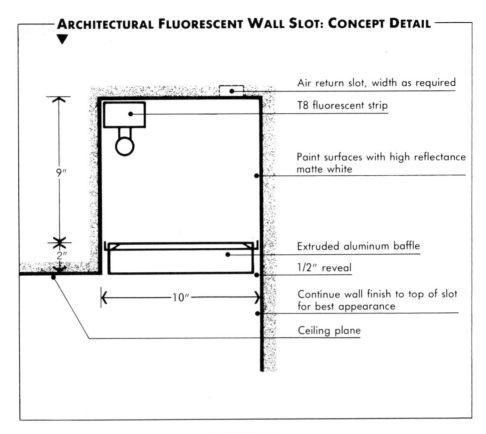

──── **ARCHITECTURAL FLUORESCENT WALL SLOT: CONCEPT DETAIL** ────
▼

Air return slot, width as required

T8 fluorescent strip

Paint surfaces with high reflectance matte white

9"

Extruded aluminum baffle

2"

1/2" reveal

←————10"————→

Continue wall finish to top of slot for best appearance

Ceiling plane

FIGURE 4–1

"dots" similarly spaced. Photometrically, the luminaire needs an asymmetric distribution to throw light far across the ceiling in a relatively uniform and soft pattern.

Custom luminaires often are just unique assemblies of various off-the-shelf components. Figure 4–3 shows a bollard concept using a standard step light mounted in some rather straightforward treated lumber segments. Figure 4–4 shows the use of standard incandescent G-lamps, a standard piece of plexiglass, and an uplight as components for a custom torchiere. This drawing led to development of the torchiere shown in Figures 5–9, 5–10, C1, and C2.

LUMINAIRE CONSTRUCTION

Luminaires are likely to remain in a given installation for fifteen years or more. Their ability to withstand the environment (indoor or out), their ability to withstand building system interaction (e.g., vibration due to mechan-

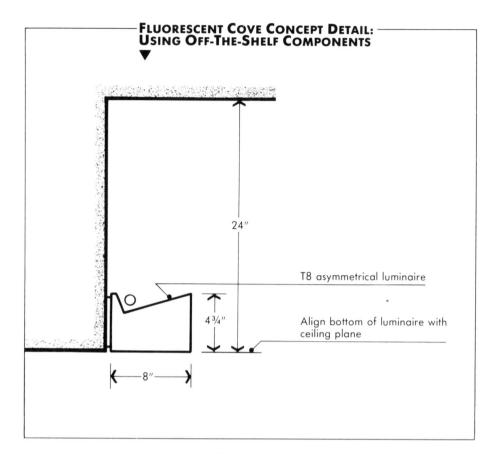

FLUORESCENT COVE CONCEPT DETAIL:
USING OFF-THE-SHELF COMPONENTS
▼

24″

T8 asymmetrical luminaire

4 ¾″

Align bottom of luminaire with
ceiling plane

8″

FIGURE 4–2

ical equipment), and their ability to withstand, indeed encourage, proper
maintenance are key construction-related qualities necessary for long life.
Heavy gauge steel and/or extruded aluminum are good base construction
methods for long-life luminaires. Connections are the most likely points of
failure in any luminaire, and mechanical fasteners (e.g., screws or rivets)
seem more permanent than tab/slot construction.

Baffles and louvers should be of sufficient gauge and/or of such cell size
as to minimize torquing. Extruded aluminum baffles or double-sided steel
(U-shaped) baffles lead to more sturdy, monolithic construction. Lenses
should be virgin acrylic, both for best performance and for greatest resistance to discoloring over time.

In order to judge luminaire construction, several techniques are available:
review the manufacturers' literature; view and handle a working sample;
construct a mockup. These techniques should be used in a linear progres-
sion toward decision making. For example, if six different manufacturers'
luminaires are under consideration, then carefully review the manufactur-

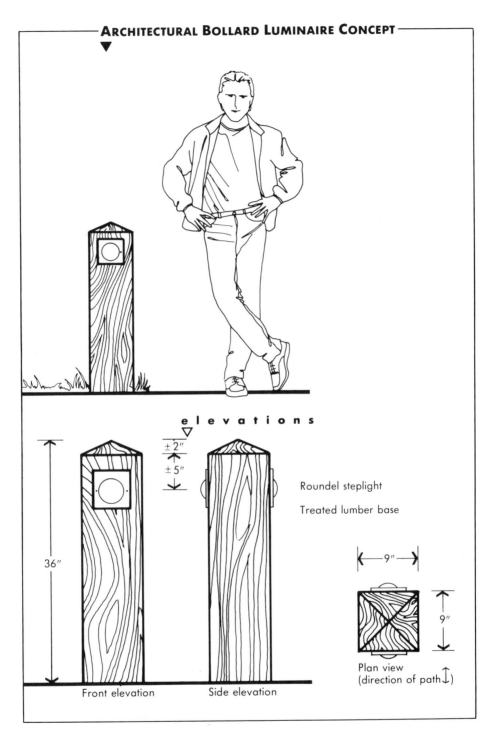

ARCHITECTURAL BOLLARD LUMINAIRE CONCEPT ▼

elevations ▽

± 2″
± 5″

36″

Roundel steplight

Treated lumber base

9″

9″

Plan view
(direction of path↕)

Front elevation   Side elevation

FIGURE 4–3

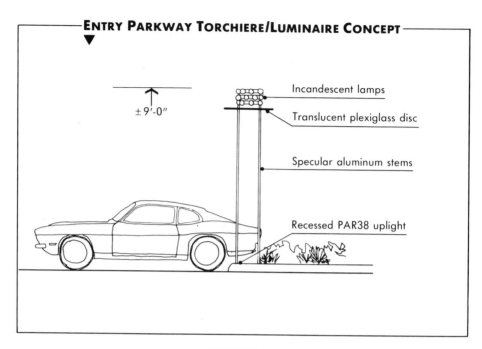

ENTRY PARKWAY TORCHIERE/LUMINAIRE CONCEPT

± 9'-0"

Incandescent lamps

Translucent plexiglass disc

Specular aluminum stems

Recessed PAR38 uplight

FIGURE 4–4

ers' literature. Of the six, perhaps three manufacturers will use heavier-gauge steel than the others. Order and review samples of the three remaining luminaires. After this review, perhaps two luminaires will surpass the third. Finally, consider a mockup to review the construction quality of the luminaires after installation by electrical contractors. The mockup also provides an excellent opportunity for one to review the quality of appearance and of photometry.

LUMINAIRE APPEARANCE

Selecting a luminaire for its appearance simply on the basis of reviewing some catalog photographs may produce surprising and disappointing results. For any luminaire it is necessary to ascertain several things firsthand: the consistency, sheen, and durability of the finish; methods of attachment to the architecture; methods of connecting various components to one another; baffle, louver, reflector, and/or refractor fit and finish; and long-run connector components. To do all of this, an actual working sample is required, or a visit to an installation using the luminaire in question. Reviewing an installation sometimes is preferable to obtaining a sample because the sample can be reviewed and "perfected" at the factory if it is known to be intended for designer review.

LUMINAIRE PHOTOMETRY

The photometry or optical performance of a luminaire is quite critical to the success of a lighting system. Even decorative luminaires need to have some sort of particular optical performance if they are to serve their decorative function. For example, crystal wall sconces look good only if small, low-wattage, clear incandescent lamps or actual candle flames are used. Only such point sources show the crystal off in a glittery, sparkly fashion.

With the exception of the more decorative luminaires, photometric information from manufacturers' data is quite useful in the design development of a project (see the lumen method example in Chapter 5).

Reviewing actual working samples, however, still is recommended. Some aspects of light distribution are not reported in published photometric data (an unintentional omission). The IES has established procedures for photometrically testing luminaires, but because of the limitations of these procedures and/or the limitations of the testing equipment, certain photometric information is difficult, if not impossible, to determine. Perhaps the most striking example is the measurement of luminaire luminances. Photometric tests may indicate that luminaire luminances are acceptable, but viewing an actual working sample may show spikes of reflected or transmitted light at peculiar, nonstandard angles that cause glare. Many parabolic luminaires exhibit a condition known as flash; that is, there is a specific area on the parabolic reflector that reflects a mirror image of the fluorescent lamp(s). As one might imagine, this is a rather disturbingly glary reflection, one that can be judged only by actually seeing a working luminaire, not by reviewing photometric data.

MANUFACTURERS' LITERATURE

Many of the better luminaire manufacturers offer a wealth of catalog information. Typically, this literature includes a photo or line drawing of the luminaire along with product features, construction, and finish, ordering information, and sometimes application ideas. Additionally, very detailed photometric data are available in the better manufacturers' literature.

To show a few of the kinds of equipment available and to illustrate the information being made available by manufacturers, a short collection of manufacturers' literature is presented here. A complete list of manufacturers of lighting equipment can be obtained from the annual lighting directories of *Lighting Design & Application (LD&A)*, *Architectural Lighting*, and *Interiors* magazines, and others.

Selected literature from Columbia, Peerless, Edison Price, and Kurt Versen illustrates the kind of luminaires, their quality, and the photometric documentation available to the designer. The literature is presented in the following order: recessed incandescent, recessed compact fluorescent, recessed standard fluorescent, and indirect fluorescent.

Figure 4–5a is a datasheet for a 5-inch-diameter, A-lamp downlight. These particular downlights are also available in several wall wash versions (to light one wall, to light two walls intersecting at a 90° angle, to light two parallel walls, or a corridor application, and to light only a small vertical segment of a wall). Hence, the size of the ceiling hole and the luminaire finish can remain consistent throughout a room, yet light distribution can be modified by various reflector modifications. Edison Price, like some other manufacturers, has a complete line of same-aperture luminaires that use different lamps, as noted in the last paragraph of the "Features" section in Figure 4–5a. Hence, low voltage PAR lamp luminaires and standard voltage PAR lamp luminaires also are available in 5-inch-diameter units. This allows for downlighting and accenting to occur in the same room without introducing different-sized and different-appearing luminaires for the different functions.

This luminaire is available in two finishes, clear natural aluminum Alzak (an Alcoa registered tradename) and champagne gold Alzak. The champagne gold finish varies from luminaire manufacturer to luminaire manufacturer; Edison Price's champagne gold is a very subtle soft finish. Manufacturers' samples should always by reviewed for color compatibility with interior space finishes.

Note that the Edison Price luminaire can be obtained with an overlap or a flush flange. The overlap flange, shown on the luminaire on the datasheet, helps to hide the irregularities of the cut hole in the ceiling material by overlapping the ceiling material. In this case, the flange is available from the manufacturer in three finishes: the finish of the reflector (clear or champagne gold), standard white (to match standard white ceiling tile), and custom colors. Custom colors and finishes are available from many manufacturers, but generally require long lead times (6 to 12 weeks) and additional cost.

Reflector finishes generally are based on two criteria: glare control and the finish complement to other luminaires' and/or surfaces' finishes. Many times, luminaire finishes are matched for a "complete look" throughout a project. Incandescent and compact fluorescent downlights' cone reflectors and trims will match the ambient lighting system (if the ambient system is direct lighting). For example, if 2 by 2 parabolic luminaires are selected for the ambient lighting (see Figure 4–13a, 4–13b, 4–14a, and 4–14b for luminaire examples, and Figure 5–17 for an application example), then clear aluminum reflector downlights may be used for a matching appearance. Figure 5–17 illustrates 2 by 2 parabolic luminaires with clear aluminum cone adjustable accent luminaires. The designer should always review any luminaire finish in a lighted sample, using the lamp that will be used in the finished space.

Darklite™A19/5

Edison Price Incorporated

Features

A 5″ diameter aperture recessed low brightness downlight designed for use with inside frosted A19 lamps (100 watt maximum). The fixture provides a shielding angle of 40°. One basic housing allows interchangeable use of the downlight and wallwash reflectors. This permits housings to be installed first and reflectors installed or changed at any time according to the required application.

The A19/5 is part of the Edison Price family of A lamp downlights and washlights which are available in five different aperture sizes. Each size is scaled for a different ceiling height, which gives the specifier the ability to match the aperture size of PAR lamp and low voltage fixtures.

Applications

The A19/5 is a small aperture fixture suitable for downlighting or wall washing in offices, stores, residences, lobbies, corridors and reception areas. Reflectors are available in clear natural aluminum Alzak® or champagne gold Alzak®

Washlight reflectors available are: wallwash (120°), corner wallwash (210°), double wallwash (2 x 120°), and half wallwash (60°).

Fixture is union made IBEW, UL listed, prewired with insulation detector and approved for ten wire 75°C branch circuit pull through wiring. Removal of the reflector allows access to the junction box.

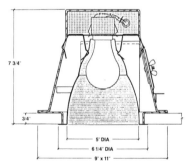

Ordering Information

For complete catalog specification, list the basic unit, and select one item from each box below.

Basic Unit: **A19/5**

Reflector Type:	Downlight:	no suffix
	Wallwash:	**WW**
	Corner Wallwash:	**CWW**
	Double Wallwash:	**DWW**
	Half Wallwash:	**HWW**

Reflector and Flange Color*		
	Overlap	Flush
Clear:	**COL**	**CFL**
Champagne Gold:	**GOL**	**GFL**

*Standard reflector flange continues reflector finish. White painted flanges and custom color painted flanges are available on special order. Add **WF** (white flange), or **CCF** (custom color flange) to catalog number.

Examples: **A19/5 COL** is the complete catalog number for a downlight with clear reflector and overlap flange. **A19/5 CWW COL WF** is the complete catalog number for a corner washlight with clear reflector and white painted overlap flange.

TM Registered Trademark of Edison Price Incorporated

12/87

FIGURE 4–5a

INCANDESCENT LUMINAIRE PHOTOMETRIC DATA
5-INCH DIAMETER ALZAK REFLECTOR
A-LAMP
▼

Darklite A19/5
Edison Price Incorporated   409 East 60 Street   New York NY 10022   212-838-5212

Photometric Report

Independent Testing Laboratories Report No. 33191.
Luminaire: Recessed incandescent
with spun aluminum reflector, specular finish.
Lamp: 100 watt A19, 1740 lumens.
Efficiency: 67.1%.
Spacing Criterion: 1.0.

Candlepower Distribution
(Candelas)

	0.0
0	1052
5	1013
15	860
25	840
35	533
45	137
55	3
65	0
75	0
85	0
90	0

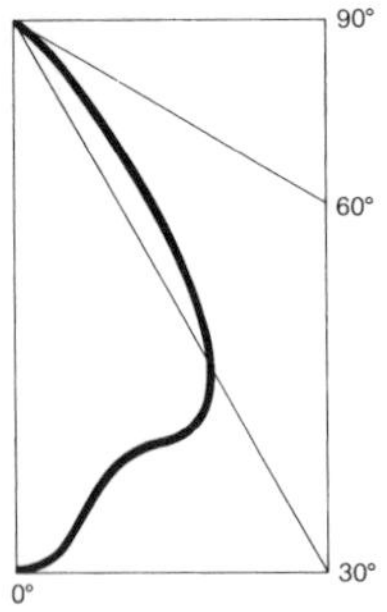

Luminance Data
(Footlamberts)

Vertical Angle	Average
45	4354.
55	118.
65	0.
75	0.
85	0.

Zonal Lumen Summary

Zone	Lumens	% Lamp	% Fixt
0- 30	724	41.6	62.0
0- 40	1053	60.5	90.1
0- 60	1167	67.1	100.0
0- 90	1168	67.1	100.0
90-180	0	0.0	0.0
0-180	1168	67.1	100.0

Coefficients of Utilization — Zonal Cavity Method
Effective Floor Cavity Reflectance 0.20

RC	80				70				50				30			10			0
RW	70	50	30	10	70	50	30	10	70	50	30	10	50	30	10	50	30	10	0
0	80	80	80	80	78	78	78	78	75	75	75		71	71	71	68	68	68	67
1	77	75	73	72	75	73	72	71	71	70	69		68	67	67	66	65	65	63
2	73	70	68	66	72	69	67	65	67	65	64		65	64	62	63	62	61	60
3	70	66	63	61	69	65	63	60	64	61	59		62	60	58	60	59	58	57
4	67	62	59	56	66	62	58	56	60	58	55		59	57	55	58	56	54	53
5	64	59	55	52	63	58	55	52	57	54	52		56	53	51	55	52	51	50
6	61	55	51	49	60	55	51	49	54	51	48		53	50	48	52	50	48	47
7	58	52	48	45	57	51	48	45	50	47	45		50	47	45	49	46	44	44
8	55	48	45	42	54	48	44	42	47	44	42		47	44	42	46	43	41	41
9	52	45	41	39	51	45	41	39	44	41	39		44	41	38	43	40	38	37
10	49	42	39	36	48	42	38	36	42	38	36		41	38	36	41	38	36	35

Darklite A19/5 WW

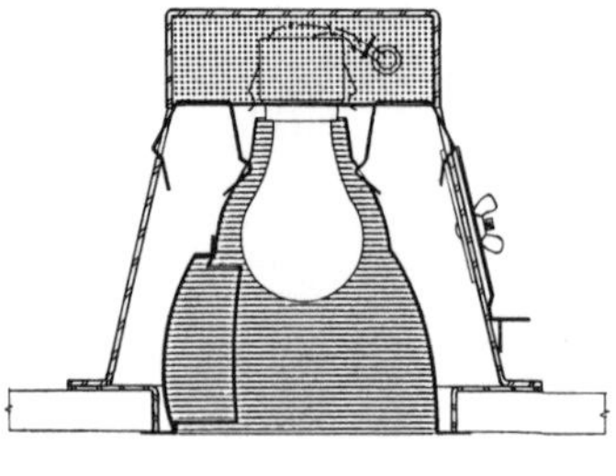

Washlight Information

All vertical footcandles listed are initial values with no
contribution from ceiling or floor reflectances.
Computation performed with a total of five washlight units.

Distance from ceiling	2'6" from wall, 2'6" o.c.		3' from wall, 3' o.c.	
	Below fixture	Between fixtures	Below fixture	Between fixtures
1 ft	9	9	5	5
2	16	15	9	9
3	22	21	13	13
4	23	23	16	15
5	20	20	16	16
6	15	15	14	14
7	12	12	11	11
8	9	9	9	9
9	7	7	7	7

FIGURE 4–5b

Figure C1. *(Top)* The Steelcase Corporate Development Center visitor entry is marked by human-scale torchieres lining the drive, with indirect cold cathode highlighting the canopy entry. The torchieres were a result of the initial concept shown in Figure 4-4 and subsequent half- and full-scale mock-ups shown in Figures 5-9 and 5-10. Photo courtesy Steelcase Inc.; photo credit: Steelcase Inc.

Figure C2. *(Above)* A nighttime view of the Steelcase Corporate Development Center shows the lantern-like effect from the torchieres. Fritted glass was used extensively throughout for glare control during daylight hours, and this frit served an additional function at night by glowing when lighted with a "facade" lighting system located inside the building. Pink cold cathode at the top identifies the facility as a landmark, and is reminiscent of the pink granite and silver/pink metal cladding on the building facade. Photo courtesy Gary Steffy Lighting Design Inc.; photo credit: Robert Eovaldi.

Figure C25. *(At Right)* This marker airbrush rendering was used to express the initial facade lighting concept for the Steelcase Corporate Development Center Project. Marker airbrushing is a relatively inexpensive and easy technique for illustrating lighting ideas for clients and fellow designers. Figure C26 shows the same elevation view of the completed project. Photo courtesy Gary Steffy Lighting Design Inc.; photo credit: Steven Kuzma Photography.

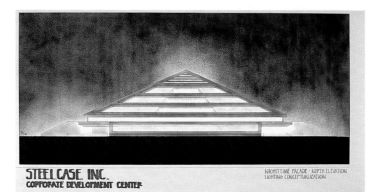

STEELCASE INC.
CORPORATE DEVELOPMENT CENTER

NIGHTTIME FACADE - NORTH ELEVATION
LIGHTING CONCEPTUALIZATION

Figure C26. *(Above)* This night facade view of the Steelcase Corporate Development Center is remarkably similar to the airbrush rendering shown in Figure C25. Note the uniform glow from the fritted skylights, which are illuminated with indirect fluorescent equipment on the inside of the building. Photo courtesy Gary Steffy Lighting Design Inc.; photo credit: Robert Eovaldi.

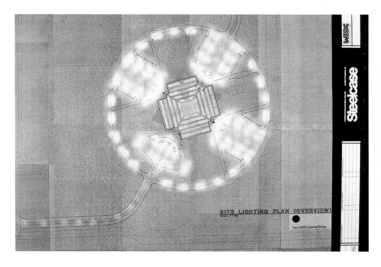

SITE LIGHTING PLAN (OVERVIEW)

Figure C27. *(At Left)* This plan-view rendering of the Steelcase Corporate Development Center site is a composite of computer plots and airbrushing. This rendering/plot was used to show the client the extent and relative intensities of proposed site lighting. Photo courtesy Gary Steffy Lighting Design Inc.; photo credit: Steven Kuzma Photography.

Figure C3. *(Above)* The two-story atrium in the Steelcase Corporate Development Center has as its centerpiece a pendulum sculpture by Dennis Jones. The pendulum pierces the building through a center shaft that is highlighted by a series of cold cathode coves. A series of 5.5-volt bullet beam lamps near the shaft opening highlights the pendulum and the pool over which it swings. Quartz wall wash luminaires are used selectively around the perimeter of the atrium to highlight artworks. Custom compact fluorescent sconces mark the corridors leading to the elevators and the office areas. Photo courtesy Peerless Lighting; photo credit: Richard Sexton.

Figure C4. *(At Right)* Cold cathode slots were used extensively throughout the Steelcase Corporate Development Center cafeteria servery to highlight vertical elements and to reinforce the food serving areas. These cold cathode slots are similar in concept to the fluorescent slot concept shown in Figure 4-1. The white glowing vertical elements serve as sign banners and are comprised of the fritted glass used on the building's skylights — hence the soft uniform glow. Photo courtesy Steelcase Inc.; photo credit: Steelcase Inc.

Figure C5. *(Above)* Wall sconces from Atelier International (AI) combined with a unique wall covering provide not only interesting luminance patterning on the wall, but with a change in viewing angle also provide a change in color. Photo courtesy Steelcase Inc.; photo credit: Steelcase Inc.

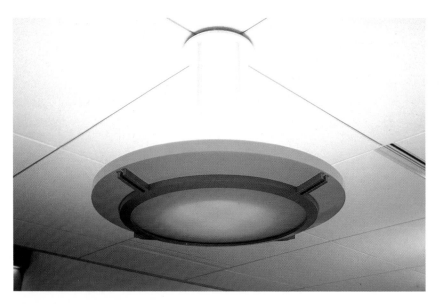

Figure C6. *(Above)* The "MD-33" nonlinear indirect luminaire conceptualized by Gary Steffy Lighting Design Inc., developed by Peerless Lighting, and shown in mockup in Figure 5-12 is seen here in its final form, as it was used in the Steelcase Corporate Development Center project. On 12-foot spacings, these luminaires provide very uniform luminances (at luminance ratios of less than 8:1), with 30 average, maintained footcandles/300 lux on the workplane. The luminaire uses 39-watt, SPX35 compact fluorescent lamps by General Electric. Photo courtesy Peerless Lighting; photo credit: Richard Sexton.

Figure C6a. *(At Left)* This view of the open plan area of the Steelcase Corporate Development Center shows the use of indirect nonlinear luminaires, supplemented with quartz wall wash lighting in the background on the core wall. Photo courtesy Peerless Lighting; photo credit: Richard Sexton.

Figure C6b. *(Above)* A skylight and loft system was designed by the architect, Don Koster, AIA, of The WBDC Group, so that nearly all of the building's occupants had a readily accessible view to the exterior. Such daylight exposure could cause serious VDT reflected glare and washout conditions. The lighting designer and architect worked on the concept of frit-coating the glass by PPG Industries in such a way that the view would be preserved, but glare would be diminished. The architect's perseverance on the frit led to very well-balanced brightnesses when combined with the soft, indirect lighting system. Vertical bulkhead lighting in the skylight wells was necessary to avoid too extreme luminance contrasts and also to provide additional ambient lighting on cloudy days and during early winter morning and late winter afternoon conditions. Photo courtesy Peerless Lighting; photo credit: Richard Sexton.

Figure C7. *(Above)* The secretarial area at the executive core on level four of the Steelcase Corporate Development Center is lighted with a cove using off-the-shelf luminaires (see Figure 4-2). The pendulum shaft is highlighted with blue-white cold cathode (color temperature of 8500K). Photo courtesy Steelcase Inc.; photo credit: Steelcase Inc.

Figure C8. *(At Right)* A conference room at the executive core of the Steelcase Corporate Development Center uses two of the special MD-33 nonlinear indirect luminaires for general lighting. A fluorescent wall slot (see Figure 4-1 for a concept detail) is used to wash one wall and to provide luminance balancing with respect to the ceiling. Two square incandescent adjustable accent luminaires are shown on the upper left, highlighting a marker board. A "typical" reflected ceiling plan for this kind of space is shown in Figure 6-2; with a "typical" switching plan shown in Figure 6-3. Recognize that the black furniture is acceptable for conversational-type activities and where image is important. For an office, however, lighter furniture is recommended (see Chapter 2, Table 2-3). Photo courtesy Peerless Lighting; photo credit: Richard Sexton.

Figure C8a. *(At Right)* This unique workroom at the Steelcase Corporate Development Center is designed to encourage freeflowing conversation and idea sessions. Particularly dramatic lighting is used to enhance these aspects. A plexiglass panel, shaped like the table and suspended, is illuminated with exposed, theatrical-appearing track luminaires to provide a floating lighted plane. Grazing fluorescent lighting is used on the specular marker board. Low-voltage PAR36 accent lights are used to highlight the artwork and dried plants in the background. Photo courtesy Peerless Lighting; photo credit: Richard Sexton.

Figure C8b. *(At Left)* Even in very functional, nonceremonial spaces at the Steelcase Corporate Development Center, attention is paid to luminance distribution. To enhance the pleasantness and spaciousness of this utilitarian corridor, basic fluorescent louvered strip lighting is used to wash the walls with light. Photo courtesy Peerless Lighting; photo credit: Richard Sexton.

Figure C8c. *(At Right)* This view out partially fritted glass at the top floor of the Steelcase Corporate Development Center clearly illustrates the concept of frit coating as shading devices. The frit is a permanent, ceramic coating that cannot be destroyed without breaking the glass. Gradations of horizontal lines of frit — heavier and closer spacings of lines at the top of the window to thinner and wider spacings of lines at the middle of the window — help control the sky luminances. Photo courtesy Peerless Lighting; photo credit: Richard Sexton.

Figure C9. *(At Right)* This showroom office at the Stow & Davis Corporate Headquarters is glass-fronted for maximum viewing exposure. To provide a sense of spatial definition and to accentuate the architectual motif developed by the architects, Ric Pulley and Julie Barnhart-Hoffman of Steelcase Design Services, low-voltage PAR36 lamps in adjustable accent luminaires highlight the etched glass pattern. Photo courtesy Steelcase Inc.; photo credit: Steelcase Inc.

Figure C10. *(Above)* Ambient lighting in the Stow & Davis Corporate Headquarters is achieved with narrow-profile, human-scale direct fluorescent luminaires. A special grid system accommodates the light and a surrounding HVAC boot to provide for a clean, monolithic appearance. Photo courtesy Steelcase Inc.; photo credit: Steelcase Inc.

Figure C11. *(At Left)* The entry to United Airlines Red Carpet Club in Denver is lighted with indirect fluorescent lighting overhead and a cold cathode lighted wall on the right. Use of a specially selected paint — selected under the cold cathode lamp under consideration — can lead to a fluorescing effect. The pale blue wall along with the cool white cold cathode provides a sense of an expansive exterior view to the sky. Photo courtesy Gary Steffy Lighting Design Inc.; photo credit: Imageworks/Ron Johnson.

Figure C12. *(Below)* The check-in lobby at the United Airlines Red Carpet Club in Denver is lit with electric "skylights" (fluorescent strip lighting above the plexiglass panels). To balance the ceiling brightness, wall brightnesses are introduced with a fluorescent slot detail (see Figure 4-1). This also contributes to a sense of spaciousness and pleasantness. The final "layer" of lighting is the accent lighting on the artwork, which consists of adjustable accent luminaires with PAR38 standard-voltage lamps. Photo courtesy Gary Steffy Lighting Design Inc.; photo credit: Imageworks/Ron Johnson.

Figure C13. *(Above)* In order to make the large United Airlines Red Carpet Club more intimate, the interior designer, Dennis St. John, introduced partial-height walls and overhead trellis works. MR-16 framing projectors located above the trellis works create the sun-light-like shadow patterns on the back wall. Indirect fluorescent lighting is achieved with widespread, asymmetric luminaires located in the ceiling "beams" using T8, 3000K lamps. Photo courtesy Gary Steffy Lighting Design Inc.; photo credit: Imageworks/Ron Johnson.

Figure C15. *(At Left)* Mirror lighting is always a challenge. Here, the client wanted a clean, unobtrusive, yet functional lighting system. Although Hollywood mirror lights are popular for makeup and/or shaving and grooming, they can seem dated and gaudy. By taking advantage of a medicine chest, stripping the silver backing from the mirror, etching the remaining glass strip, and then putting a strip fluorescent light or an incandescent Lumiline lamp behind the etched glass, one can achieve wonderful-quality facial lighting. Photo courtesy Powell/Kleinschmidt; photo credit: copyright 1985, Peter Aaron/ESTO, all rights reserved.

Figure C16. *(At Right)* In this Michigan residence, the living room is divided from the dining room by a unique millwork element, on top of which are theatrical footlights aimed at the high ceiling. These footlights, where lamps are a repeating linear array of red, blue, and amber, can be dimmed to any position and thus create any color of light on the ceiling. Adjustable accent luminaires with PAR38 lamps are used to highlight the divider, and are used to highlight the artwork in the background. The specular fireplace marble wall is lighted with an incandescent slot similar to the detail shown in Figure 3-5, but with specially designed reflectors by Edison Price. Photo courtesy Gary Steffy Lighting Design Inc. and Bob Wine Architect; photo credit: Balthazar Korab.

Figure C14. *(Facing Page, Bottom)* The residence of Donald Powell is lighted to accentuate the architectural finishes and features and to contribute to a sense of spaciousness. Adjustable accent luminaires with PAR 38 lamps highlight the wood room divider and the stainless steel mesh fabric wall covering on the left. Small, discrete luminaires using R14 lamps provide downlighting at the cocktail table. (Fill light was used to highlight the sofa on the left.) Photo courtesy Powell/Kleinschmidt; photo credit: copyright 1985, Peter Aaron/ESTO, all rights reserved.

Figure C17. *(At Right)* The table center-piece in the dining area of the Michigan residence is highlighted by two adjustable accent luminaires, each using a 5.5-volt bullet beam PAR36 lamp. Photo courtesy Gary Steffy Lighting Design Inc. and Bob Wine Architect; photo credit: Balthazar Korab.

Figure C18. *(Below)* This action area at the Steelcase Western Division Headquarters uses two layers of lighting: an ambient layer of high-level lighting is achieved with fluorescent pendent tubes with radial baffles, above which there is an accent layer of PAR 38 gimbal ring luminaires on track. This lighting helps provide a dramatic focus on this special display area. Photo courtesy Steelcase Inc.; photo credit: Steelcase Inc.

Figure C19. *(Above)* Lighting along the walls of the core of the Steelcase Western Division Headquarters is accomplished with a fluorescent wall slot similar to the detail shown in Figure 4-1. One should recognize the importance of wall lighting with medium- to dark-toned wall materials. The architectural kiosks also provide light to enhance the functional difference between the open office area and core spaces, as well as to introduce visual interest. The traditional furniture-integrated ambient lighting works best in high ceiling spaces (in this case the ceiling is 10 feet 6 inches above the floor), and where furniture will not be moved much. Task lights on the desk and under the binder bins are necessary for appropriate lighting levels on paper tasks and to prevent shadowing from the furniture. Indirect lighting tends to be less glary and less shadowy than direct lighting. Photo courtesy Steelcase Inc.; photo credit: Steelcase Inc.

Figure C20. *(Above)* Private offices at the Steelcase Western Division Headquarters are lighted similarly to the open office areas. Some indirect lighting along with wall lighting is used to provide a softer, less harsh light to the space. Instead of desk-mounted task lights, task lighting is achieved with downlighting from the pendent luminaires. Photo courtesy Steelcase Inc.; photo credit: Steelcase Inc.

Figure C21. *(At Left)* The Steelcase Western Division Headquarters private dining room is lighted similarly to the remainder of the facility—indirectly. For the appropriate level of brightness and for some color, cold cathode was used in cove elements made of drywall. Adjustable accent luminaires using MR-16 lamps highlight the artwork and the table centerpiece. Photo courtesy Archigraphics Inc.; photo credit: Rick Mendoza.

Figure C22. *(Below)* Exposed cold cathode outlines the curvilinear wall surrounding the presentation room at the Steelcase Western Division Headquarters, and attracts attention to this "entertainment" space. Inside the presentation room, cold cathode placed above ceiling plates provides an indirect glow for general lighting. Adjustable accent luminaires with PAR 38 lamps provide task lighting and can be dimmed for notetaking during presentations. Photo courtesy Steelcase Inc.; photo credit: Steelcase Inc.

Figure C23. *(Above)* Facade lighting for this office building in Southfield, Michigan, is done without washing the entire facade with a blast of light. Instead, the curvilinear facade is enhanced with incrementally shorter runs of blue cold cathode. The cathode is aligned to a band of blue brick (see Figure C24). To complete the facade lighting, the interior surfaces of the atrium were finished in light colors by the architect, Neumann-Smith, and then lighted with fluorescent luminaires. Photo courtesy Gary Steffy Lighting Design Inc., photo credit: Robert Eovaldi

Figure C24. *(Above)* A closeup of the blue brick band highlighted with blue cold cathode on the office building shown in Figure C23. The cold cathode tube is clear when not energized, allowing the blue brick to read through during the daylight hours. Photo courtesy Gary Steffy Lighting Design Inc., photo credit: Robert Eovaldi.

Photometric data for the Edison Price downlight are shown in Figure 4–5b. These data are for a specific lamp. The luminaire efficiency is reported at the upper left along with the spacing criterion. Luminaire efficiency is the percentage of lamp lumens that exit the luminaire. Obviously, some lumens are lost in absorption in the reflector. Luminaire efficiency is important, but it is by no means the sole criterion by which a luminaire should be selected.

The spacing criterion is discussed in Chapter 5. Candlepower distribution is particularly important for performing point method calculations, discussed in Chapter 5. Candlepower, reported in candelas, is the intensity of the light in a specific direction. The coefficients of utilization (CU) are necessary for performing lumen method calculations, discussed in Chapter 5. A candlepower curve is shown to the left of the CU table to give the designer a sense of the light distribution pattern from the luminaire.

Finally, because this particular luminaire is available in a wall wash version, some vertical illuminance data (illuminance on a vertical—wall—surface) are reported at the bottom of the sheet. When the wall wash luminaires are placed on 3-foot centers and 3 feet from the wall, the vertical illuminance is quite uniform. The intensity, however, is somewhat decreased, resulting in a less bright wall wash effect.

There are times when mechanical or structural clearance limits the permissible height of recessed downlights. By side-mounting the lamp, as shown in the datasheet of Figure 4–6a, the luminaire height can be reduced by several inches.

Because the lamp is not placed vertically on the central axis of the luminaire, the candlepower distribution is no longer axially symmetric—symmetrical all the way around. Therefore, a much larger candlepower distribution table is listed (Figure 4–6b). The vertical column of angular values of zero through 90° indicates the angle from nadir (straight down) at which candlepower was measured. The horizontal row of angular values of zero to 180.0° indicates the angle of the plane of candlepower measurement in plan view.

Figure 4–7a is a catalog datasheet for two versions of an R-lamp downlight. These luminaires by Kurt Versen are available in two aperture sizes, one for R–20 lamps and the other for R–30 lamps. They are part of a family of luminaires of the same finish and similar size. These luminaires can be relamped from below or from the top (via access screws). Reflectors are available in specular clear natural aluminum or in black, gold, bronze, or pewter. These luminaires, like many downlights, are available modified for sloped ceilings so that the lamp sits perpendicular to the floor, even in cathedral ceilings. For use in outdoor canopies, a damp label is available.

Photometric data for the Kurt Versen luminaires are shown in Figure 4–7b. Illuminance data are given for typical floor-to-ceiling heights for single

Darklite™A19/5S

Edison Price Incorporated

Section 1

Features

An extremely shallow 5″ diameter recessed low brightness downlight designed for use with inside frosted A19 lamps (100 watt maximum). The fixture provides a shielding angle of 40°. One basic housing allows interchangeable use of the downlight and wall-wash reflectors. This permits housings to be installed first and reflectors installed or changed at any time according to the required application. Recessed depth is only 5 11/16″.

The A19/5S is part of the Edison Price family of A lamp downlights and washlights which are available in five different aperture sizes. Each size is scaled for a different ceiling height, which gives the specifier the ability to match the aperture size of PAR lamp and low voltage fixtures.

Applications

The A19/5S is a small aperture fixture suitable for downlighting or wall washing in offices, stores, residences, lobbies, corridors and reception areas. Reflectors are available in clear natural aluminum Alzak® or champagne gold Alzak®.

Washlight reflectors available are: wallwash (120°), corner wallwash (210°), double wallwash (2 x 120°), and half wallwash (60°).

Fixture is union made IBEW; UL listed; prewired with insulation detector and approved for ten wire 75°C branch circuit pull through wiring. Removal of the reflector allows access to the junction box.

Ordering Information

For complete catalog specification, list the basic unit, and select one item from each box below.

Basic Unit: **A19/5S**

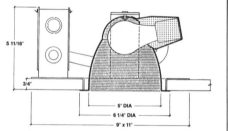

Reflector Type:	Downlight:	no suffix
	Wallwash:	**WW**
	Corner Wallwash:	**CWW**
	Double Wallwash:	**DWW**
	Half Wallwash:	**HWW**

Reflector and Flange Color*		
	Overlap	Flush
Clear:	**COL**	**CFL**
Champagne Gold:	**GOL**	**GFL**

*Standard reflector flange continues reflector finish. White painted flanges and custom color painted flanges are available on special order. Add **WF** (white flange), or **CCF** (custom color flange) to catalog number.

Examples: **A19/5S COL** is the complete catalog number for a downlight with clear reflector and overlap flange. **A19/5S CWW COL WF** is the complete catalog number for a corner washlight with clear reflector and white painted overlap flange.

5 11/16″
3/4″
5″ DIA
6 1/4″ DIA
9″ x 11″

FIGURE 4–6a

INCANDESCENT LUMINAIRE PHOTOMETRIC DATA
5-INCH DIAMETER ALZAK REFLECTOR
SIDE-MOUNTED A-LAMP
▼

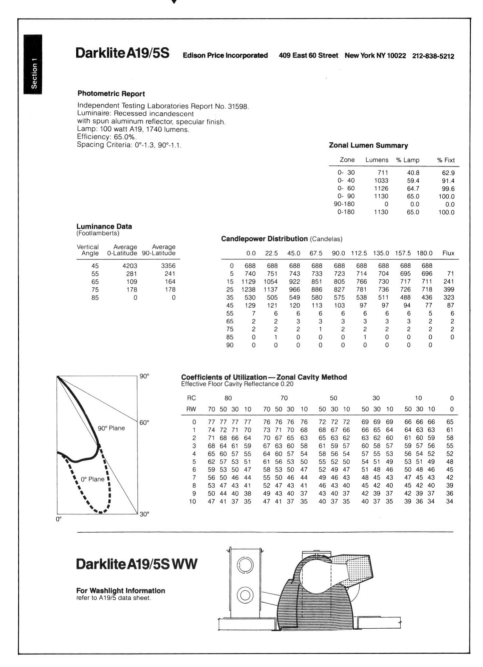

Darklite A19/5S   Edison Price Incorporated   409 East 60 Street   New York NY 10022   212-838-5212

Photometric Report

Independent Testing Laboratories Report No. 31598.
Luminaire: Recessed incandescent
with spun aluminum reflector, specular finish.
Lamp: 100 watt A19, 1740 lumens.
Efficiency: 65.0%.
Spacing Criteria: 0°-1.3, 90°-1.1.

Zonal Lumen Summary

Zone	Lumens	% Lamp	% Fixt
0- 30	711	40.8	62.9
0- 40	1033	59.4	91.4
0- 60	1126	64.7	99.6
0- 90	1130	65.0	100.0
90-180	0	0.0	0.0
0-180	1130	65.0	100.0

Luminance Data
(Footlamberts)

Vertical Angle	Average 0-Latitude	Average 90-Latitude
45	4203	3356
55	281	241
65	109	164
75	178	178
85	0	0

Candlepower Distribution (Candelas)

	0.0	22.5	45.0	67.5	90.0	112.5	135.0	157.5	180.0	Flux
0	688	688	688	688	688	688	688	688	688	
5	740	751	743	733	723	714	704	695	696	71
15	1129	1054	922	851	805	766	730	717	711	241
25	1238	1137	966	886	827	781	736	726	718	399
35	530	505	549	580	575	538	511	488	436	323
45	129	121	120	113	103	97	97	94	77	87
55	7	6	6	6	6	6	6	6	5	6
65	2	2	3	3	3	3	3	3	2	2
75	2	2	2	1	2	2	2	2	2	2
85	0	1	0	0	0	1	0	0	0	0
90	0	0	0	0	0	0	0	0	0	

Coefficients of Utilization — Zonal Cavity Method
Effective Floor Cavity Reflectance 0.20

RC		80				70				50			30			10			0
RW	70	50	30	10	70	50	30	10	50	30	10	50	30	10	50	30	10	0
0	77	77	77	77	76	76	76	76	72	72	72	69	69	69	66	66	66	65
1	74	72	71	70	73	71	70	68	68	67	66	66	65	64	64	63	63	61
2	71	68	66	64	70	67	65	63	65	63	62	63	62	60	61	60	59	58
3	68	64	61	59	67	63	60	58	61	59	57	60	58	57	59	57	56	55
4	65	60	57	55	64	60	57	54	58	56	54	57	55	53	56	54	52	52
5	62	57	53	51	61	56	53	50	55	52	50	54	51	49	53	51	49	48
6	59	53	50	47	58	53	50	47	52	49	47	51	48	46	50	48	46	45
7	56	50	46	44	55	50	46	44	49	46	43	48	45	43	47	45	43	42
8	53	47	43	41	52	47	43	41	46	43	40	45	42	40	45	42	40	39
9	50	44	40	38	49	43	40	37	43	40	37	42	39	37	42	39	37	36
10	47	41	37	35	47	41	37	35	40	37	35	40	37	35	39	36	34	34

Darklite A19/5S WW

For Washlight Information
refer to A19/5 data sheet.

FIGURE 4–6b

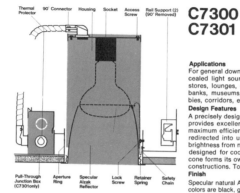

Thermal Protector   90° Connector   Housing   Socket   Access Screw   Rail Support (2) (90° Removed)

Pull-Through Junction Box (C7301 only)   Aperture Ring   Specular Alzak Reflector   Lock Screw   Retainer Spring   Safety Chain

C7300
C7301

C1

Applications
For general downlighting or highlighting when a concealed light source is desired. Use in auditoriums, stores, lounges, churches, transportation terminals, banks, museums, hotels, schools, restaurants, lobbies, corridors, etc.

Design Features
A precisely designed specular Alzak conoid reflector provides excellent performance characteristics with maximum efficiency. Spill light is gathered and then redirected into useful zones. The result is very low brightness from normal viewing angles. Housings are designed for cool lamp operating temperatures. The cone forms its own minimum trim, and fits all ceiling constructions. Top or bottom service.

Finish
Specular natural Alzak reflectors are standard. Optional colors are black, gold, bronze, pewter. Housing is matte black. Steel parts are thoroughly processed and phosphate conditioned for corrosion resistance prior to spraying and baking.

General
Fixtures are union made IBEW, pre-wired, thermally protected as required by NEC. C7300 is UL listed for eight wire 75°C through wiring. C7301 is UL listed for eight wire 75°C pull-through wiring. Mounting attachments and instructions are included. Access above ceiling required for C7300.

Accessories
For 27" support rails, add R2 to catalog number.
For 52" support rails. add H5 to catalog number.
For specular black reflector, add B to catalog number.
For specular gold reflector, add G to catalog number.
For specular pewter reflector, add Y to number.
For specular bronze reflector, add Z to number.
For sloped ceilings see model C7310.
For damp label, add DL to catalog number.

Brightness

Catalog Number	Lamp	80°	70°	60°	50°
C7300	30W R-20 WFL	1	2	3	5
C7300	50W R-20 WFL	1	2	3	7
C7301	75W R-30 Spot	2	3	6	30
C7301	75W R-30 Flood	3	6	14	55

Footlamberts, clear cone. See Performance Datacharts for colored cone multipliers.

Dimensions and Lamps

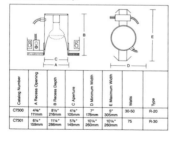

B   C   A   E   D

Catalog Number	Recess Opening	Recess Depth	Aperture	D Minimum Width	E Maximum Width	Watts	Type
C7300	4⅜" 111mm	8½" 216mm	4⅛" 105mm	7" 178mm	5" 305mm	30-50	R-20
C7301	6¼" 159mm	11¼" 286mm	5⅞" 149mm	10¼" 260mm	10¼" 260mm	75	R-30

kurt versen ✪
Kurt Versen Company   Point Source Lighting
Westwood, New Jersey 07675

FIGURE 4–7a

INCANDESCENT LUMINAIRE PHOTOMETRIC DATA
4½-INCH DIAMETER ALZAK REFLECTOR
R-LAMP
▼

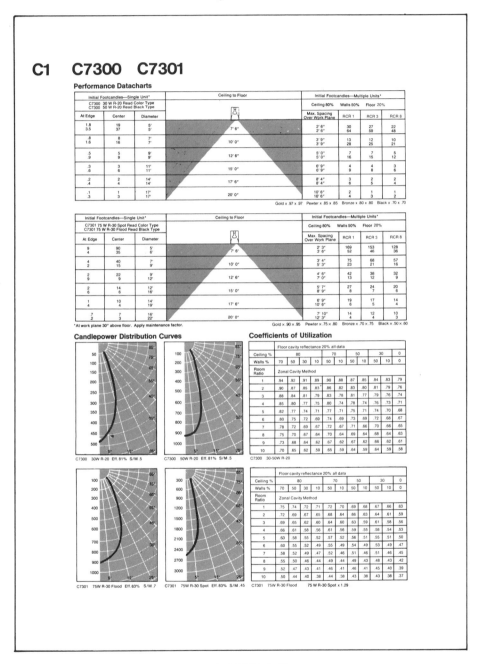

C1   C7300   C7301

Performance Datacharts

Initial Footcandles—Single Unit*			Ceiling to Floor	Initial Footcandles—Multiple Units*			
C7300 30 W R-20 Read Color Type / C7300 50 W R-20 Read Black Type				Ceiling 80% Walls 50% Floor 20%			
At Edge	Center	Diameter		Max. Spacing Over Work Plane	RCR 1	RCR 3	RCR 8
1.8 / 3.5	19 / 37	5' / 5'	7' 6"	2' 6" / 2' 6"	30 / 64	27 / 59	22 / 48
.8 / 1.6	8 / 16	7' / 7'	10' 0"	3' 9" / 3' 9"	13 / 28	12 / 25	10 / 21
.5 / .9	5 / 9	9' / 9'	12' 6"	5' 0" / 5' 0"	7 / 16	7 / 15	5 / 12
.3 / .6	3 / 6	11' / 11'	15' 0"	6' 9" / 6' 9"	4 / 9	4 / 8	3 / 6
.2 / .4	2 / 4	14' / 14'	17' 6"	8' 4" / 8' 4"	3 / 6	2 / 5	2 / 4
.1 / .3	1 / 3	17' / 17'	20' 0"	10' 6" / 10' 6"	2 / 4	1 / 3	1 / 2

Gold x .97 x .97   Pewter x .85 x .85   Bronze x .80 x .80   Black x .70 x .70

Initial Footcandles—Single Unit*			Ceiling to Floor	Initial Footcandles—Multiple Units*			
C7301 75 W R-30 Spot Read Color Type / C7301 75 W R-30 Flood Read Black Type				Ceiling 80% Walls 50% Floor 20%			
At Edge	Center	Diameter		Max. Spacing Over Work Plane	RCR 1	RCR 3	RCR 8
9 / 4	90 / 35	5' / 6'	7' 6"	2' 3" / 3' 6"	169 / 52	153 / 46	128 / 36
4 / 2	40 / 15	7' / 9'	10' 0"	3' 4" / 5' 3"	75 / 23	68 / 21	57 / 16
2 / .9	22 / 9	9' / 12'	12' 6"	4' 6" / 7' 0"	42 / 13	38 / 12	32 / 9
2 / .6	14 / 6	12' / 16'	15' 0"	5' 7" / 8' 9"	27 / 8	24 / 7	20 / 6
1 / 4	10 / 4	14' / 19'	17' 6"	6' 9" / 10' 6"	19 / 6	17 / 5	14 / 4
.7 / .2	7 / 3	16' / 22'	20' 0"	7' 10" / 12' 3"	14 / 4	12 / 4	10 / 3

*At work plane 30" above floor. Apply maintenance factor.   Gold x .90 x .95   Pewter x .75 x .80   Bronze x .70 x .75   Black x .50 x .60

Candlepower Distribution Curves

C7300 30W R-20 Eff. 81% S/M .5

C7300 50W R-20 Eff. 81% S/M .5

C7301 75W R-30 Flood Eff. 63% S/M .7

C7301 75W R-30 Spot Eff. 83% S/M .45

Coefficients of Utilization

C7300 30-50W R-20

	Floor cavity reflectance 20% all data									
Ceiling %	80			70			50		30	0
Walls %	70	50	30	10	50	10	50	10	50	10	0
Room Ratio	Zonal Cavity Method									
1	.94	.92	.91	.89	.90	.88	.87	.85	.84	.83	.79
2	.90	.87	.85	.83	.86	.82	.83	.80	.81	.79	.76
3	.88	.84	.81	.79	.83	.78	.81	.77	.79	.76	.74
4	.85	.80	.77	.75	.80	.74	.78	.74	.76	.73	.71
5	.82	.77	.74	.71	.77	.71	.75	.71	.74	.70	.68
6	.80	.75	.72	.69	.74	.69	.73	.69	.72	.68	.67
7	.78	.72	.69	.67	.72	.67	.71	.66	.70	.66	.65
8	.75	.70	.67	.64	.70	.64	.69	.64	.68	.64	.63
9	.73	.68	.64	.62	.67	.62	.67	.62	.66	.62	.61
10	.70	.65	.62	.59	.65	.59	.64	.59	.64	.59	.58

C7301 75W R-30 Flood   75 W R-30 Spot x 1.29

	Floor cavity reflectance 20% all data									
Ceiling %	80			70			50		30	0
Walls %	70	50	30	10	50	10	50	10	50	10	0
Room Ratio	Zonal Cavity Method									
1	.75	.74	.72	.71	.72	.70	.69	.68	.67	.66	.63
2	.72	.69	.67	.65	.68	.64	.66	.63	.64	.61	.59
3	.69	.65	.62	.60	.64	.60	.63	.59	.61	.58	.56
4	.66	.61	.58	.56	.61	.56	.61	.56	.58	.54	.53
5	.63	.58	.55	.52	.57	.52	.56	.51	.55	.51	.50
6	.60	.55	.52	.49	.55	.49	.54	.49	.53	.49	.47
7	.58	.52	.49	.47	.52	.46	.51	.46	.51	.46	.45
8	.55	.50	.46	.44	.49	.44	.49	.43	.48	.43	.42
9	.52	.47	.43	.41	.46	.41	.46	.41	.45	.40	.39
10	.50	.44	.40	.38	.44	.38	.43	.38	.43	.38	.37

FIGURE 4–7b

units and multiple units. Candlepower curves also are shown, along with coefficients of utilization.

Not all downlights are made with aluminum reflectors. For many years, the black milligroove baffle downlight was quite popular. An example of such a luminaire is shown in Figure 4–8a. Although black milligroove luminaires are not as efficient as the clear aluminum units, they do offer the possibility of various painted finishes from some manufacturers. Some designers will want to avoid the "swiss cheese" look of black holes in a white ceiling, but, at the same time, it is not desirable to introduce the bright, glary reflections that might result from using white reflectors. Hence light-to-medium gray baffles are being used. When lighted, these baffles have luminances that tend to match those of white ceilings, particulary in areas with indirect fluorescent lighting as the ambient source.

In any case, for best glare control, direct view of the lamp should be minimized as much as possible. This generally requires the use of deeper downlights, such as the Edison Price and Kurt Versen units shown in Figures 4–5a, 4–6a, 4–7a, and 4–8a. With downlights, efficiency and glare control usually are diametrically opposed criteria. To gain efficiency, the lamp is best left exposed, with no reflector or shielding. To gain glare control, the lamp should be recessed into a reflector housing and/or fitted with some shielding. Obviously, human energy is the most precious resource; so glare control should take precedence over lamp efficiency.

With the introduction of compact fluorescent lamps, some downlight manufacturers have been designing and making available luminaires that take advantage of the lamp's long life and good color. These luminaires, two of which are illustrated in Figures 4–9a and 4–9b (Kurt Versen) and Figures 4–10a and 4–10b (Columbia), work best when specifically designed around compact fluorescent lamps. A-lamp reflectors retrofitted with compact fluorescent lamps *do not* provide efficient, effective lighting. In fact, retrofitted reflectors usually will reflect a telltale "rainbow"—an effect known as iridescence. Low-iridescence reflectors do not exhibit this effect, which is also known as "oil-canning" because the rainbow resembles the effect of light reflecting from an oil film.

The Kurt Versen luminaire (Figure 4–9a and 4–9b) is available in a variety of beam spreads (the "Wide Beam" is shown), which indicates that the manufacturer has very carefully designed the luminaire optics for maximum efficiency while minimizing glare by using a relatively deep housing and by using the low-brightness Alzak finish on reflectors.

These kinds of luminaires are particularly appropriate where the look of incandescent lighting is desirable, but the maintenance and operating costs are especially important.

The lower right portion of Figure 4–9a includes an "Energy Operating Data" table, which indicates ballast losses for the 9- and 13-watt lamps.

Incandescent Luminaire Datasheet
6-Inch Diameter Milligroove Baffle
R/PAR Lamp
▼

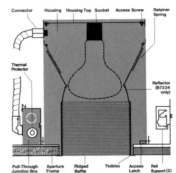

B7222
B7224

B5

Connector · Housing · Housing Top · Socket · Access Screw · Retainer Spring

Thermal Protector

Reflector (B7224 only)

Pull-Through Junction Box · Aperture Frame · Ridged Baffle · Tinitrim · Access Latch · Rail Support (2)

Applications
For general downlighting in medium and high ceiling areas where a concealed light source is desired. Use in auditoriums, stores, lounges, churches, transportation terminals, lobbies, banks, museums, hotels, schools, restaurants

Design Features
A one piece heavy wall aluminum ridged baffle traps spill light and greatly reduces aperture brightness at normal viewing angles. Deeply grooved sharp ridges break up peripheral light and are seen as a soft side wall glow. This construction is unaffected by lamp heat and will last indefinitely. The unique contour of Kurt Versen's ridges produce unparalleled brightness control compared to other grooved baffle designs. Top or bottom service.

Finish
Exposed parts are durable white enamel, inside is matte black. All metal is thoroughly processed and phosphate conditioned for corrosion resistance prior to spraying and baking. This assures better paint adhesion and a built-up protective finish of superior quality and durability.

General
Fixtures are union made IBEW, pre-wired, thermally protected as required by NEC. UL listed for eight wire 90°C branch circuit pull-through wiring. Aperture frame, mounting attachments and installation instruction sheets are included with each unit.

Accessories
For 27″ support rails, add R2 to catalog number.
For 52″ support rails, add R5 to catalog number.
For sloped ceilings see model D7424.
For damp label, add DL to catalog number.

Brightness

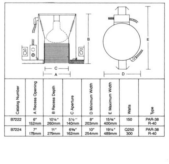

Catalog Number	Lamp	80°	70°	60°	50°
B7222	150W R-40 Flood	2	7	14	66
	150W PAR-38 Flood	7	2	5	7
B7224	300W R-40 Flood	2	4	7	128
	Q250W PAR-38 Flood	.4	1	2	9

Data in footlamberts

Dimensions and Lamps

Catalog Number	A. Recess Opening	B. Recess Depth	C. Aperture	D. Minimum Width	E. Maximum Width	Watts	Type
B7222	6″ 152mm	10¼″ 260mm	5½″ 140mm	8″ 203mm	15¾″ 400mm	150	PAR-38 R-40
B7224	7″ 178mm	11″ 279mm	6⅜″ 162mm	10″ 254mm	19¼″ 489mm	Q250 300	PAR-38 R-40

kurt versen
Kurt Versen Company   Point Source Lighting
Westwood, New Jersey 07675

FIGURE 4–8a

INCANDESCENT LUMINAIRE PHOTOMETRIC DATA
6-INCH DIAMETER MILLIGROOVE BAFFLE
R/PAR LAMP
▼

B5   B7222   B7224

Performance Datacharts

Initial Footcandles—Single Unit*			Ceiling to Floor	Initial Footcandles—Multiple Units*			
B7222 150 W R-40 Flood Read Color Type B7222 150 W PAR-38 Flood Read Black Type				Ceiling 80% Walls 50% Floor 20%			
At Edge	Center	Diameter		Max. Spacing Over Work Plane	RCR 1	RCR 3	RCR 8
2.1 6.2	21 61	11' 7'	10' 0"	6' 0" 4' 6"	19 45	19 40	14 32
1.2 3.4	12 34	14' 9'	12' 6"	8' 0" 6' 0"	12 25	11 23	8 18
.8 2.2	8 22	17' 11'	15' 0"	10' 0" 7' 6"	8 16	7 15	5 11
.5 1.5	5 15	21' 14'	17' 6"	12' 0" 9' 0"	5 11	5 10	4 8
.4 1.1	4 11	25' 17'	20' 0"	14' 0" 10' 6"	4 8	4 7	3 6
.3 .9	3 8	28' 19'	22' 8"	16' 0" 12' 0"	3 6	3 6	2 4

Initial Footcandles—Single Unit*			Ceiling to Floor	Initial Footcandles—Multiple Units*			
B7224 300 W R-40 Flood Read Color Type B7224 Q250W PAR-38 Flood Read Black Type				Ceiling 80% Walls 50% Floor 20%			
At Edge	Center	Diameter		Max. Spacing Over Work Plane	RCR 1	RCR 3	RCR 8
2.4 6.5	24 61	14' 9'	12' 6"	8' 6" 6' 6"	30 62	26 56	21 44
1.5 4.2	16 39	17' 11'	15' 0"	10' 8" 8' 2"	19 39	18 36	12 28
1.1 2.8	11 27	21' 14'	17' 6"	12' 9" 9' 9"	13 28	13 25	9 19
.8 2.1	8 20	25' 17'	20' 0"	14' 10" 11' 5"	10 20	9 18	6 14
.5 1.3	5 12	32' 21'	25' 0"	19' 2" 14' 8"	6 12	6 11	4 9
.3 .8	3 8	38' 24'	30' 0"	23' 5" 17' 10"	4 7	4 6	3 5

* At work plane 30" above floor. Apply maintenance factor.

Candlepower Distribution Curves

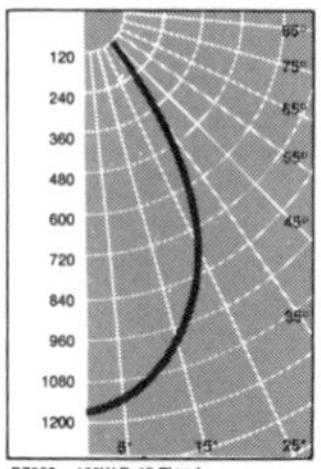

B7222 150W R-40 Flood Eff. 33% S/M .8

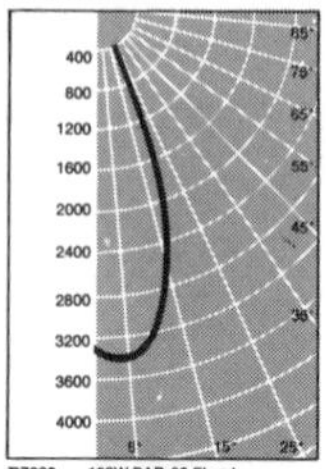

B7222 150W PAR-38 Flood Eff. 45% S/M .6

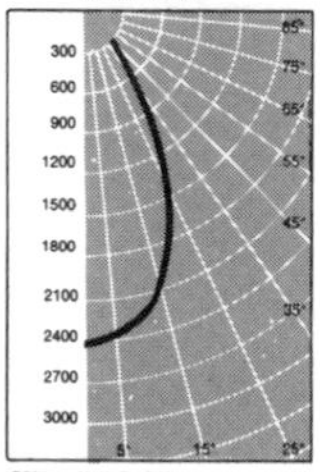

B7224 300W R-40 Flood Eff. 54% S/M .85

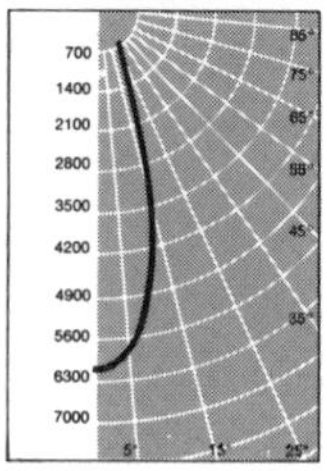

B7224 Q250W PAR-38 Flood Eff. 66% S/M .65

Coefficients of Utilization

	Floor cavity reflectance 20% all data									
Ceiling %	80				70			50		30	0
Walls %	70	50	30	10	50	10	50	10	50	10	0
Room Ratio	Zonal Cavity Method										
1	.53	.52	.51	.51	.51	.50	.49	.48	.48	.47	.45
2	.51	.49	.48	.46	.48	.46	.47	.45	.46	.44	.42
3	.49	.47	.45	.44	.46	.43	.45	.43	.44	.42	.
4	.47	.45	.43	.41	.44	.41	.43	.40	.42	.40	.39
5	.45	.42	.40	.39	.42	.38	.41	.38	.40	.38	.37
6	.44	.41	.39	.37	.40	.37	.40	.37	.39	.36	.36
7	.42	.39	.37	.35	.39	.35	.38	.35	.38	.35	.34
8	.41	.37	.35	.34	.37	.33	.37	.33	.36	.33	.33
9	.39	.35	.33	.32	.35	.32	.35	.32	.34	.31	.31
10	.37	.34	.31	.30	.33	.30	.33	.30	.33	.30	.29

B7222 150W PAR-38 Flood   B7224 Q250W PAR-38 Flood x 1.44

	Floor cavity reflectance 20% all data									
Ceiling %	80				70			50		30	0
Walls %	70	50	30	10	50	10	50	10	50	10	0
Room Ratio	Zonal Cavity Method										
1	.62	.61	.60	.59	.60	.58	.58	.56	.56	.54	.52
2	.59	.57	.55	.53	.56	.52	.54	.51	.53	.50	.48
3	.57	.53	.51	.49	.53	.48	.51	.48	.50	.47	.45
4	.54	.50	.47	.45	.49	.44	.48	.44	.47	.43	.42
5	.51	.47	.43	.41	.46	.41	.45	.41	.44	.40	.39
6	.49	.44	.41	.38	.43	.38	.43	.38	.42	.38	.37
7	.46	.41	.38	.36	.41	.36	.40	.35	.39	.35	.34
8	.44	.38	.35	.33	.38	.33	.37	.33	.37	.33	.32
9	.41	.36	.32	.30	.35	.30	.35	.30	.34	.30	.29
10	.38	.33	.30	.28	.33	.27	.32	.27	.32	.27	.27

B7224 300W R-40 Flood   B7222 150W R-40 Flood x .65

FIGURE 4–8b

DIRECT FLUORESCENT LUMINAIRE DATASHEET
8¾-INCH DIAMETER ALZAK REFLECTOR
COMPACT LAMP
▼

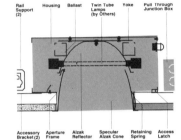

Rail Support (2) | Housing | Ballast | Twin Tube Lamps (by Others) | Yoke | Pull Through Junction Box

Accessory Bracket (2) | Aperture Frame | Alzak Reflector | Specular Alzak Cone | Retaining Spring | Access Latch

P346
P347
Twin Tube Wide Beam

P7

Applications
For corridors and transient spaces. Long life 10,000 hour lamps indicate use where relamping is difficult. Shallow recess depth permits installation when plenums are limited. For low level softly diffused lighting anywhere. Superb output for minimal energy expenditure.

Design Features
A high purity semi-specular Alzak primary reflector gathers and directs lamp output through a parabolic conoid baffle cone. Distribution is extremely broad with a soft pattern edge. A full steel housing protects the optical system and ensures a constant relationship between reflectors for dependable performance. A two inch deep aperture throat permits installation in varying thickness ceilings without special modification. Lamp and ballast service from below.

Finish
Specular Alzak natural cones are standard. Optional colors are black, bronze, gold, pewter and umber. Cones are processed to minimize iridescence or ''rainbow effect.'' On deeper cone colors it is virtually eliminated. Housing and internal steel parts are phosphate conditioned for corrosion resistance prior to spraying and baking optical matte black.

General
Fixtures are union made IBEW, pre-wired and UL listed for eight wire 75°C pull through wiring. Mounting attachments and instructions are included.

Accessories
For specular black cone add B to catalog number.
For specular bronze cone add Z to catalog number.
For specular gold cone add G to catalog number.
For specular pewter cone add Y to catalog number.
For specular umber cone add R to catalog number.
For 27" support rails add R2 to catalog number.
For 52" support rails add R5 to catalog number.
For high power factor ballast add HP to catalog number.
For damp label add DL to catalog number.

Dimensions and Lamps

Catalog Number*	A Recess Opening	B Recess Depth	C Aperture	D Minimum Width	E Maximum Width	Lamps
P346	8³/₄" 222mm	8¾" 222mm	8³/₈" 213mm	14¹/₄" 362mm	21½" 546mm	Two 9W Twin tube T4
P347	8³/₄" 222mm	8¾" 222mm	8³/₈" 213mm	14¹/₄" 362mm	21½" 546mm	Two 13W Twin tube T4

*Add 120 or 277 to catalog number for proper voltage.

Energy Operating Data

	120V		277V	
	2x9W	2x13W	2x9W	2x13W
Ballast loss	7.80	8.30	9.50	9.30
Total fixture draw	25.80	34.30	27.50	35.30
Starting amps	.29	.52	.27	.50
Operating amps	.24	.38	.18	.30
Volt amps, primary	29.60	46.40	49.90	83.10

Data is for normal power factor, High power factor is available, see Accessories.
For HPF multiply starting, operating and volt amps above by .5.

Brightness

Catalog Number	Lamp	80°	70°	60°	50°
P346	Two 9W Twin tube	8	23	80	1051
P347	Two 13W Twin tube	9	26	83	1401

Footlamberts, clear cone. See Performance Datachart for colored cone multipliers.

kurt versen
Kurt Versen Company   Point Source Lighting
Westwood, New Jersey 07675

FIGURE 4–9a

DIRECT FLUORESCENT LUMINAIRE PHOTOMETRIC DATA
8¾-INCH DIAMETER ALZAK REFLECTOR
COMPACT LAMP
▼

P7   P346   P347   Twin Tube Wide Beam

Performance Datacharts

Initial Footcandles—Single Unit*			Ceiling to Floor	Initial Footcandles—Multiple Units*			
P346 Two 9W Twin tube				Ceiling 80% Wall 50% Floor 20%			
At Edge	Center	Diameter		Max Spacing Over Work Plane	RCR 1	RCR 3	RCR 8
1.2	12	10'	7'6"	9'0"	15	11	6
1.0	10	11'	8'0"	9'11"	12	10	5
.7	7	13'	9'0"	11'8"	9	7	4
.5	5	15'	10'0"	13'6"	7	5	3
.4	4	17'	11'0"	15'4"	5	4	2
.3	3	20'	12'6"	18'0"	4	3	2

Initial Footcandles—Single Unit*			Ceiling to Floor	Initial Footcandles—Multiple Units*			
P347 Two 13W Twin tube				Ceiling 80% Wall 50% Floor 20%			
At Edge	Center	Diameter		Max Spacing Over Work Plane	RCR 1	RCR 3	RCR 8
1.7	17	12'	7'6"	9'0"	15	11	6
1.4	14	13'	8'0"	9'11"	12	10	5
1.0	10	15'	9'0"	11'8"	9	7	4
.7	8	18'	10'0"	13'6"	7	5	3
.6	6	27'	11'0"	15'4"	5	4	2
.4	4	24'	12'6"	18'0"	4	3	2

*At work plane 30" above floor. Apply maintenance factor.   Black x.50   Bronze x.75   Gold x.95   Pewter x.80   Umber x.75

Corridor Footcandles

Ceiling Height	Spacing Ratio 1.0						
	C/L	2'	4'	6'	8'	10'	12'
8'0"	11	11	12	11	11	11	12
8'6"	9	10	11	10	9	10	11
9'0"	9	9	10	9	9	9	9
	Spacing Ratio 1.5						
8'0"	7	7	8	9	8	7	7
8'6"	6	6	7	8	8	7	6
9'0"	5	6	7	7	7	6	5

Ceiling Height	Spacing Ratio 1.0						
	C/L	2'	4'	6'	8'	10'	12'
8'0"	17	16	16	16	17	16	7
8'6"	15	14	15	14	15	14	8
9'0"	13	13	13	13	13	13	5
	Spacing Ratio 1.5						
8'0"	10	10	12	13	12	10	10
8'6"	9	9	11	12	11	9	9
9'0"	8	8	9	11	10	9	8

P346 Two 9W Twin tube
On centerline of floor. Corridor width 5 feet. For 7 foot corridor x.95.
Reflectances: Ceiling 80%, walls 50% floor 20%.

P347 Two 13W Twin tube
On centerline of floor. Corridor width 5 feet. For 7 foot corridor x.95.
Reflectances: Ceiling 80%, walls 50% floor 20%.

Candlepower Distribution Curves

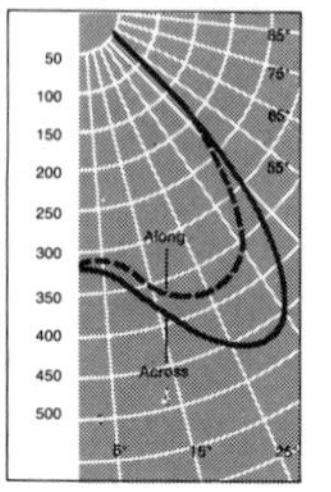

P346 Two 9W Twin tube
Eff. 64% S/M 1.7

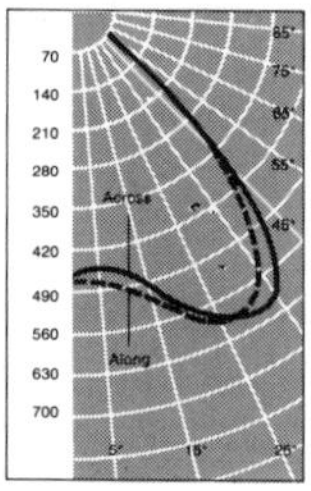

P347 Two 13W Twin tube
Eff. 67% S/M 1.8

Brightness data expressed in footlamberts are shown on the reverse of this page.

Coefficients of Utilization

Floor cavity reflectance 20% all data										
Ceiling %	80			70		50		30		0
Walls%	70	50	30	10	50	10	50	10	50	10	0
Room Ratio	Zonal Cavity Method									
1	.69	.67	.65	.63	.66	.61	.63	.59	.60	.58	.55
2	.64	.59	.55	.52	.58	.51	.55	.50	.53	.49	.46
3	.58	.52	.47	.44	.51	.43	.50	.43	.47	.42	.39
4	.53	.46	.42	.37	.45	.37	.44	.36	.43	.36	.33
5	.49	.41	.36	.31	.41	.31	.39	.31	.38	.30	.29
6	.45	.37	.31	.27	.36	.27	.35	.27	.33	.26	.25
7	.42	.33	.28	.23	.33	.23	.31	.23	.30	.23	.22
8	.38	.29	.24	.21	.29	.21	.28	.20	.28	.20	.19
9	.35	.27	.21	.17	.25	.17	.25	.17	.24	.17	.16
10	.33	.24	.19	.15	.23	.15	.23	.15	.22	.15	.14

P346 Two 9W Twin tube x.95
P347 Two 13W Twin tube

FIGURE 4–9b

DIRECT FLUORESCENT LUMINAIRE DATASHEET
1 x 1 PARABOLIC
COMPACT LAMP
▼

T1100
Twin Tube Fluorescent

Type _____ Voltage _____

Description

Nondirectional ten inch or twelve inch square parabolic louver luminaire is offered in one, two or three compact fluorescent lamp combinations. Cell configurations are 4 cell - available with 1, 2 or 3 lamps, 9 cell - available with 2 or 3 lamps and 16 cell - available with 3 lamps only. T1100 series fixtures are designed for esthetic compatibility with Columbia's fluorescent Parabolume or to be used separately as low brightness recessed light sources.

Luminaire is designed for flush mounting in recessed opening and held in place by either two adjustable mounting bars for "fit-in" ceiling or a support shroud for "lay-in" ceiling. Lay-in support shroud is finished with matte white as standard. The T1100 series features a "self trimming" louver assembly with minimum exposed lip at ceiling line.

Construction

Basic construction of code gauge steel. Steel mounting bars provide vertical adjustment and leveling with finished ceiling. Louver is of formed interlocked anodized aluminum and is self trimming. Louver is retained in fixture by two snap-in spring steel latches and is secured when open by a concealed safety tether.

Finish

Fixture housing and upper reflector are finished with baked gloss white enamel. Louver finish is iridescence suppressing semi-specular (No. 49) anodized aluminum. Alternate louver finishes are specular aluminum (No. 42), specular ferric gold (No. 47) or semi-specular champagne (No. 48).

Labels and Electrical

Fixture bears appropriate recessed labels for compact fluorescent lamps. Fixture is available with a J-Box for branch circuit wiring or a flex adapter plate for rapid wiring connection without opening the fixture or wireway. Standard fixtures include 120V high power factor ballast; 277V HPF ballast is available as an option. Fixtures use one, two or three 13W compact fluorescent lamps or one 16W Octron U-lamp. Lamps by "others ".

Installation

"Fit-in" option is provided with slip-in adjustable hanger bars that are shipped unattached for field installation. "Lay-in" ceiling support shroud and Tee bar clips are provided with fixture. Support shroud is installed at factory. Luminaire fits in a 9⅝" square recessed opening, template provided. Fixture leveling screws are accessible through the fixture body. Louver is then snapped into place and retained on a safety tether. No tools required for lamping or maintenance.

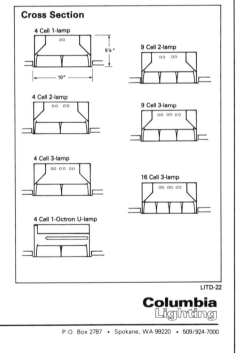

Cross Section

4 Cell 1-lamp

9 Cell 2-lamp

4 Cell 2-lamp

9 Cell 3-lamp

4 Cell 3-lamp

16 Cell 3-lamp

4 Cell 1-Octron U-lamp

LITD-22

Columbia Lighting

P.O. Box 2787 • Spokane, WA 99220 • 509/924-7000

USI LIGHTING

FIGURE 4–10a

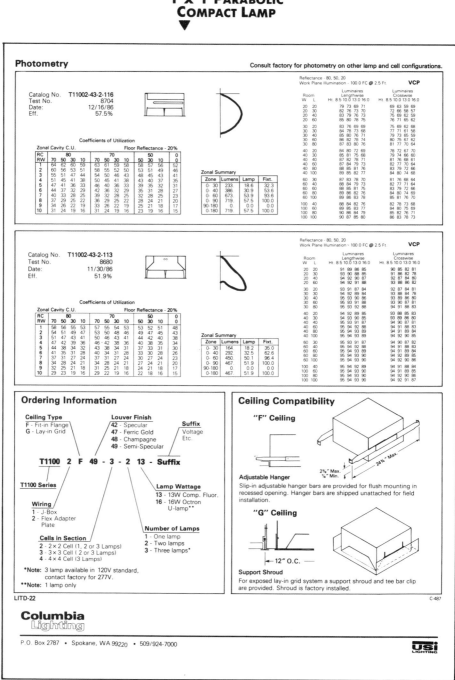

FIGURE 4–10b

Note that more efficient, high-power-factor ballasts are now available for the lower-wattage compact fluorescent lamps.

Photometric and application data are shown in Figure 4–9b for the Kurt Versen compact fluorescent luminaire. On the candlepower curves in the lower left, the "Along" curve indicates the luminaire candlepower on a plane through the luminaire along (or parallel with) the length of the lamps. The "Across" curve indicates the luminaire candlepower on a plane through the luminaire across (or perpendicular to) the length of the lamps. This terminology is used for any luminaire using a tubular-shaped lamp where the lighted length of the lamp is longer than the lighted width of the lamp.

An extension of the classic direct fluorescent parabolic luminaire is shown in Figures 4–10a and 4–10b. Using compact fluorescent lamps, the manufacturer has designed a very small-scale square parabolic luminaire. A variety of lamping types and configurations and louver cell sizes are available, as shown in the lower right of Figure 4–10a. Various finishes are available on the louvers, and the luminaire can be made to fit a variety of ceiling systems. Coefficient of utilization data for the luminaire are shown in Figure 4–10b, along with VCP data. VCP, or visual comfort probability, data sometimes are used to assess the general glare conditions of a given lighting system. The VCP methodology is based on research dating to the late 1950s and early 1960s, and, as such, its appropriateness has come under considerable question for today's lighting systems and illuminance conditions. The methodology's major fault is its inability to flag luminaire flash (see above discussion of "Luminaire Photometry"). Typically, luminaires with VCP of 80 or greater are considered appropriate for VDT installations. Note, however, that this means low-brightness luminaires, which may result in a space that seems too dark to occupants unless the designer uses soft wall lighting or accenting. Also, the flash zone may be at such an angle and of such an intensity that it causes reflected glare and/or reflected image problems on the VDT screen. Only mockups can help the designer assess whether these conditions exist and, if so, their severity.

With louvered luminaires, a key quality issue is the integrity, strength, and appearance of the louver. Gaps at the louver cross-piece intersections are unsightly and can slightly interfere with the luminaire's optics. The top of the louver (the top end of the "V"-shaped louver blade) can be a light trap if the aluminum does not return over the top to close the "V."

Figures 4–11a and 4–11b illustrate a Columbia 1 by 4 parabolic luminaire that uses one lamp. Figure 4–11c shows an installation of 1 by 4, one-lamp parabolic luminaires. These luminaires offer the possibility of introducing various air handling capabilities; hence, the black reveal around the perimeter of the luminaire.

One way to quickly assess a parabolic luminaire's glare control is to check the depth and cell size of the louver or baffle. The Columbia luminaire in Figures 4–11a and 4–11b has a baffle depth greater than 3 inches and a baffle

DIRECT FLUORESCENT LUMINAIRE DATASHEET
1 x 4 PARABOLIC (1-LAMP)
TUBULAR LAMP
▼

P4 Parabolume
1'×4' 1-Lamp

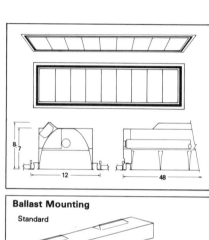

Description

P4 Parabolume is a high performance luminaire designed to optimize fluorescent lighting distribution for maximum spacing and comfort. Fixtures may be tandem wired or ballasted individually. Controlled widespread distribution maximizes spacing while preserving high visual comfort. Parabolic louver is surrounded by a uniform black reveal.

Construction

Luminaire housing and endcaps of die-formed code gauge CR steel. Reflecting surface of specular anodized reflector matches precise parabolic contours of louver. Ballast "bubbles" atop fixture housing are located for non-interference with cross-over air diffuser. Anodized aluminum louver is secured in open or closed position by die-formed steel hinges. Louver hinges from either side. Latches are finger-tip actuated, positive-feed type, fabricated of spring steel and concealed in black reveal.

Finish

Painted parts are treated with a five-stage phosphate bonding process and finished with a high temperature baked enamel after fabrication. Louvers are semi-specular natural anodized (No. 43) aluminum as standard. Also available in specular (No. 42), Ferric Gold (No. 47) and Champagne Gold (No. 48).

Ceiling Compatibility

P4 Parabolumes are available to fit most standard ceiling systems in NEMA type G (lay-in), type F (overlapping flange) and type M (fit-in flange). Also available for Slot Grid and Concealed Grid ceilings on special order with or without tile protecting shrouds - see P4 brochure. Luminaires for concealed suspension ceilings are furnished with necessary clips and/or wing hangers. For information on compatibility with specific ceilings, contact your Columbia representative.

Ballast Mounting

Standard

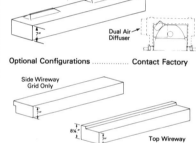

Dual Air Diffuser

Optional Configurations .... Contact Factory

Side Wireway Grid Only

Top Wireway

Air Handling

All supply/return functions and air extract are shown at left and are available as a specified option. Directional control vanes and/or extract dampers must be specified. Extract holes are located out of sight directly above lamp. See air removal data on reverse side of this sheet.

Installation

For fast wiring connections without the necessity of opening fixture or wireway, a flex connector adapter plate is furnished with each luminaire. Plastic dust cover which eliminates construction dust and protects lamps is included as standard.

Labels & Electrical

Luminaires bear appropriate U.L. recessed fixture labels. Completely wired with standard Class "P" C.B.M. ballast 120V standard. Each luminaire equipped with one 240W ballast unless otherwise specified.

Ordering Guide

Description	Ordering Number	Ship. Wt.	Lamps
Lay-in	P4-141G-43193-*	20	1-F40
Flanged	P4-141F-43193-*	21	1-F40
Modular	P4-141M-43193-*	21	1-F40

*Air Handling Functions
Ordering Number must be suffixed with one of the following nine numerals which will indicate specific air function(s).

1 - Static
2 - Supply/Return (no vanes)
3 - Supply/Return (with vanes)
4 - Supply/Return/Extract (no vanes or dampers)
5 - Supply/Return/Extract (with vanes - no dampers)
6 - Supply/Return/Extract (no vanes - with dampers)
7 - Supply/Return/Extract (with vanes and dampers)
8 - Extract Only (no dampers)
9 - Extract Only (with dampers)

P4-8

Columbia
Lighting

P.O. Box 2787 • Spokane, WA 99220-2787 • 509/924-7000

FIGURE 4–11a

Direct Fluorescent Luminaire Photometric Data
1 x 4 Parabolic (1-Lamp)
Tubular Lamp

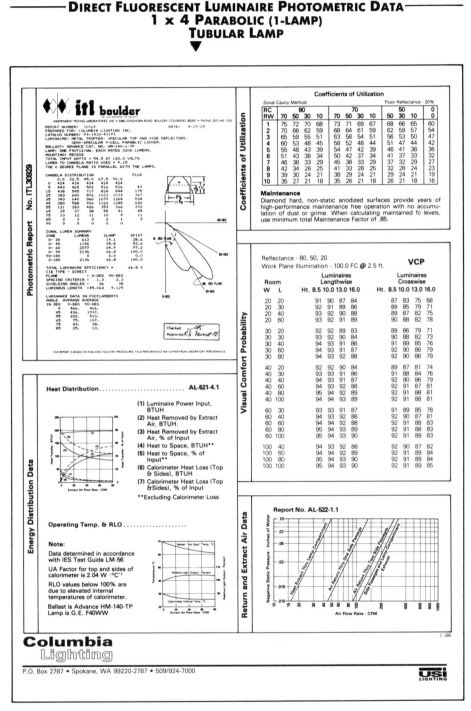

FIGURE 4–11b

FIGURE 4–11c.
A very uniform level of light and resultant uniform brightnesses were achieved by using a lot of low-lumen package luminaires (one-lamp, 1 × 4 parabolic luminaires). Wall accenting is used to prevent the space from becoming too dark in appearance (a common problem with parabolic lighting systems) and to balance the brightness of the daylight on the back wall. Photo courtesy of GE Company.

spacing of about 5 inches, resulting in good glare control. Louvers that are shallower than 3 inches in depth and greater than 6 inches in spacing should be carefully reviewed for glare.

Some manufacturers have various ballast wireway configurations that permit the designer to use the deeper, less glary luminaires in tight plenum spaces. For example, the standard Columbia luminaire shown in Figure 4–11a has off-center, dual ballast "bubbles" that result in a total luminaire height of 8 inches. If structural steel, HVAC ductwork, or sprinkler pipes squeeze the plenum to only 8 inches in clear height in some areas, then the side-mounted wireway option still permits the designer to use the Columbia luminaire. The overall height is reduced to 7 inches by reconfiguring the wireway. Note that there are shallow parabolic luminaires available with wireways on top of the luminaire housing. These units, however, use shallower baffles/louvers, resulting in increased glare potential.

In Figure 4–11b, the photometric data include complete candlepower information for the Columbia luminaire, as well as CU data and VCP information. Additionally, for the mechanical engineer, some HVAC data are included. The graph in the lower left, on operating temperature and RLO (relative light output), indicates that returning air through the luminaire can actually increase its total light output. Approximately a 5 percent gain can be achieved.

Figure 4–12a shows a two-lamp sister luminaire to the one-lamp unit shown in Figure 4–11a. Here, the two lamps are stacked in what is commonly referred to as an over-under arrangement. This allows two-level switching without the drawbacks of turning off half of the lamps. If the top lamp is left off or turned off, the occupants still see a uniformly lighted baffle and reflector. If the lamps were mounted side by side, turning off one lamp would result in half of the luminaire going dark. These luminaires are particularly useful in offices or conference rooms where it has been determined that the ambient lighting should consist of parabolic luminaires, but two-level lighting is desired.

Figures 4–13a and 4–13b are the datasheet and photometric data, respectively, for a 2 by 2 parabolic luminaire. The louver is comprised of nine cells, compared to the sixteen-cell version shown in Figures 4–14a and 4–14b.

Parabolic luminaires have been in existence in some form for nearly twenty-five years. Direct glare was a significant problem in the mid–1960s, when 100 to 200 footcandles/1000 to 2000 lux was a common goal for lighting of task areas in offices. Four-lamp, 2 by 4 lensed luminaires were the popular, cheap way to achieve such illuminances. For the few employers who cared and the few architects who fought the battle, parabolic luminaires were a welcome reprieve from the glare of lensed luminaires. By the mid–1980s, however, three- and four-lamp parabolic luminaires began to lose favor. The energy crises and the electronic office revolution had both pushed illuminances lower. Engineers, in an attempt to maximize illuminance, minimize connected load, and minimize first costs, were laying out parabolic lighting systems that resulted in dark, cavelike spaces, and/or inflexible open plan offices (see Figure 4–14c), and/or severe VDT screen washout problems (when a VDT happened to be located under a three- or four-lamp parabolic luminaire). Using up to two or three times as many parabolic luminaires, with each luminaire having one-half to one-third as much light output, results in more uniform, less locally harsh, and improved VDT-viewing lighting. This can be done without an increase in energy, but generally requires higher initial costs. Figure 4–11c is an example of such a uniform, improved VDT-viewing parabolic lighting system.

Where ceiling heights are greater than 9 feet (preferably 10 feet or more), indirect lighting can provide virtually glare-free conditions while giving the impression of brightness. Obviously, just as with parabolic luminaires, this depends on lamping and spacing or layout. Another aspect of indirect light-

DIRECT FLUORESCENT LUMINAIRE DATASHEET
1 x 4 PARABOLIC (2-LAMP/OVER-UNDER)
TUBULAR LAMP
▼

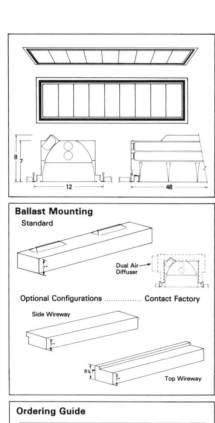

P4 Parabolume
1'×4' 2-Lamp
3¼" Louver

Description

P4 Parabolume is a high performance luminaire designed to optimize fluorescent lighting distribution for maximum spacing and comfort. Fixtures may be tandem wired for two level switching or ballasted individually. Controlled widespread distribution maximizes spacing while preserving high visual comfort. Parabolic louver is surrounded by a uniform black reveal.

Construction

Luminaire housing and endcaps of die-formed code gauge CR steel. Reflecting surface of specular anodized reflector matches precise parabolic contours of louver. Ballast "bubbles" atop fixture housing are located for non-interference with cross-over air diffuser. Anodized aluminum louver is secured in open or closed position by die-formed steel hinges. Louver hinges from either side. Latches are finger-tip actuated, positive-feed type, fabricated of spring steel and concealed in black reveal.

Finish

Painted parts are treated with a five-stage phosphate bonding process and finished with a high temperature baked enamel after fabrication. Louvers are semi-specular natural anodized (No. 43) aluminum as standard. Also available in specular (No. 42), Ferric Gold (No. 47) and Champagne Gold (No. 48).

Ceiling Compatibility

P4 Parabolumes are available to fit most standard ceiling systems in NEMA type G (lay-in), type F (overlapping flange) and type M (fit-in flange). Also available for Slot Grid and Concealed Grid ceilings on special order with or without tile protecting shrouds - see P4 brochure. Luminaires for concealed suspension ceilings are furnished with necessary clips and/or wing hangers. For information on compatibility with specific ceilings, contact your Columbia representative.

Air Handling

All supply/return functions and air extract are shown at left and are available as a specified option. Directional control vanes and/or extract dampers must be specified. Extract holes are located out of sight directly above lamp. See air removal data on reverse side of this sheet.

Installation

For fast wiring connections without the necessity of opening fixture or wireway, a flex connector adapter plate is furnished with each luminaire. Plastic dust cover which eliminates construction dust and protects lamps is included as standard.

Labels & Electrical

Luminaires bear appropriate U.L. recessed fixture labels. Completely wired with standard Class "P" C.B.M. ballast 120V standard. Each luminaire is equipped with one each 240W ballast unless otherwise specified.

P4-9

Columbia Lighting

P.O. Box 2787 • Spokane, WA 99220-2787 • 509/924-7000

USI LIGHTING

Ordering Guide

Description	Ordering Number	Ship. Wt.	Lamps
Lay-in	P4-142G-43193-*	20	2-F40
Flanged	P4-142F-43193-*	21	2-F40
Modular	P4-142M-43193-*	21	2-F40

*Air Handling Functions
Ordering Number must be suffixed with one of the following nine numerals which will indicate specific air function(s).

1 - Static
2 - Supply/Return (no vanes)
3 - Supply/Return (with vanes)
4 - Supply/Return/Extract (no vanes or dampers)
5 - Supply/Return/Extract (with vanes - no dampers)
6 - Supply/Return/Extract (no vanes - with dampers)
7 - Supply/Return/Extract (with vanes and dampers)
8 - Extract Only (no dampers)
9 - Extract Only (with dampers)

FIGURE 4–12a

DIRECT FLUORESCENT LUMINAIRE PHOTOMETRIC DATA
1 x 4 PARABOLIC (2-LAMP/OVER-UNDER)
TUBULAR LAMP
▼

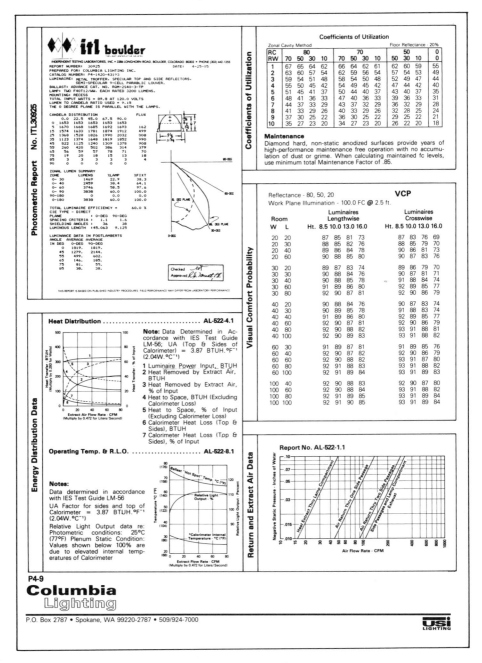

FIGURE 4–12b

DIRECT FLUORESCENT LUMINAIRE DATASHEET
2 x 2 PARABOLIC (9-CELL LOUVER)
4-LAMP
▼

Parabolume

2'x 2' U-Lamp

Description: Two foot square Parabolume is designed for use with two U-lamps which are powered by a single "industry standard" 240 watt ballast. The 2' × 2' is compatible with most modular ceiling systems and the nonlinear appearance complements any arrangement of office furnishings. Good looks, low energy consumption, quality construction and a "fit anywhere" design have made the 2' × 2' Parabolume a most versatile and highly popular luminaire.

Construction: Fixture housings constructed of die formed code gauge steel. Baffled door assemblies feature positive acting steel hinges and latches which hinge from either side. Latch side scribed for identification. Baffled door assemblies are formed aluminum. Precise parabolic contours held rigidly in place to assure snug-fit corners, maximum light control and rattle-free assemblies.

Finish: Painted parts are treated with a five-stage phosphate bonding process and finished with a high temperature baked enamel. Regress slots are flat black. Baffled door assembles are semi-specular anodized aluminum. For more detailed information or custom anodized finishes (such as specular gold) contact your Columbia representative.

Labels & Electrical: Fixtures bear appropriate U.L. label and I.B.E.W. label. Completely wired with Class "P" C.B.M. ballasts - 120V standard.

Ceiling Compatibility: Recessed Parabolumes are available to fit most standard ceiling systems in NEMA type G (lay-in), F (flanged) and type M (fit-in). For information on compatibility with specific ceilings contact your Columbia representative. Fixtures for concealed suspension ceilings are furnished with necessary clips or wing hangers. Designed for mounting individually or in continuous rows.

Air Handling: All recessed models are available with U.L. labels as air supply units; air return units; with heat extract functions; or static. Heat Extract option (removing room air through lamp compartment) must be specified. Compatible air diffusers by Columbia, Anemostat, Barber Colman, Krueger, Titus or Tuttle & Bailey. For air supply information, see Columbia catalog Page 92-31.

Installation: For fast wiring connections without the necessity of opening fixture or wireway, a Flex Connector Adapter Plate kit is furnished with each luminaire. Self adhering mylar overlay to protect lamps and eliminate construction dust is available as an option.

Maintenance: Diamond hard, non-static Coilzak® surfaces provide years of high-performance maintenance free operation with no accumulation of dust or grime. When calculating maintained fc levels, use minimum total Maintenance Factor of .85.

Surface or Pendant Mount: Attractive surface mount luminaires - designed for compatibility with comparable recessed models - are also available as standard stock. Construction features completely enclosed steel housing finished in baked white enamel or custom finishes to meet your needs. These luminaires require only minimal maintenance and match the performance of recessed Parabolumes.

® Registered Tradename - ALCOA

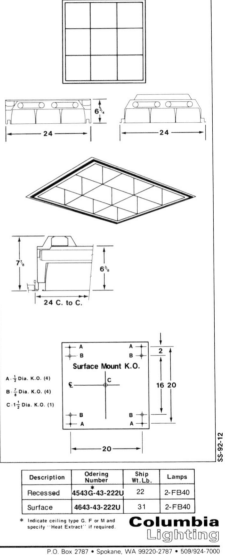

Description	Odering Number *	Ship Wt.Lb.	Lamps
Recessed	4543G-43-222U	22	2-FB40
Surface	4643-43-222U	31	2-FB40

* Indicate ceiling type G. F or M and specify "Heat Extract" if required.

Columbia Lighting

P.O. Box 2787 • Spokane, WA 99220-2787 • 509/924-7000

USI LIGHTING

SS-92-12

FIGURE 4–13a

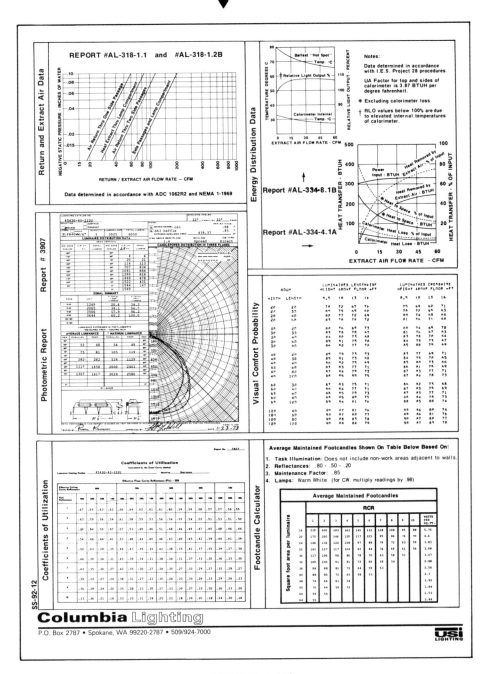

FIGURE 4–13b

DIRECT FLUORESCENT LUMINAIRE DATASHEET
2 x 2 PARABOLIC (16-CELL)
U-LAMP
▼

Parabolume

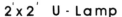

Description: Two foot square Parabolume is designed for use with two U-lamps which are powered by a single "industry standard" 240 watt ballast. The 2'×2' is compatible with most modular ceiling systems and the nonlinear appearance complements any arrangement of office furnishings. Good looks, low energy consumption, quality construction and a "fit anywhere" design have made the 2'×2' Parabolume a most versatile and highly popular luminaire.

Construction: Fixture housings constructed of die formed code gauge steel. Baffled door assemblies feature positive acting steel hinges and latches which hinge from either side. Latch side scribed for identification. Baffled door assemblies are formed aluminum. Precise parabolic contours held rigidly in place to assure snug-fit corners, maximum light control and rattle-free assemblies.

Finish: Painted parts are treated with a five-stage phosphate bonding process and finished with a high temperature baked enamel. Regress slots are flat black. Baffled door assembles are semi-specular anodized aluminum. For more detailed information or custom anodized finishes (such as specular gold) contact your Columbia representative.

Labels & Electrical: Fixtures bear appropriate U.L. label and I.B.E.W. label Completely wired with Class "P" C.B.M. ballasts - 120V standard.

Ceiling Compatibility: Recessed Parabolumes are available to fit most standard ceiling systems in NEMA type G (lay-in), F (flanged) and type M (fit-in). For information on compatibility with specific ceilings contact your Columbia representative. Fixtures for concealed suspension ceilings are furnished with necessary clips or wing hangers. Designed for mounting individually or in any desired pattern.

Air Handling: All recessed models are available with U.L. labels as air supply units; air return units; with heat extract functions; or static. Heat Extract option (removing room air through lamp compartment) must be specified. Compatible air diffusers by Columbia, Anemostat, Barber Colman, Krueger, Titus or Tuttle & Bailey. For air supply information, see Columbia catalog Page 92-31.

Installation: For fast wiring connections without the necessity of opening fixture or wireway, a Flex Connector Adapter Plate kit is furnished with each luminaire. Self adhering mylar overlay to protect lamps and eliminate construction dust is available as an option.

Maintenance: Diamond hard, non-static Collzak ® surfaces provide years of high-performance maintenance free operation with no accumulation of dust or grime. When calculating maintained fc levels, use minimum total Maintenance Factor of .85.

Surface or Pendant Mount: Attractive surface mount luminaires - designed for compatibility with comparable recessed models - are also available as standard stock. Construction features completely enclosed steel housing finished in baked white enamel or custom finishes to meet your needs. These luminaires require only minimal maintenance and match the performance of recessed Parabolumes.

® Registered tradename - ALCOA

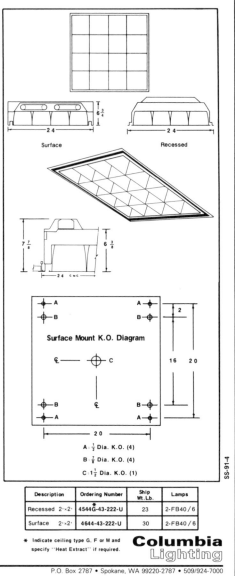

Description	Ordering Number	Ship Wt.Lb.	Lamps
Recessed 2'×2'	4544G-43-222-U	23	2-FB40/6
Surface 2'×2'	4644-43-222-U	30	2-FB40/6

＊ Indicate ceiling type G, F or M and specify "Heat Extract" if required.

Columbia Lighting

USI LIGHTING

P.O. Box 2787 • Spokane, WA 99220-2787 • 509/924-7000

FIGURE 4–14a

DIRECT FLUORESCENT LUMINAIRE PHOTOMETRIC DATA
2 x 2 PARABOLIC (16-CELL)
U-LAMP
▼

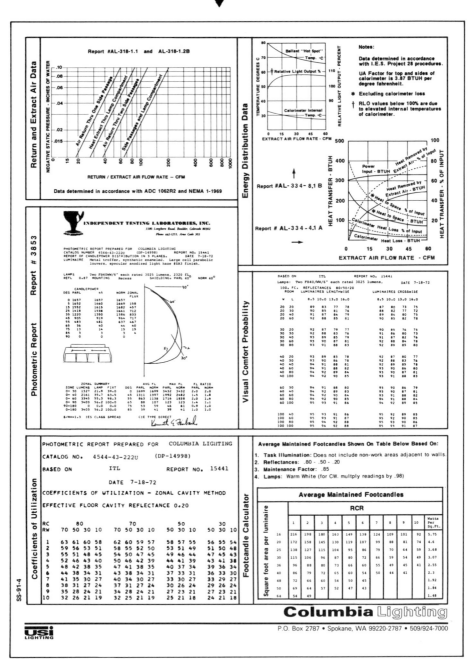

FIGURE 4–14b

FIGURE 4–14c.
An "engineered" approach to lighting failed to consider all of the pertinent criteria.
By simply attempting to maximize illuminance while minimizing connected
load, designs using parabolic lighting can cause inflexible space usage. Note the
"dark" office near the middle left and the "bright" office at the far left.

ing, which varies significantly from manufacturer to manufacturer, is luminaire optics. In fact, the better the optics, generally the lower the ceiling
height can be for indirect lighting consideration, and/or the shorter the
mounting distance between the ceiling and luminaires.

Figure 4–15a is a datasheet for a widespread distribution indirect luminaire. The lensed upper side helps to provide for a widespread distribution
of light across the ceiling and also provides some direct glow from the luminaire. This direct glow helps to introduce some direct brightness, thereby
minimizing the sense of haze and dinginess that is characteristic of very
uniform low-to-moderate brightnesses. At the same time, however, this
glow must not be too bright; otherwise luminaire disturbances will reflect
from the VDT screen.

With today's needs for uniform, moderate levels of light in open plan offices, it is no longer true that direct lighting systems are always more efficient at delivering illuminance than indirect lighting systems. As the datasheets indicate, indirect luminaires can be quite efficient. These luminaires
are available in T8 fluorescent versions. Also, there are variations available
that use the higher-wattage compact fluorescent lamps.

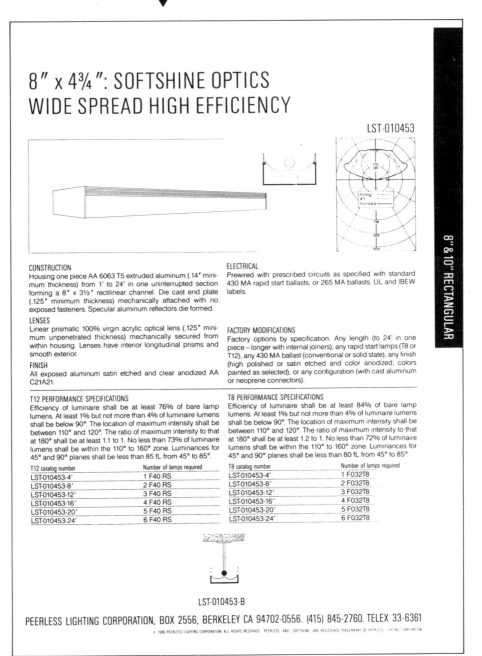

8" x 4¾": SOFTSHINE OPTICS
WIDE SPREAD HIGH EFFICIENCY

LST-010453

8" & 10" RECTANGULAR

CONSTRUCTION
Housing one piece AA 6063 T5 extruded aluminum (.14" minimum thickness) from 1' to 24' in one uninterrupted section forming a 8" x 3½" rectilinear channel. Die cast end plate (.125" minimum thickness) mechanically attached with no exposed fasteners. Specular aluminum reflectors die formed.

LENSES
Linear prismatic 100% virgin acrylic optical lens (.125" minimum unpenetrated thickness) mechanically secured from within housing. Lenses have interior longitudinal prisms and smooth exterior.

FINISH
All exposed aluminum satin etched and clear anodized AA C21A21.

ELECTRICAL
Prewired with prescribed circuits as specified with standard 430 MA rapid start ballasts, or 265 MA ballasts. UL and IBEW labels.

FACTORY MODIFICATIONS
Factory options by specification. Any length (to 24' in one piece – longer with internal joiners), any rapid start lamps (T8 or T12), any 430 MA ballast (conventional or solid state), any finish (high polished or satin etched and color anodized; colors painted as selected), or any configuration (with cast aluminum or neoprene connectors).

T12 PERFORMANCE SPECIFICATIONS
Efficiency of luminaire shall be at least 76% of bare lamp lumens. At least 1% but not more than 4% of luminaire lumens shall be below 90°. The location of maximum intensity shall be between 110° and 120°. The ratio of maximum intensity to that at 180° shall be at least 1.1 to 1. No less than 73% of luminaire lumens shall be within the 110° to 160° zone. Luminances for 45° and 90° planes shall be less than 85 fL from 45° to 85°.

T12 catalog number	Number of lamps required
LST-010453-4'	1 F40 RS
LST-010453-8'	2 F40 RS
LST-010453-12'	3 F40 RS
LST-010453-16'	4 F40 RS
LST-010453-20'	5 F40 RS
LST-010453-24'	6 F40 RS

T8 PERFORMANCE SPECIFICATIONS
Efficiency of luminaire shall be at least 84% of bare lamp lumens. At least 1% but not more than 4% of luminaire lumens shall be below 90°. The location of maximum intensity shall be between 110° and 120°. The ratio of maximum intensity to that at 180° shall be at least 1.2 to 1. No less than 72% of luminaire lumens shall be within the 110° to 160° zone. Luminances for 45° and 90° planes shall be less than 80 fL from 45° to 85°.

T8 catalog number	Number of lamps required
LST-010453-4'	1 F032T8
LST-010453-8'	2 F032T8
LST-010453-12'	3 F032T8
LST-010453-16'	4 F032T8
LST-010453-20'	5 F032T8
LST-010453-24'	6 F032T8

LST-010453-B

PEERLESS LIGHTING CORPORATION, BOX 2556, BERKELEY CA 94702-0556. (415) 845-2760. TELEX 33-6361

FIGURE 4–15a

INDIRECT FLUORESCENT LUMINAIRE PHOTOMETRIC DATA
RECTILINEAR PROFILE, WIDESPREAD DISTRIBUTION
TUBULAR LAMP (T12)

▼

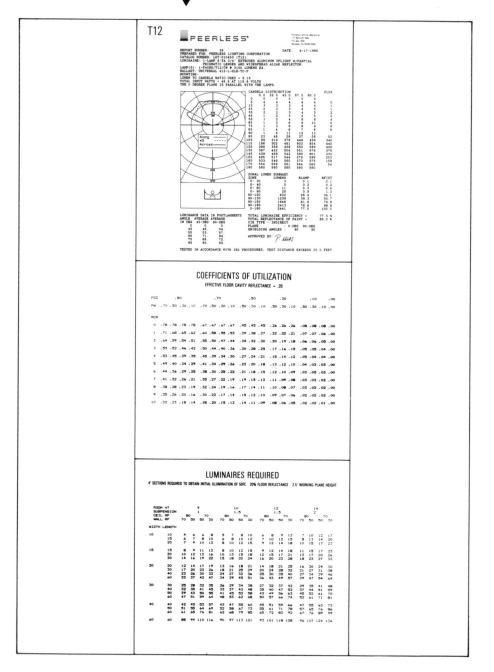

FIGURE 4–15b   (Top)

FIGURE 4–15c   (Middle)

FIGURE 4–15d   (Bottom)

—INDIRECT FLUORESCENT LUMINAIRE PHOTOMETRIC DATA— RECTILINEAR PROFILE, WIDESPREAD DISTRIBUTION TUBULAR LAMP (T8)
▼

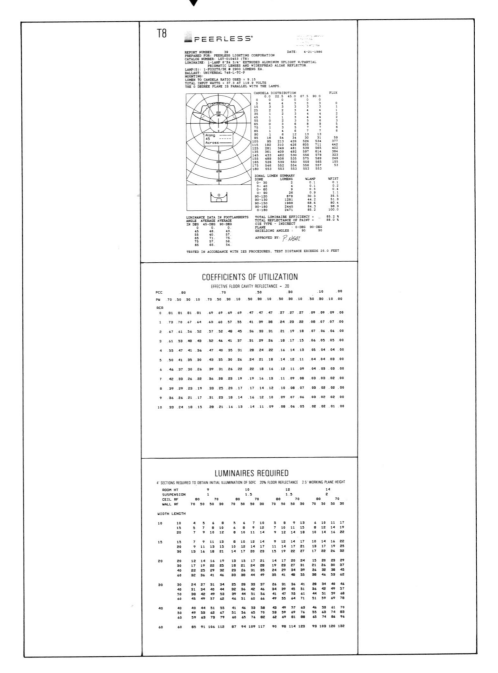

FIGURE 4–15e   (Top)

FIGURE 4–15f   (Middle)

FIGURE 4–15g   (Bottom)

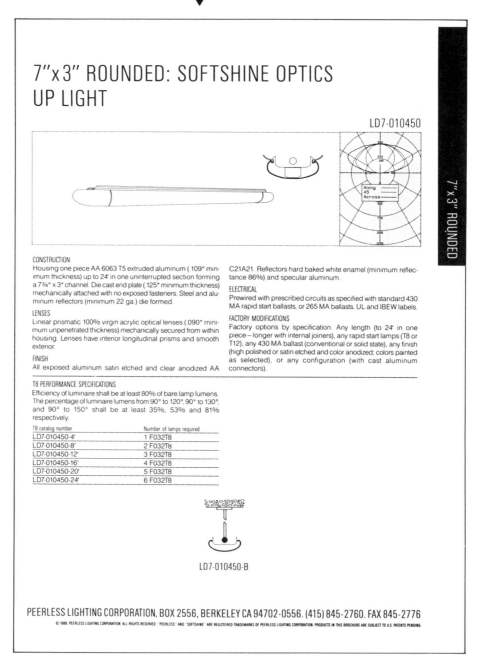

7"x3" ROUNDED: SOFTSHINE OPTICS
UP LIGHT

LD7-010450

7"x3" ROUNDED

CONSTRUCTION
Housing one piece AA 6063 T5 extruded aluminum (.109" min-imum thickness) up to 24' in one uninterrupted section forming a 7¾" x 3" channel. Die cast end plate (.125" minimum thickness) mechanically attached with no exposed fasteners. Steel and alu-minum reflectors (minimum 22 ga.) die formed.

LENSES
Linear prismatic 100% virgin acrylic optical lenses (.090" mini-mum unpenetrated thickness) mechanically secured from within housing. Lenses have interior longitudinal prisms and smooth exterior.

FINISH
All exposed aluminum satin etched and clear anodized AA

C21A21. Reflectors hard baked white enamel (minimum reflec-tance 86%) and specular aluminum.

ELECTRICAL
Prewired with prescribed circuits as specified with standard 430 MA rapid start ballasts, or 265 MA ballasts. UL and IBEW labels.

FACTORY MODIFICATIONS
Factory options by specification. Any length (to 24' in one piece — longer with internal joiners), any rapid start lamps (T8 or T12), any 430 MA ballast (conventional or solid state), any finish (high polished or satin etched and color anodized; colors painted as selected), or any configuration (with cast aluminum connectors).

T8 PERFORMANCE SPECIFICATIONS
Efficiency of luminaire shall be at least 80% of bare lamp lumens. The percentage of luminaire lumens from 90° to 120°, 90° to 130°, and 90° to 150° shall be at least 35%, 53% and 81% respectively.

T8 catalog number	Number of lamps required
LD7-010450-4'	1 F032T8
LD7-010450-8'	2 F032T8
LD7-010450-12'	3 F032T8
LD7-010450-16'	4 F032T8
LD7-010450-20'	5 F032T8
LD7-010450-24'	6 F032T8

LD7-010450-B

PEERLESS LIGHTING CORPORATION, BOX 2556, BERKELEY CA 94702-0556. (415) 845-2760. FAX 845-2776
© 1988. PEERLESS LIGHTING CORPORATION. ALL RIGHTS RESERVED. "PEERLESS" AND "SOFTSHINE" ARE REGISTERED TRADEMARKS OF PEERLESS LIGHTING CORPORATION. PRODUCTS IN THIS BROCHURE ARE SUBJECT TO U.S. PATENTS PENDING.

FIGURE 4–16a

——INDIRECT FLUORESCENT LUMINAIRE PHOTOMETRIC DATA—— ROUNDED THIN PROFILE, WIDESPREAD DISTRIBUTION TUBULAR LAMP ▼

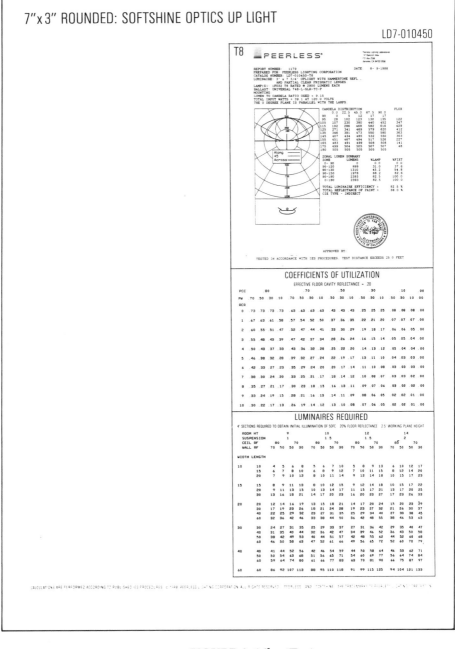

FIGURE 4–16b (Top)

FIGURE 4–16c (Middle)

FIGURE 4–16d (Bottom)

Figure 4–15b is the candlepower report for the T12 version of the Peerless widespread luminaire; Figure 4–15c gives the CU data; and Figure 4–15d is a quick application reference table, designed to indicate approximately the number of luminaires required to meet certain illuminance criteria under certain design conditions.

For the T8 version of the Peerless widespread luminaire, Figure 4–15e provides candlepower data, Figure 4–15f gives CU data, and Figure 4–15g provides a quick application reference.

As more designers and employers recognize the virtues of indirect lighting for today's offices, the need arises for thinner-profile equipment as well as nonlinear solutions. Figures C6, C6a, C6b, and C7 illustrate the latest in a trend toward nonlinear lighting. Using the 39-watt compact fluorescent lamp by GE, Peerless developed the MD–33 luminaire as conceptualized by Gary Steffy Lighting Design Inc.

Thinner-profile indirect linear luminaires also provide an alternative to the standard rectilinear luminaires. Figure 4–16a shows such an alternative. The rounded sides combined with a shallower depth result in a sleek, high-performance luminaire. Candlepower data are shown in Figure 4–16b, with CU data in Figure 4–16c and a quick application reference in Figure 4–16d.

Operating samples of all luminaires should be reviewed prior to their specification. Hanging indirect luminaires in a mockup setting (see Figure 5–12) helps the designer better undertand the limit of luminance variations possible with various manufacturers' equipment.

These luminaires and their datasheets and photometry have been presented here to indicate the scope and scale of luminaires available and the information available on them. There is no need to guess about lighting equipment or optics. There is no reason to use generic luminaires as provided by the IES or in other texts for purposes of design and calculation. "Lazy design" is no substitute for design. The designer should treat every project as fresh and new, and should research criteria, concepts, and solutions accordingly.

CHAPTER FIVE

DESIGN TOOLS

INTRODUCTION

The design development phase of a project cannot be considered complete unless it is known that the proposed solution(s) will work. To know this requires considerable experience and/or quantifiable documentation. Because considerable experience can be gained only over a significant period of time, this text deals with the quantifiable documentation aspects.

There comes a time on a project when both the designer and the client wish to be assured or reassured that a proposed solution will indeed meet most or all of the needs, most or all of the time. The most definite way to determine a proposed solution's success is to build it. This is also an extremely costly method of testing a solution.

Most design tools are part of an iterative process; that is, the design comes first, then a test. If the test does not work, some reevaluation of the design occurs, which usually leads to some sort of redesign, then another test, and so on. Design tools can be classified into qualitative tools and quantitative tools. Qualitative tools allow the designer to assess the lighting quality aspects of a design. For example, will a particular design really lead to an impression of spaciousness? A small-scale model may help test this design aspect. On the other hand, quantitative tools allow the designer to assess the lighting quantities—luminances, luminance ratios, and illuminances, to name a few.

QUALITATIVE DESIGN TOOLS

Before one gets bogged down in all sorts of technical data and calculations, it is desirable to know if the lighting design will be successful in meeting the softer, more subjective or psychological criteria. It is relatively easy to achieve certain luminances and illuminances—this is a matter of selecting the appropriate lamps and luminaires. It is much more difficult to decide how the space ought to look and feel *and to further decide what areas should be light, dark, or in between to achieve said look and feel.* Two-dimensional and three-dimensional visualizing provides the most appropriate qualitative design tools, including mood shots, light renderings, models, and mockups.

MOOD SHOTS

Sometimes clients are clearly most comfortable after having seen examples of work that is similar to the work being proposed. Photos and magazine images can serve this purpose, but this technique must be used with great care. Often the photos and magazine images contain the photographer's fill light, which makes the scene especially attractive as photo art. Obviously, the fill light will not occur in a real environment; so the photo misleads the client. Some photographers have taken the time and patience to educate themselves on these aspects and are able to provide photographic images that in and of themselves are attractive, while portraying space and light realistically.

Another difficulty in using mood shots to convey lighting techniques is the fact that not only the lighting but also color, finishes, composition, and spatial form contribute to the way a space "feels" or "reads" in a photograph. In a photo of an upscale restaurant used to illustrate art accent lighting, the client may see an elegant, attractive dining environment, while the designer only "sees" the art accent lighting. The client may approve the lighting because he or she approves of the upscale restaurant photo, and may be quite disappointed in the space that actually is built. To avoid this problem, use photos of similar space, style, taste, and budget to the client's, and/or clearly state that only the lighting effect is being considered.

LIGHT RENDERINGS

Expressing a sense of light and dark, shade and shadow to a client is a necessity if the client is uninitiated in lighting, or if new techniques or modified applications are to be used on a project. Although some expression can be conveyed in written form, being "there" (through mockups) or seing a pic-

FIGURE 5–1.
A light rendering of a corridor space used during the design process to confirm to the designer that the lighting concept was appropriate, and to convince the client that this was a reasonable solution to lighting a long, narrow corridor. Figure 5–2 shows the completed project.

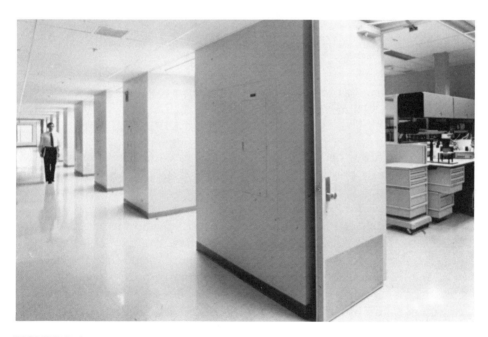

FIGURE 5–2.
This corridor lighting was accomplished by placing recessed, direct parabolic louver luminaires in the door pockets, providing a wash across the corridor and alleviating the usual "tunnel" effect achieved by placing luminaires down the middle of the corridor. Figure 5–1 was used as a design tool to confirm the design approach before specification.

FIGURE 5–3.
This light rendering was done in an effort to convince the client that the lighting of the coffered ceiling was an appropriate method.

ture (light rendering) of "there" will be the most expeditious means of convincing a client of your intentions. Recognize that light renderings are also excellent learning tools. They help the designer to better visualize the space or area and allow for exploration of more appropriate solutions.

Light renderings can take many forms. Relatively simple pencil sketches can address spatial form and shade and shadow. Figure 5–1 illustrates a rather straightforward corridor space. Typically, a no-thought solution would involve some sort of fluorescent luminaires running down the center of the corridor ceiling. Such an application may be inexpensive, but it shows no attempt to minimize the impact of the corridor's length. Recessing luminaires into the ceiling above the door pockets costs no more (uses the same recessed fluorescent luminaires), but helps provide visual relief and approaches a side-window, daylighted appearance. The light rendering of Figure 5–1 was used to convince the client that such a low-cost yet unique solution could enhance one's impression of the space. Figure 5–2 shows the completed project.

In a more complicated space, the structure and architecture must be care-

FIGURE 5–4.
Fluorescent lighting located in the left fascia washes across the coffers to provide an indirect lighting system. By lighting the ceiling, the height of the space is enhanced.

fully reviewed so that the lighting will enhance both. A two-story, sweeping curved circulation and lounge space with an exterior window wall can create quite a challenge. Figure 5–3 shows a light rendering of such a space. To accentuate the height of the space and to articulate the structure, a lighting scheme that highlights the overhead structural coffers was deemed appropriate. Figure 5–3 was used to sell the client on the concept. Luminaires are placed along the building side of each coffer bulkhead. These luminaires then wash light across the ceiling coffer between each beam. The completed installation is shown in Figure 5–4.

Pencil and charcoal sketches can be quick and effective. The key, of course, is understanding what light will do—how it will shade, shadow, highlight, sparkle, wash, streak, and so on. This can be learned only through observation (see Chapter 1, under "Lighting Education"). A journal (sketchbook) of observations is a convenient reference for such work. Pencil and charcoal are limited to monochromatic renderings, but can be used quite effectively to illustrate the effect of lighting. Figure 5–5 is an all-pencil rendering on white paper, and Figure 5–6 is a charcoal rendering on a neutral gray board. Note how the white charcoal can be most effective in showing highlight and reflection. To illustrate color, an effective and rather convenient technique is airbrushing with markers.

A rather inexpensive marker airbrush tool allows the designer greater range in both shade and color intensity in a much shorter time than color renderings. Figure C25 shows an airbrush rendering of a nighttime view of a building facade. The facade floodlighting concept is based on lighting specially coated glass (frit pattern glass; see Chapter 3, under "Daylight Sources") from within the building for a subtle glow, with some neon hidden in the HVAC vents at the building's peak for a hint of color. Both "subtle glow" and "hints of color" can be readily shown with the marker airbrush technique. The finished project, from a similar view to that used for the airbrush marker rendering, is shown in Figure C26. Figure C27 shows a composite light rendering plan using the marker airbrush technique to render the building along with computer output plots of parking areas and the entry drive. This provides a "satellite" view of the site.

As presentations are made to upper management, and as the criticality of the decision tends to increase, it may be necessary to spend more time on developing refined presentation renderings. This usually means hiring a renderer for the express purpose of producing high-quality presentation images. Many times these renderers prefer to render in "total daylight" or in "extreme contrast." Total daylight tends to show spatial form, colors, and finishes as if they were lighted by total daylight from all directions. Extreme contrast tends to show space as it is rendered by brilliant sun or moon, so that severe shadows add drama to the rendering. Both techniques make for attractive renderings, but they unfortunately do not render the proposed lighted space in even a reasonably accurate fashion. Uninitiated decision makers like many of the renderings for art's sake; so they make major approvals based on these inaccurate representations, only to discover upon construction completion that colors are not nearly so lively, shadows are not nearly so contrasty, and walls are generally darker than anticipated. The designer employing a renderer should clarify before retaining the renderer that extra care and caution will be necessary to portray spatial brightness and surface colors and finishes as realistically as possible. Obviously, this means that the designer must carefully explain how light will be used throughout the space(s).

Figure 5–7 shows a professional rendering where the renderer paid particular attention to wall lighting effects and the light from the architectural

FIGURE 5–5.
This rather complex rendering was made with pencil and was used for presentation to the upper management of a development group.

kiosks. Although the light patterns are not perspectively accurate, they at least provide clues to how light will strike room surfaces and the relative intensity of those light patterns. This rendering was used to help sell management on the architectural concept of the core office details (horizontal banding, mullioned doors and sidelights, floor materials, kiosks as circulation elements). Figure 5–8 (also see Figure C19) shows the constructed space.

Light renderings can be a convenient method, requiring only a small investment of money and time to illustrate lighting concepts for the design team's edification and for client comprehension. A variety of techniques are available, which lend themselves to black/white/gray value studies or to color renderings. Although light renderings can be a good way to capture the look of a space, a good sense of how a space may feel and function cannot be acquired through renderings.

FIGURE 5–6.
Charcoal used on a neutral gray board is very effective in presenting lighting concepts. Notice the attention to highlight detail on the brick wall surface on the left.

MODELS

Models have long been used to establish architectural cadence and form. With some innovation, models also can be used to illustrate day and electric lighting effects. Models are particularly effective in conveying a look and in providing additional insight into the subjective aspects of a design. Photographs, especially slides or video, of models can be very effective communication devices for the client. Also, not much time or money is necessary to achieve a good model design tool.

Models can be used to show both interior and exterior lighting concepts. For example, they can be used to highlight select vertical surfaces, define corners with light, and identify graphics with light. One type of model may tend to show low light levels and, using mostly perimeter lighting, to put people in silhouette, leading to a relaxed, pleasant setting (see Chapter 2, under "Subjective Impressions"). Another may show the interior lighting concept of generally washing an entire space or area uniformly with light. Such models actually can be used to argue against proposed solutions and begin to "quantify" the qualitative aspects of design solutions (for the client, to whom "seeing is believing").

MOCKUPS

Mockups are very effective qualitative techniques, and can sometimes be used for quantitative purposes. Mockups need not be full-scale or highly

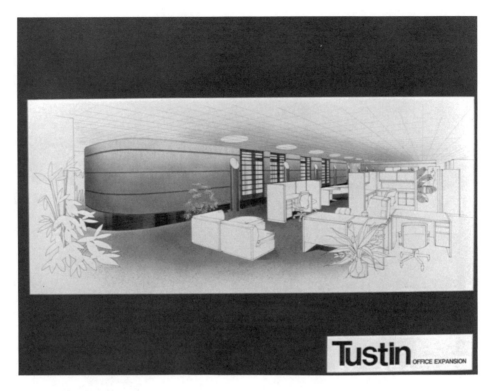

FIGURE 5–7.
This professional rendering is sensitive to the lighting effects being proposed for the given project. Sometimes professional renderings are nothing more than "100%" daylit renderings with full brightness and color throughout the entire rendering. Photo courtesy Steelcase Inc.

detailed, and they sometimes can be done with less than a hundred dollars' worth of materials. Figure 5–9 shows a half-scale mockup of a torchiere idea. The point with such a mockup was to determine if a series of etched or milk-white plastic planes suspended one above the other could be an effective light source and "lantern." Slides of the mockup were used to convince the client of the technique's potential, and led to a more detailed, full-scale mockup, shown in Figure 5–10, with the resultant completed installation shown in Figures C1 and C2.

Sometimes mockups can be quite useful when made of simple foam board forms lighted to illustrate a concept. Figure 5–11 shows such a mockup, made of white foam board and white sheets.

Many mockups are done primarily for aesthetic reasons, but there are times when mockups are necesary for quantitative reasons. A circular, pendent-mounted indirect fluorescent luminaire was developed using this mockup approach for a specific project. Figure 5–12 shows the mockup, which was used to gather illuminance and luminance data and to "feel" the

FIGURE 5–8.
The end-result of the project proposed in the rendering in Figure 5–7 shows that the wall lighting and the kiosk lighting were indeed rendered rather realistically, allowing the client to make an intelligent, informed decision on the concept. Photo courtesy Steelcase Inc.

comfort level and brightnesses of such a lighting system in a given space. This mockup and others like it helped in developing the luminaire shown in Figures C6, C6a, C6b and C8.

Full-scale mockups may sound grand and expensive, but in the context of a 20-million- to 100-million-dollar project, spending a fraction of a percent of the project budget on a mockup is generally well worth it. This not only helps to ensure that various technical criteria are met, but also helps the client and designers decide on the appropriateness of the proposed system and facilitates systems integration.

QUANTITATIVE DESIGN TOOLS

There comes a time when the designer and the client need to know how, and then if, the proposed design will meet the luminance and illuminance

FIGURE 5–9.
This half-scale mockup of a proposed torchiere helped the designers understand the lighting optics that could be achieved and the appearance of such a concept. This led to a full-scale mockup of a later version, shown in Figures 5–10, C1, and C2. Photo courtesy Gary Steffy Lighting Design Inc.; photo credit: Steven Kuzma Photography.

criteria. Specifically, it is necessary to assess maximum and minimum luminances; luminance ratios; maximum, minimum, and average vertical illuminances; maximum, minimum, and average horizontal illuminances; relative visual performance; and visual comfort probability (for direct luminaires). The designer need not be a calculus or computer whiz, but simply needs to know which criteria are important for a given project and what specific target values should be achieved. Final, in-depth calculations can be performed by engineering consultants or by manufacturers.

For those designers who wish to perform some basic calculations that can steer them toward probable solutions, and for those who wish to perform all of the lighting design duties on a given project, this section will discuss and give examples of such calculations (from easiest to more difficult). Al-

FIGURE 5–10.
A full-scale mockup of the luminaire concept proposed in Figure 5–9 was necessary to convince the client that the lighting concept would work and look attractive. Also, this full-scale mockup allowed the lighting designers to review manufacturing methods and quality control. Photo courtesy Gary Steffy Lighting Design Inc.; photo credit: Jeff Brown.

though computer calculations are actually the easiest ones (the computer does the calculation work, and the designer interprets the data), many computer calculations are based on some rather basic techniques, which we should consider first. Therefore, this text will review quantitative design tools in the following order: templates; the lumen or zonal cavity method; the point method (inverse square method); computer calculations.

TEMPLATES

Templates can be useful in establishing a preliminary equipment layout. Primarily used for site lighting, templates are available for some interior lighting equipment as well. These templates usually consist of iso-contour lines of footcandle/lux values printed on white paper. By overlaying tracing paper or vellum onto the white paper template, the designer can begin to lay out luminaire spacings based on illuminance criteria. The illuminance criteria usually must be assumed as a minimum value because average values are not readily available from quick template layouts. Although tem-

FIGURE 5–11.
A simple, inexpensive, and quick mockup can be achieved with foam board and sheets. This mockup was done during renovation work to show the client one of several lighting options for a lobby. Photo courtesy GE Company.

plates are a quick technique, they are not very accurate; and they also are rather misleading because they allow the designer to design to a single criterion, illuminance, but the impression of authenticity and accuracy they produce leads the designer to believe the job of calculations is complete after spending half an hour with the templates. Table 5–1 elaborates on the characteristics of templates and other calculation techniques.

LUMEN METHOD

The lumen method, or zonal cavity method, of calculation is no doubt the simplest method of establishing a uniform luminaire layout based on horizontal illuminance criteria (typically at desk height). Although lots of factors, coefficients, lamp lumen data, and other values must be sought from a variety of references, the calculation itself entails nothing more than multiplication and division. Because this technique does require some research time to collect the data necessary to perform the calculation, and because the calculation is rather cumbersome (thus giving the appearance of scientific accuracy), many designers believe it is the extent of lighting design. Figure 5–13 shows the result of such thinking. Considering the lumen

FIGURE 5–12.
A new luminaire proposed for a large open office project was tested and retested
in various mockups with actual ceiling material, using sheets to define space and
reflect some light back into the mockup area—an effect similar to having a lot of
luminaires continue in all directions. Photo courtesy Peerless Lighting; photo
credit: Richard Sexton.

method to be the be-all and end-all to lighting design is an incorrect assumption; *the Lumen Method is only a single-criterion compliance technique
and only for uniform layouts* (see Figure 5–14). The lumen method is primarily an illuminance-only design tool. Table 5–1 outlines the characteristics of the lumen method calculation technique.

The single greatest benefit of the lumen method is its general ease of use
in establishing preliminary lighting layouts for initial budget projections
and initial module development. If some "tricks" are used, the lumen
method can serve as a fairly accurate layout tool. The lumen method is
somewhat more accurate for direct lighting equipment, but still is of sufficient accuracy for indirect lighting equipment to qualify as a "rough cut"
design tool. Final, more accurate computer calculations should be performed prior to the development of layouts for contract documents for both
direct and indirect lighting.

The lumen method was so named for the axiom that illumination on a
large surface is equal to the total lumens incident on that surface divided
by the area of that surface. In its initial form, then, the lumen method is
simply the total number of lumens reaching a work surface divided by the

FIGURE 5–13.
The result of doing "calculation" design is a sea of ambient luminaires, with no accents. Surfaces that all have the same tonal quality also contribute to a monotonous look.

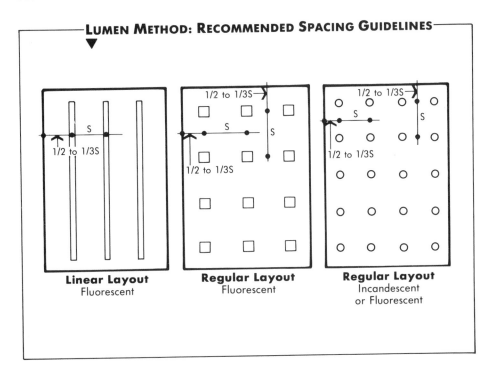

FIGURE 5–14

Table 5-1.
Quantitative design tools.

Characteristic	Templates	Lumen Method	Point Method	Flux Transfer
Technique	Hand	Hand/computer	Hand/computer	Hand/computer
Luminances	No	No	Yes	Yes
Horizontal illuminances	Yes	Yes	Yes	Yes
Vertical illuminances	No	No	Yes	Yes
Accuracy	• Poor for interior • Fair for exterior	• Fair to good	• Good to excellent	• Good to excellent
Advantages	• Quick	• Quick	• More accurate	• Most accurate • Quick by computer
Disadvantages	• Single criterion compliance	• Single criterion compliance	• Very time-consuming • No interreflection	• Limited by data input • False sense of security

- Not very accurate
- Limited to assumptions used in establishing template
- No interreflection
- Assumes empty room condition for interior
- May not include maintenance factor

- Average value basis
- Assumes uniformity
- Assumes empty room conditions
- No body shadow

- Assumes point source (must discretize large sources—complicates calculation and increases time consumption)

- False sense of accuracy[1]
- In most cases cannot account for furniture or partitions

Uses

- Exterior and interior uniform or nonuniform layouts
- Establishing preliminary layout
- Budget estimating

- Interior uniform layouts
- Establishing preliminary layout
- Budget estimating
- Final layout for noncritical spaces
- Fair for indirect
- Good for direct

- Exterior and interior uniform or nonuniform layouts
- Establishing exact layout for accent lighting
- Establishing exact layout

- Exterior and interior uniform or nonuniform layouts
- Establishing exact layout

[1] With any of these calculation techniques, it is easy to be caught up in the "correctness" of the answer, but in most cases it will be difficult ever to measure to within 10%.

area of the work surface. Note that the limitations of the general lumen method are such that the work surface is actually the area of the room under consideration. The lumen method can be used in a number of ways, to find: (1) the initial average illuminance on a horizontal surface to be expected from a proposed layout; (2) the maintained average illuminance (average illuminance to be expected over time, compensating for dirt buildup and depreciation factors) to be expected from a proposed layout; (3) the quantity of lamps required in a given space in order to achieve a specific average maintained illuminance on a horizontal surface; or (4) the quantity of luminaires required in a given space in order to achieve a specific average maintained illuminance on a horizontal surface. These four lumen method procedures are formulated in Table 5–2. Table 5–3 describes the various factors required for one to undertake a lumen method calculation: maintained illuminance target value; work area; initial lamp lumens; recoverable light loss factors; nonrecoverable light loss factors; and coefficient of utilization.

The maintained illuminance target value is the illuminance criterion that has been established for a particular space. This target value is reported in lux or footcandles, and is to be *maintained* over the life cycle of the lamps and between cleaning of the lighting equipment. Illuminance targets may be obtained from the *IES Handbook Application Volume*, the client's inhouse

Table 5–2.
Lumen method formulations.

The Lumen Method technique can be used in one of four ways:

- To determine initial average illuminance (E_i) from a given layout:

$$E_i = \frac{\text{Initial lamp lumens} \times CU \times NRLLF}{\text{Work area}}$$

- To determine maintained average illuminance (E_m) from a given layout:

$$E_m = \frac{\text{Initial lamp lumens} \times CU \times RLLF \times NRLLF}{\text{Work area}}$$

- To determine the quantity of lamps required for a given room and illuminance target:

$$\text{Number of lamps} = \frac{E_m \times \text{Work area}}{CU \times RLLF \times NRLLF \times \text{Lumens per lamp}}$$

- To determine the quantity of luminaires required for a given room and illuminance target:

$$\text{Number of luminaires} = \frac{E_m \times \text{Work area}}{CU \times RLLF \times NRLLF \times \text{Lumens per lamp} \times \text{Lamps per luminaire}}$$

Where: CU = coefficient of utilization; $RLLF$ = recoverable light loss factor; $NRLLF$ = nonrecoverable light loss factor.

Table 5–3.
Lumen method factors.

Factors required to perform lumen method calculation	Source for determining factor precisely	Rough estimate
• Maintained illuminance target value (E_m in footcandles or lux)	• IES illuminance selection procedure • Client criteria • Experience • Codes and/or ordinances	• Office ambient lighting (35 to 45 fc/350 to 450 lx) • Office tasklighting (50 to 75 fc/500 to 750 lx) • Lobby ambient lighting (5 to 15 fc/50 to 150 lx) • Lobby task lighting (25 to 50 fc/250 to 500 lx) • Corridor lighting (5 to 15 fc/50 to 150 lx)
• Work area (horizontal surface in square feet or square meters)	• Floor plan • Measurements (for renovation)	• From plan
• Initial lamp lumens (lumens)	• Lamp manufacturers' catalogs	• 90-watt halogen TB lamp = 1750 lumens • 90-watt halogen PAR lamp = 1250 lumens • 13-watt compact fluorescent triphosphor lamp = 900 lumens • 32-watt T8 fluorescent triphosphor lamp = 2900 lumens • 40-watt T12 fluorescent triphosphor lamp = 3300 lumens • 40-watt T12 U-bent triphosphor lamp = 2900 lumens
• Recoverable light loss factor (RLLF) (unit less) 　—Lamp lumen depreciation	• Lamp manufacturers' data	• Incandescent = 0.95 • Fluorescent (rapid start) = 0.90 • Mercury/metal halide = 0.65
—Luminaire dirt depreciation	• *IES Handbook Reference Volume* • Experience	• For most newer commercial spaces = 0.97

(Continued)

Table 5–3. (Continued)

Factors required to perform lumen method calculation	Source for determining factor precisely	Rough estimate
—Room surface dirt depreciation	• *IES Handbook Reference Volume* • Experience	• For most commercial spaces = 0.97
• Nonrecoverable light loss factors (NRLLF—unitless)		
—Voltage factor	• Electrical engineer/*IES Handbook Reference Volume*	• For most commercial spaces = 1.0
—Ballast factor	• Ballast manufacturers	• For CBM-certified ballasts = 0.93
—Thermal factor	• Luminaire or lamp manufacturers	• Assume 0.95
—Partition factor	• Not readily available	• See Table 5–4
• Coefficient of utilization (CU)	• Manufacturers' data • See appropriate figures in Chapter 4	• NA (must use manufacturers' data) • *IES Handbook Reference Volume*

guidelines, the experience obtained from a variety of similar projects, and/or codes and ordinances. For many open plan offices where task lights will be provided on each desk, a typical maintained illuminance target value will be in the range of 35 to 45 footcandles/350 to 450 lux. For many open plan offices where task lights are not used, a typical maintained illuminance target value will be in the range of 50 to 75 footcandles/500 to 750 lux. Refer to Chapter 2, under *Illuminance*," for additional discussion of maintained illuminance target values.

The work area, which, for lumen method calculations, is the horizontal workplane, generally comprises the area of the entire space. If the lumen method is to be used for determining the quantity of luminaires required in a 10-foot by 20-foot office, then the work area is set at 10 times 20 or 200 square feet. As is discussed in the *IES Handbook Reference Volume*, the work area can be smaller than the room area, and the lumen method still can be used as a reasonable design tool.

Initial lamp lumens are reported by the lamp manufacturers in catalog literature.

Recoverable light loss factors (RLLF—see Table 5–3) include all of the light loss factors that can be "recovered." As discussed in Chapter 3, lamps lose some light output over time. This is barely perceptible with incandescent lamps, but is noticable with fluorescent lamps, and is significant with mercury vapor and metal halide lamps. This particular recoverable factor is known as lamp lumen depreciation. By group-relamping all lamps on a predetermined periodic basis (generally at 70 percent or so of rated lamp life), lamp lumen depreciation (LDD) can be recovered. Such group relamping is generally quite cost-effective in terms of both energy cost (electricity expended for a particular light level) and maintenance cost (money expended to change all lamps one at a time on an on-call basis). A second RLLF is luminaire dirt depreciation (LDD). As a building is operated over time, dust collects on luminaire lenses, louvers, and reflectors. The *IES Handbook Reference Volume* contains graphs for establishing the LDD for specific lighting equipment in specific building types.

The IES information is based on empirical data collected in the 1950s and 1960s, which may not be very accurate for today's building systems. In any event, a predetermined schedule should be established for cleaning lighting equipment. This is usually based on the group relamping schedule. For example, if lamps are group-replaced every three years, then a luminaire cleaning schedule based on eighteen months would be appropriate. Finally, room surface dirt depreciation (RSDD) also is a recoverable factor. As room surfaces age, they collect dirt; and although this is certainly a secondary factor compared to lamp lumen depreciation or luminaire dirt depreciation, it can have some impact on reducing reflected light. By repainting and/or refinishing walls, floors, and ceilings from time to time, this factor is minimized.

Nonrecoverable light loss factors (NRLFF—see Table 5–3) include all those factors that negatively impact the lighting system and are permanent. These are the factors that account for real-world conditions that are not part of the lamps' and luminaires' laboratory testing standards. During photometric testing of lamps and luminaires, very specific voltages, standard reference ballasts, and ambient temperatures are used. Such reference standards are necessary if a designer is to compare one manufacturer's lamp or luminaire performance to another manufacturer's. Once placed in a real-world situation, however, those reference standard conditions generally are not met, and usually there is some performance reduction.

The voltage factor is a result of the nominal voltage to the lamp and/or ballast not being maintained. Voltage drop, voltage surges, and primary voltages above or below those expected can reduce the light output.

The ballast factor accounts for the differences experienced when operating a given fluorescent lamp on a ballast other than the standard reference ballast used to photometrically test the lamp. Off-the-shelf 30- and 40-watt ballasts manufactured by members of Certified Ballast Manufacturers (CBM) have ballast factors of 0.93 or greater.

The thermal factor is a nonrecoverable factor accounting for the difference in luminaire ambient temperature from the testing lab to the real world. A reasonable thermal loss is about 5 percent, for a thermal factor of 0.95.

Perhaps the most troublesome and frequently overlooked nonrecoverable factor is the partition factor, which is considered in those spaces where partial height partitions are used to subdivide space. Generally, the lower the ceiling and the higher the partition, the lower (the worse) the partition factor is. Partition factors usually are lower (worse) for direct, well-controlled luminaires and usually higher (better) for indirect, widespread distribution luminaires. Table 5–4 outlines some approximate partition factors for various ceiling heights and partition heights, and Figure 5–15 graphically illustrates the effects of partitions on light reaching a worksurface. To accommodate this effect, it is necessary to design with more luminaires closer together, with less light coming from each luminaire to produce more uniform, ambient lighting.

It is conceivable for a typical fluorescent lighting system for a commercial installation with partial height partitions to have an RLLF of 0.85, an NRLLF of 0.88, and a PF of 0.95. This yields a total light loss factor of 0.71. In other words, over a two- to three-year period, it is quite possible to have 29 percent less light than the lighting system could potentially produce under optimum, "new" conditions.

Coefficients of utilization (CUs) are an expression of the lighting system's efficiency in producing lumens on the work surface, reported in decimal

Table 5-4.
Partition factors.

Ceiling height	Partition height	Approximate partition factor (PF)[1]
Between 8'6" and 9'0"	Less than 42"	1.0
	43" to 54"	0.95
	55" to 65"	0.85
	66" to 80"	0.75
Between 9'0" and 9'6"	Less than 42"	1.0
	43" to 54"	0.97
	55" to 65"	0.90
	66" to 80"	0.80
Between 9'6" and 10'0"	Less than 42"	1.0
	43" to 54"	0.97
	55" to 65"	0.95
	66" to 80"	0.85

[1]For widespread indirect luminaires, the partition factor may well be 5 points better for 43" and higher partitions. For example, the PF for a widespread indirect lighting system in a room with an 8'6" ceiling height and 43" to 54" partitions is likely to by 1.0.

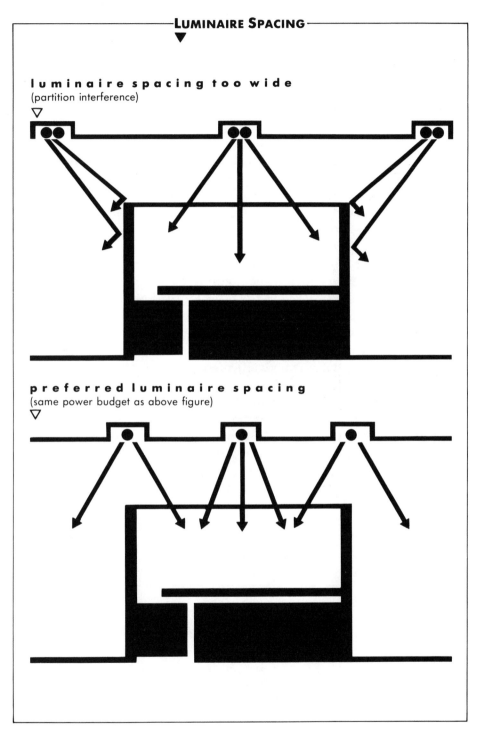

LUMINAIRE SPACING

luminaire spacing too wide
(partition interference)

preferred luminaire spacing
(same power budget as above figure)

FIGURE 5–15

form. Some light output (lumens) from the lamps is absorbed by the luminaire, walls, and ceiling. The CU depends on: (1) efficiency of the luminaire; (2) distribution of light from the luminaire (narrow, medium, or widespread); (3) room surface reflectances; and (4) geometry (size and proportions) of the room. CU values are found in manufacturers' data. Reported in tabular form, CUs are determined by the designer, on the basis of given room proportions and room surface reflectances. Figures 4–5b, 4–6b, 4–7b, 4–8b, 4–9b, 4–19b, 4–11b, 4–12b, 4–13b, 4–14b, 4–15c, 4–15f, and 4–16c are various manufacturers' photometric reports for specific luminaires, in which CU data can be found.

Room proportions for CU data are identified by a single number, known as the room cavity ratio, or RCR. Figure 5–16 illustrates the variables that affect the room cavity ratio. This ratio, whose formula may look complicated, is actually quite simple. One only needs a mathematical constant (2.5), the room length and width, and the height of the cavity from the workplane (which could be the floor) to the bottom of the luminaires in order to determine RCR. See Figure 5–16 for the formula that is used.

After one determines the RCR, the room surface reflectances must be estimated. For purposes of using the lumen method as an estimator, and because the floor reflectance has little impact on the illuminance level on the workplane, the floor reflectance can always be assumed to be 20 percent. Walls and ceilings can be categorized according to their tone: light, medium, or dark. See Table 5–5 for typical surface reflectance estimations.

Now the CU can be determined from the manufacturer's data. Find the CU table, and locate the appropriate ceiling reflectance zone and the wall reflectance column within the zone. Then locate the RCR column (generally the left-most column) and read down to the RCR for the room in question. Read across from the appropriate RCR and down the appropriate ceil-

Table 5–5.
Surface reflectance estimations.

Surface	Tone	Estimated reflectance, %
Walls	Light (light paint colors)	50
	Medium (light woods, light fabrics, and medium paint)	30
	Dark (dark woods, medium-to-dark fabrics, and dark paint)	10
Ceilings	Light (commercial white tile)	80
	Medium (commercial neutral tile and light paint)	50
	Dark (commercial fabric tile and medium paint)	30

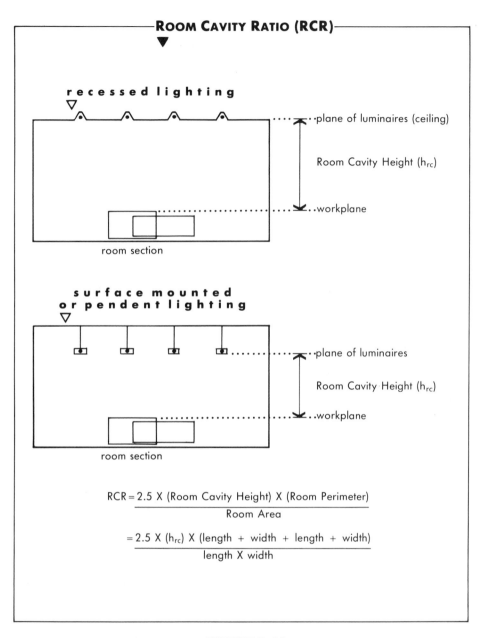

FIGURE 5–16

ing/wall reflectance to find the coefficient of utilization. The CU must be given in decimal form to be used in the lumen method formula.

Refinements can be made for more accurate calculations based on specific wall, floor, and ceiling reflectances, and based on floor cavities (the cavity between the workplane and the floor plane if they are not identical) and ceiling cavities (the cavity between the plane of light and the ceiling if they are not identical). Typically, however, these are tedious and cumbersome calculations, which generally result in mathetically insignificant changes.

LUMEN METHOD EXAMPLE

Figure 5–17 shows a space—a training room—that has a general lighting system layout based on a lumen method calculation. A schematic floor plan is shown in Figure 5–18. Information about the space that was known at the time of design also is given in Figure 5–18. Such information is useful in establishing a lighting concept prior to equipment selection. Based on this information, the following concept was developed:

Training Room Lighting Concept:
Controlled Overhead Lighting (Low Brightness)

- Allow for transparency projection without switching lights off
- Allow view into CAD area without screen washout
- Minimum glare

FIGURE 5–17.
The lumen method was used to help lay out the ambient lighting system in this training room. Note the addition of wall lighting for subjective purposes. Photo courtesy Gary Steffy Lighting Design Inc.; photo credit: Steven Kuzma Photography.

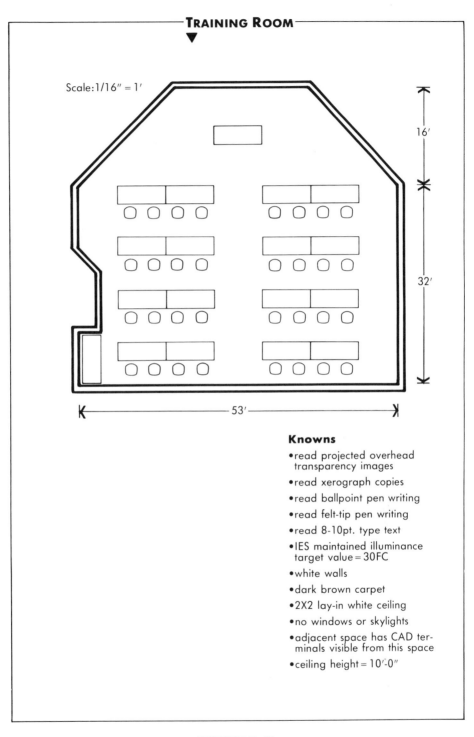

TRAINING ROOM

Scale: 1/16″ = 1′

16′

32′

53′

Knowns

•read projected overhead
  transparency images

•read xerograph copies

•read ballpoint pen writing

•read felt-tip pen writing

•read 8-10pt. type text

•IES maintained illuminance
  target value = 30FC

•white walls

•dark brown carpet

•2X2 lay-in white ceiling

•no windows or skylights

•adjacent space has CAD terminals visible from this space

•ceiling height = 10′-0″

FIGURE 5–18

Perimeter Wall Lighting

- Promote sense of spaciousness
- Introduce peripheral brightness missing due to lack of windows
- Balance room/task brightness
- Establish multilevel lighting (switch overhead system independently of wall system)
- Avoid gloomy, cavelike feeling often associated with just overhead, low brightness lighting

The lumen method can be used to establish the quantity of low-brightness luminaires required to meet the illuminance target value of 30 footcandles. Figures 4–14a and 4–14b show a manufacturer's datasheet and photometric information for a low-brightness luminaire, in this case a Columbia 2 by 2, 16-cell parabolic luminaire. Figure 5–19 shows the CU data for the Columbia luminaire. The 2 by 2 luminaire can be conveniently integrated with a 2 by 2 ceiling system. Also, a 2 by 2 unit is more human-scale than a 2 by 4 unit.

From Table 5–3, a list of factors needed for the lumen method can be developed. For the training room example, these factors are:

Lumen Method Training Room Example Summary

Factor	Value
• Maintained illuminance target (IES)	30 FC
• Work area (Figure 5–20)	2288 SF
• Initial lamp lumens	3000 lumens
• Recoverable light loss factor	0.85
• Nonrecoverable light loss factor	0.88
• RCR (Figure 5–21)	1.5
• Coefficient of utilization (Figure 5–19)	0.59

Figure 5–19 shows the CU determination. Therefore, the number of luminaires required is:

$$\frac{E_m \times \text{Work area}}{CU \times RLLF \times NRLLF \times \text{Lumens per lamp} \times \text{Lamps per luminaire}}$$

which is, by substitution:

$$\frac{30 \times 2288}{0.59 \times 0.85 \times 0.88 \times 3000 \times 2}$$

which equals 26 luminaires.

─────── **TRAINING ROOM: CU DETERMINATION** ───────
▼

Columbia Lighting Catalog No. 4544-43-222U
Based on ITL Report No. 15441
Coefficients of Utilization-Lumen Method
Effective Floor Cavity Reflectance=20%

RC(%) Ceiling Reflectance	80				70				50			30		
RW(%) Wall Reflectance	70	50	30	10	70	50	30	10	50	30	10	50	30	10
RCR 1	.63	.61	.60	.58	.62	.60	.59	.57	.58	.57	.55	.56	.55	.54
Room Cavity 2	.59	.56	.53	.51	.58	.55	.52	.50	.53	.51	.49	.51	.50	.48
Ratio 3	.55	.51	.48	.45	.54	.50	.47	.45	.49	.46	.44	.47	.45	.43
4	.52	.46	.43	.40	.50	.46	.42	.39	.44	.41	.39	.43	.41	.38
5	.48	.42	.38	.35	.47	.41	.38	.35	.40	.37	.34	.39	.36	.34
6	.44	.38	.34	.31	.43	.38	.34	.31	.37	.33	.31	.36	.33	.30
7	.41	.35	.30	.27	.40	.34	.30	.27	.33	.30	.27	.33	.29	.27
8	.38	.31	.27	.24	.37	.31	.27	.24	.30	.26	.24	.29	.26	.24
9	.35	.28	.24	.21	.34	.28	.24	.21	.27	.23	.21	.27	.23	.21
10	.32	.26	.21	.19	.32	.25	.21	.19	.25	.21	.18	.24	.21	.18

Knowns

White ceiling~80% reflectance

White walls~50% reflectance

Floor~20% reflectance
(for lumen method calculations, assume floor reflectance of 20% since floor does not dramatically affect light on work surface)

RCR=1.5

CU

Interpolate between 1 and 2—add the CU value for RCR of 1 to the CU value for RCR of 2 and divide by two

FIGURE 5–19

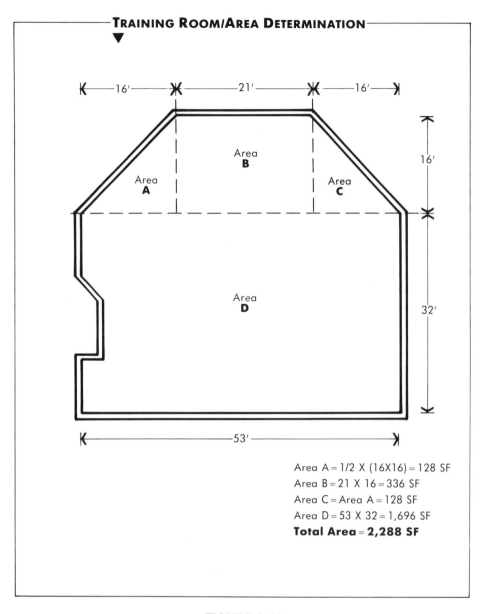

TRAINING ROOM/AREA DETERMINATION

Area A = 1/2 X (16X16) = 128 SF
Area B = 21 X 16 = 336 SF
Area C = Area A = 128 SF
Area D = 53 X 32 = 1,696 SF
Total Area = 2,288 SF

FIGURE 5–20

This calculation permits the establishment of an appropriate preliminary equipment layout and cost budget and provides a starting point for developing more accurate computer calculations, if desired.

Doing a lighting layout requires that one complete at least two additional steps after determining the number of luminaires. Each step is more or less a check on the other. One step is the area-per-luminaire process; another is the spacing-to-mounting-height process.

The area-per-luminaire process simply entails dividing the area of the

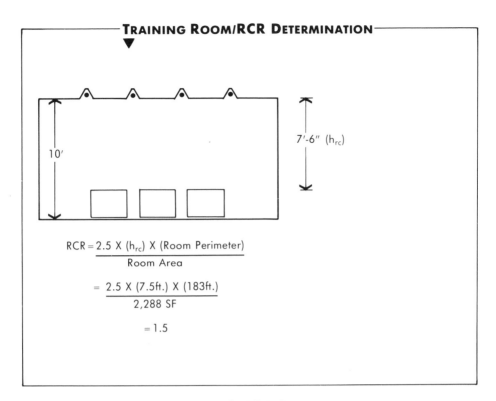

TRAINING ROOM/RCR DETERMINATION

$$RCR = \frac{2.5 \times (h_{rc}) \times (\text{Room Perimeter})}{\text{Room Area}}$$

$$= \frac{2.5 \times (7.5\text{ft.}) \times (183\text{ft.})}{2,288 \text{ SF}}$$

$$= 1.5$$

FIGURE 5–21

worksurface used in the lumen method by the number of luminaires determined by the lumen method. This yields a certain amount of square feet per luminaire, and the square root of this value can be the basis for spacing layouts. For example, in the training room illustration the number of luminaires required to light 2288 SF of space is 26; so each luminaire could cover about 88 SF of space. Thus, a reasonable basis for spacing is the square root of 88 SF, or 9 to 10 feet.

Another way to help ensure uniform lighting is to follow the manufacturers' spacing-to-mounting-height ratios (S/MH). These values are usually part of the photometric report and are indeed the maximum suggested ratio of spacing distance to mounting height. In the training room example, the photometric data (Figure 4–14b) indicate that the S/MH should not exceed 1.3. Because the training room has a mounting height (h_{rc}) of 7.5 feet, the maximum spacing suggested is 9 feet 9 inches.

In any case, Figure 5–14 illustrates the general spacing guidelines that should be followed in order to obtain uniform illuminance levels and to maximize wall darkness.

As can be seen in Figure 5–17, the spacing guideline for the luminaire-to-wall distance was exceeded. This is permissible when other lighting is added to prevent walls from becoming too dark, and when the perimeter of the room is not a major task area. The work area illuminance approaches 40 footcandles/400 lux, maintained, because luminaires are closer together and the illuminance throughout the room is no longer uniform from wall to wall and corner to corner.

POINT METHOD

Although the lumen method is most widely used to establish a preliminary quantity of luminaires to be used in a space to achieve an average uniform light level, the point method is most often used as an illuminance check technique for a specific point or points in a room. Figures 5–22 and 5–23 illustrate the variables involved in the point method and the available formulas for horizontal and vertical illuminance.

The point method generally is used as a hand-calculation technique to analyze accent lighting. For downlighting applications, however, using the point method as a hand technique usually is quite tedious. Here computer assistance is appropriate.

Interreflection (light reflected from walls and ceiling to the point of interest) is not accounted for in the point method. Also, the point method is based on the assumption that the luminaire is relatively pointlike, or small. This may mean that large luminaires must be discretized (divided up into smaller segments). Typically, the distance (d) between the luminaire and the point of interest should be between four and five times the largest dimension of the luminaire. So, for a 2 by 4 luminaire to be considered a point source, the luminaire should be 16 to 20 feet away from the point of calculational interest.

By including the RLLF and NRLLF values (discussed above for the lumen method) in the point method, one can find the maintained illuminance.

The point method is particularly accurate for exterior lighting calculations and for interior spaces with very low surface reflectances (little or no interreflection component).

COMPUTER CALCULATIONS

There are quite a few software programs available for computer calculation of design problems. These programs, in many instances, are not much more than lumen method procedures. Therefore, the calculation may be quick, but it is no more accurate than the lumen method calculations done by hand. There are also programs based on the point method, whose accuracy generally is good; and certainly the speed of the computer is helpful in analyzing the effects of many luminaires on many points in a space. A few programs are based on more serious and rigorous mathematical models of

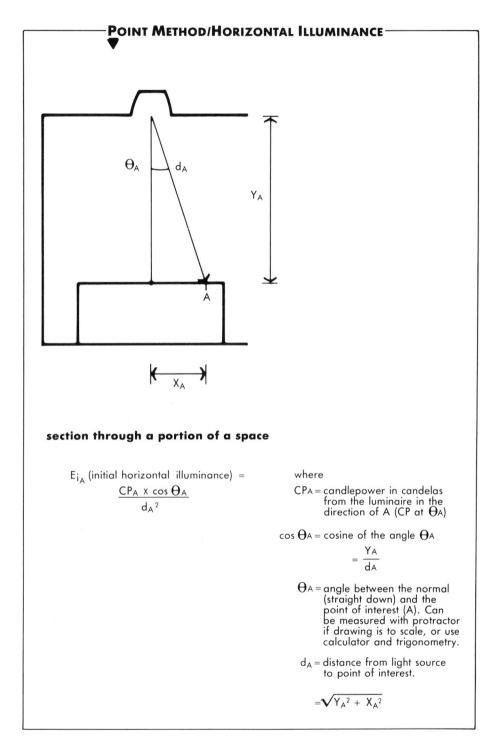

section through a portion of a space

E_{i_A} (initial horizontal illuminance) =

$$\frac{CP_A \times \cos \Theta_A}{d_A{}^2}$$

where

CP_A = candlepower in candelas from the luminaire in the direction of A (CP at Θ_A)

$\cos \Theta_A$ = cosine of the angle Θ_A

$$= \frac{Y_A}{d_A}$$

Θ_A = angle between the normal (straight down) and the point of interest (A). Can be measured with protractor if drawing is to scale, or use calculator and trigonometry.

d_A = distance from light source to point of interest.

$$= \sqrt{Y_A{}^2 + X_A{}^2}$$

FIGURE 5–22

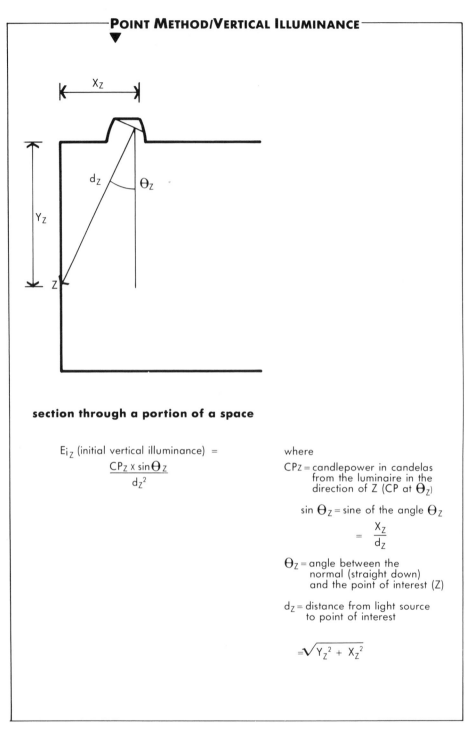

POINT METHOD/VERTICAL ILLUMINANCE

section through a portion of a space

E_{i_Z} (initial vertical illuminance) =

$$\frac{CP_Z \times \sin\Theta_Z}{d_Z{}^2}$$

where

CP_Z = candlepower in candelas from the luminaire in the direction of Z (CP at Θ_Z)

$\sin\Theta_Z$ = sine of the angle Θ_Z

$$= \frac{X_Z}{d_Z}$$

Θ_Z = angle between the normal (straight down) and the point of interest (Z)

d_Z = distance from light source to point of interest

$$= \sqrt{Y_Z{}^2 + X_Z{}^2}$$

FIGURE 5–23

lighting, and they tend to be the most accurate ones because they include the interreflected component of light.

Because the computer spews forth reams of printed input and output data, computer calculations often give the misimpression of flawless finality. First and foremost, the accuracy of computer calculations is limited by the accuracy of the input data. Second, as mentioned previously, the computer software may not be much more than simple hand techniques put on a machine. Third, the accuracy of any calculation technique is difficult to ascertain because measured light levels usually are only within 10 to 20 percent of calculated values. This is so primarily because of meter inaccuracies, voltage fluctuations, room surface reflectance characteristics, and so on.

Whenever computer calculations are made, the RLLF and NRLLF values discussed in the lumen method section are applicable and should be used. This is especially important when a third party (manufacturer or engineer) runs computer calculations for the designer. Such third parties may use light loss factors different from those reported in Table 5–3, or may elect to use no light loss factors or may only use selected light loss factors. Room surface reflectance assumptions can significantly affect the calculations. Many people use the IES-recommended 80 percent ceiling reflectance, 50 percent wall reflectance, and 20 percent floor reflectance; and doing this can change light levels from 10 to 30 percent. The designer is responsible for communicating the appropriate variables and assumptions to be used by third parties.

CHAPTER SIX

LIGHTING DESIGN DOCUMENTATION

INTRODUCTION

The contract documents typically contain detailed, dimensioned, and accurate architectural reflected ceiling plans, elevations, sections, details, and specifications needed to convey design information to a contractor. These documents also include shop drawing review and disposition. Any particular project is only as good as the contract documents. Typically, the reflected ceiling plans contain information indicating the luminaire type or designation, the luminaire location and or spacing, and, if necessary, the luminaire orientation or direction of light throw.

Elevations and sections are shown for lighting purposes when luminaires are floor– or wall–mounted or have a unique profile or inner optical characteristic that must be illustrated.

Details are used to convey the exact architectural dimensions and construction necessary for a particular luminaire or lighting effect.

Specifications are perhaps the most critical aspect of any lighting design, as they outline the expected duties of the contractor, indicate specific lamp, ballast, transformer, and luminaire requirements, and cite applicable code requirements.

Shop drawings are used as a verification step to assure the design team that the contractor has properly interpreted and will be executing the specification as written for the specific project.

REFLECTED CEILING PLANS

Reflected ceiling plans are so named because they are a mirror–image (reflected) view of the ceiling. Imagine that you are looking down onto a mirror inserted as a plane about 4 feet above the floor, and the luminaires and various ceiling elements are all visible in this mirror. This view constitutes a reflected ceiling plan.

To develop reflected ceiling plans, the designer needs to know equipment locations, spacings, and focus or aiming directions (if applicable). Symbols are needed to provide a cohesive indication of specific luminaires throughout a project.

The ANSI (American National Standards Institute) standards for lighting symbols are quite limited. To make drawings more meaningful at initial glance to both designers and contractors, a more diverse and realistic representation of luminaires might be appropriate. Figures 6–1 and 6–1b illustrate various possible luminaire symbols. These symbols are appropriate for the architectural or electrical reflected ceiling plans that typically are used to show lighting, and they usually are drawn roughly to the scale of the reflected ceiling plan.

Figure 6–2 illustrates a reflected ceiling plan. Note that luminaires are clearly and boldly indicated so that they will not be easily missed. Also note the identification of all luminaires (see "Luminaire/Lamp/Ballast Schedule" section in this chapter). This identification designation (series of alphanumerics) usually is located adjacent to the luminaire, and no parenthetical description is given (Figure 6–2 was laid out, and descriptors were added for clarity). For luminaires located in the center of tiles in lay–in ceilings, it is not necessary to give luminaire dimensions, but it is desirable to provide them to avoid any misunderstanding. Field layouts of the grid may move up to 12 inches from the point of origin that the designer used for laying out the luminaires. For drywall ceilings, dimensions are a necessity. The contractor should not be permitted to scale dimensions from drawings, as this can lead to serious error.

DESIGN DETAILS

The concept details developed during design development (discussed in Chapter 4) now must be firmly detailed. Exact dimensions, appropriate supports, connections, integration details, and finishes must be identified. These details need to be placed on drawings as well as in specifications. The registered professional (architect or engineer) on the project is responsible for the final development and specification of the mechanics of the details.

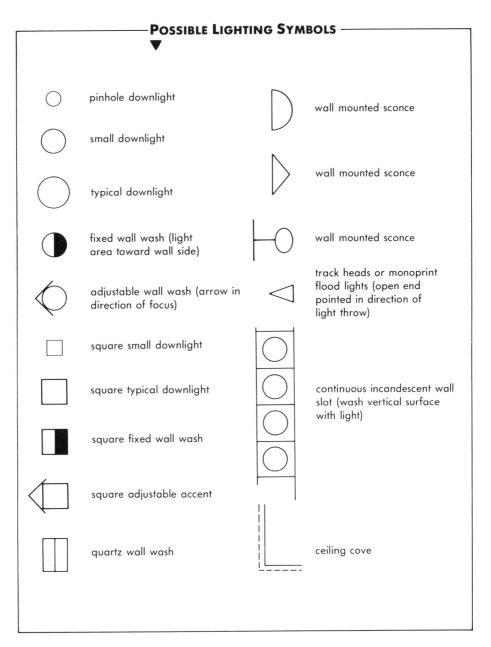

FIGURE 6–1

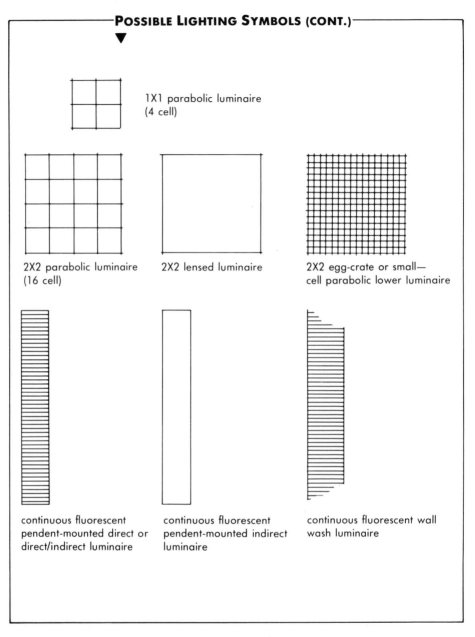

FIGURE 6–1b

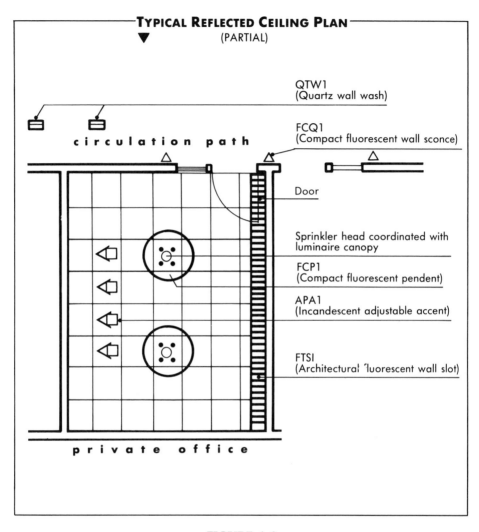

FIGURE 6–2

THE SPECIFICATION

Section 16500 of the total project specification is the "Lighting Specification." The architect and/or the engineer may adopt the lighting designer's specification—in which case this is now a legal document. As such, the specification must clearly and concisely outline the expected responsibilities of the contractor and clearly describe the luminaires that have been selected to meet the specific criteria for the respective project. Typically, the specification will include at least five sections and sometimes six or seven, plus a one– or two–sentence foreword. These sections fall under the following headings: General; Substitutions; Lamps—General; Transformers/Ballasts; Luminaire/Lamp/Ballast Schedule; and sometimes Control Devices.

FOREWORD

The foreword is generally quite short, simply indicating the project name and address to which the specification applies. This is also an appropriate place to discuss revisions and how revisions may be identified in future documents. The following is a sample foreword:

Specification
Lighting Systems Specification of Luminaires and Lamps for the John Doe Company Headquarters, Kansas City, Kansas.
This Specification is generated to assure design compliance with lighting criteria. This is not intended nor does it presume to cover mechanical, electrical, or structural engineering issues. These areas are to be addressed by the respective disciplines.
Revisions to this specification will be indicated by asterisks (*) in the margins.

GENERAL

The general section outlines the general responsibilities expected of the contractor. This includes whether or not the contractor is to provide the equipment described in the specification (actually buy it for the owner) and/or to receive and/or store the specified equipment. The general section also indicates code requirements. Other items that are appropriate for the general section are those general items that apply to a broad range of equipment or practices that the contractor is expected to undertake. A rather typical general section might read:

1. *General*
The contractor shall provide, receive, unload, uncrate, store, protect, and install lamps, luminaires, and switches as specified herein. Lamps for miscellaneous equipment shall be provided and installed by the contractor according to equipment manufacturers' guidelines.
All equipment, wiring, and installation shall be in accordance with the National Electric Code and applicable local codes and shall be thermally protected where necessary.
All fluorescent luminaires using straight T8, T10, or T12 lamps shall be equipped with knife–edge sockets only. No other socket type shall be acceptable.

Contractor shall be responsible for installation of all fluorescent luminaires so that all lamps in all luminaires are parallel to each other except where expressly noted.

Contractor shall be responsible for sealing all outdoor luminaires for wet locations (i.e., all knockouts, all pipe and wire entrances, etc.) as is standard industry practice to prevent water from entering luminaires.

SUBSTITUTIONS

Some contractors, in an effort to increase their profit, will attempt to submit alternatives to the specified equipment. Although very few alternative submittals will ever equal the specified equipment, this practice continues today because of loose specifications and contractors' low regard for meeting criteria (and proving same) that the design team was retained to establish on the client's behalf. Specifications should be written firmly ("tightly"), outlining exact requirements of lighting equipment. Also, specifications should hold the contractor responsible for providing evidence that any alternatives will meet criteria and/or that the contractor will pay for all subsequent design revisions due to use of the alternate equipment.

The designer should personally know the manufacturers' representatives for various equipment in the geographic region of the designer's home office. Keeping reps informed about those projects' specifications in which their equipment is specified will help to alleviate contractor substitutions.

Because most alternatives generated by the contractor or distributor or manufacturer are usually an effort to increase their profits, one method of "holding" the specification is to report estimated prices to the owner. Typically, a 10 percent markup for a distributor and a 10 percent markup for a contractor are reasonable. The designer is responsible for providing the owner with a cost estimate and then following up at bid time to be certain that excessive markups have not occurred. In any event, a tight specification and constant followup by the designer can lead to good–quality, cost–effective lighting. A substitutions section might look like this:

2. *Substitutions*

The lighting equipment specified herein has been carefully chosen for its ability to meet the luminous environment requirements of this project. Calculations are generally performed to determine luminances, luminance ratios, horizontal and vertical illuminances. Equipment which has been shown to comply with established criteria is specified herein. Substitutions in all likelihood will be unable to meet all of the same criteria as the specified equipment.

Where permitted, substitution submittals shall consist of a physical description, dimensioned drawing, and complete photometric and electric data of the proposed lamp and luminaire. Working samples of lamp and luminaire substitutions must also be supplied for visual check of finish and operating characteristics. Photometric reports must list the actual candela values of the luminaire's distribution in at least three planes. Candela curve, footcandle and lumen tables, and isofootcandle contours are not acceptable. The contractor shall be responsible for negotiating with the client, lighting designer, electrical engineer, and architect prior to substitution submittal to assure fees are available to redesign project based on contractor's proposed substitutions; or contractor shall produce all design and calculation documentation for review by lighting designer and electrical engineer. NO SUBSTITUTIONS WILL BE CONSIDERED WITHOUT COMPLIANCE WITH THIS PARAGRAPH.

LAMPS—GENERAL

A general section on lamps should discuss the mixing and matching of various manufacturers' lamps, an initial replacement supply of lamps, and testing procedures for assuring the quality of lamps. The mixing of various lamps from different manufacturers is not recommended. Only a few lamps have ANSI requirements that they must meet; otherwise, a specific GE fluorescent lamp may not exactly match a specific Sylvania fluorescent lamp even though each manufacturer may consider its lamp "equal" to the other. An entire roomful of such lamp mixing can produce a variegated appearance.

Specifying a replacement lamp stock that is to be supplied by the contractor and left behind for the owner helps to assure that during the first half-year or so the owner will have replacement lamps on hand. In the fuss and confusion of moving in, it is sometimes difficult to sort out lamp requirements and have the purchasing department order replacement lamps during the initial months of occupancy.

Nationally recognized testing procedures are in place that assure specific lamp operating characteristics. Many of these procedures are ANSI standards. Any reputable lamp manufacturer will test lamps according to the specific procedures established in these standards. By specifying lamps that have been tested accordingly, the designer is assuring appropriate quality.

The following is an example of a general section on lamps:

3. *Lamps—General*
   NOTE: For color consistency, lamp maintenance consistency, and light output consistency, DO NOT MIX LAMPS FROM DIFFERENT

MANUFACTURERS, AND DO NOT MIX "ENERGY SAVER" LAMPS WITH "STANDARD" LAMPS (this has the same effect as mixed die lots on fabrics—when placed side by side, they may not have the same appearance.) Use one brand and type for each of the different lamps specified.

Lamps which fail within 90 days after acceptance shall be replaced at no cost to the owner.

Contractor shall supply a quantity of lamps equal to 5% of each lamp type required for each old and new luminaire, but no less than 6 of each lamp type and not more than 48 lamps of each type. These lamps shall constitute the owner's initial replacement stock.

Lamps shall conform to ANSI C78 Series Dimensional and Electrical Characteristics of Lamps.

Lamp performance (initial lumen output, life, color, and lumen maintenance) shall be as specified in the schedule.

Initial lumen output shall be as measured after 100 hours of operation.

Lamp color for light sources shall be as specified in either color temperature (degrees Kelvin) or CIE chromaticity coordinates measured by means of spectroradiometry.

Lumen depreciation, lamp life, and initial lumen output shall be reported in accordance with the following guides:

Incandescent
    IES Approved Method for Life Performance Testing of General Lighting Incandescent Filament Lamps, LM–49.
    IES Approved Method for Electrical and Photometric Measurements of General Service Incandescent Filament Lamps, LM–45.
Fluorescent
    IES Approved Method for Life Performance Testing of Fluorescent Lamps, LM–40.
    IES Approved Method for the Electrical and Photometric Measurements of Fluorescent Lamps, LM–9.
High Intensity Discharge
    IES Approved Method for Life Testing of High Intensity Discharge Lamps, LM–47.
    IES Approved Method for Photometric Measurements of High Intensity Discharge Lamps, LM–51.
Neon/Cold Cathode
    Cold cathode lighting shall provide color specified in tube sizes specified in this schedule.
    Cold cathode, where specified, shall provide look of continuous light run without shadows, hot spots, or scallops.
    End sections shall be cleaned and shall have all foreign objects re-

moved to make a clean joint. All bends shall be made in a workmanlike manner, maintaining constant tube diameter and not allowing any flattening that will distort illuminated gas.

Tubes shall terminate with electrodes in each end. Tubes shall be bombarded to proper heat and checked for leaks. Gas shall be pumped into the unit properly and precisely measured, with each tube sealed correctly.

Tubes shall be aged 24 hours after pumping to insure proper color and no leaks.

Tubes shall be installed with all necessary supports, housings, cables, leads, and transformers according to cold cathode manufacturer.

Neon/Cold Cathode Warranty: Lamps that fail within one year under normal operating conditions shall be replaced with no cost to the owner. Manufacturer shall work closely with lighting designer to ensure best quality and longest life lamps while maintaining light output levels required to meet design intent.

All neon and cold cathode work is to be performed by a manufacturer approved by lighting designers.

As required, all adjustable accent luminaires shall be aimed by the contractor under the direction of the lighting designer or designated representative of the lighting designer. Contractor shall be responsible for notifying lighting designer of appropriate time for final luminaire adjustment, and contractor shall supply personnel for final luminaire adjustment.

All fluorescent lamps, unless otherwise stated, shall be General Electric SP35 Series, Sylvania D35 Series, or Philips SPEC 35, 3500K color temperature, of diameters and lengths appropriate to the luminaires being used.

TRANSFORMERS/BALLASTS

This section usually describes the general characteristics of transformers for low voltage lamps, ballasts for fluorescent and HID lamps, and transformers for cold cathode lamps. Typically, warranties are discussed, as are the ANSI standards or other qualifications that transformers and ballasts are expected to meet. The transformers/ballasts section might read as follows:

4. *Transformers/Ballasts*
Low Voltage Incandescent
    Transformers shall have a two–year warranty which shall include replacement labor allowance.

All transformers shall be high power factor and shall operate at 120 volts.

Fluorescent

Electronic and electromagnetic ballasts shall have a two–year warranty which shall include replacement labor allowance.

All ballasts shall conform to UL935 Fluorescent Lamp Ballasts Standard, and shall be UL listed with class P thermal protection.

Ballasts shall be CBM certified, and shall conform to ANSI C82 Series Specification for Ballasts.

All Ballasts shall have a minimum power factor of 0.9 or greater.

All ballasts shall contain no PCB.

All ballasts shall have a minimum sound rating of A.

All electromagnetic fluorescent ballasts shall be premium energy–saving type suitable for operating lamps as specified and shall be by Advance or Universal for maximum energy efficiency, minimum flicker, and minimum noise. All luminaires shall be fused on the primary side of the ballast.

High Intensity Discharge

All ballasts shall conform to ANSI 824 Series Specifications for HID ballasts, and to UL 1029 High Intensity Discharge Ballasts.

HID luminaires shall be protected by Type KTK fuses of sizes recommended by luminaire manufacturer.

Ballast coil shall be class H rated.

Ballast capacitor shall be rated at least 85 degrees C hot spot temperature at specified voltage and frequency.

Neon/Cold Cathode

Transformers shall be UL listed and selected for proper operation of specified neon/cold cathode lighting. Transformers shall be remote-located in well–ventilated easily accessible areas and shall be sound-isolated from occupied working environments.

LUMINAIRE/LAMP/BALLAST SCHEDULE

Once luminaires have been selected, their description in the Specification must be completed to avoid misunderstandings among manufacturers, contractors, and designers. Table 6–1 lists the major factors that are to be addressed by the specification description. Consider using this table as a checklist to assure that pertinent descriptors are included in the specification.

Luminaire optical characteristics should be conveyed in the specification. This may mean as short a statement as "glass opal lens shall be used to diffuse light," or one as long as a complete paragraph describing special re-

Table 6–1.

Luminaire specification outline: some of the items that should be considered in the specification of luminaires.

- Nominal luminaire dimensions
  - Length
  - Width
  - Height
  - Diameter
- Intended mounting
  - Recessed
  - Surface
  - Suspended
    - Stem
    - Aircraft cable
  - Wall mount
  - Furniture mount
- Intended ceiling application
  - Lay-in
    - Standard "T"
    - Narrow "T"
    - Concealed spline
  - Drywall/plaster
  - Metal pan
  - Linear metal
  - Concrete
- Thermal requirements
  - Insulation contact
  - Insulation nearby
  - No insulation
- Flange requirements
  - Overlap trim
    - White
    - Clear aluminum
    - Custom color
  - Flangeless
- Reflector requirements
  - Shape
    - Parabolic
    - Ellipsoidal
  - Finish
    - White
    - Clear aluminum
    - Custom color
- Lensing (always specify virgin acrylic)
  - Standard pattern 12
  - KSH 19
  - KSH 20
  - High-efficiency
  - Low-brightness
  - Flush or regress
  - Reveal-edge

- Orientation
  - Direct
    - Fixed-orientation
    - Adjustable
  - Indirect
  - Direct/indirect
- Distribution
  - Widespread
  - Narrow-spread
  - Medium-spread
  - Cut-off requirements
- Maximum luminaire luminances
- Lamping
  - Number of lamps
  - Orientation of lamps
  - Switching of lamps
  - Color temperature
  - Color rendering
  - Lumen output
  - Life
- Ballasts
  - Voltage
  - Sound requirements
  - Number of lamps controlled
  - Electromagnetic vs. electronic
  - Dimming vs. nondimming
  - Size and fit within luminaire
  - Location
    - Remote
    - In luminaire
  - High power factor vs. low power factor
  - Thermal requirements (class P)
- Transformers
  - Primary voltage
  - Secondary voltage
  - Sound requirements
  - Access requirements
  - Dimming vs. nondimming
  - Remote location
  - Milliamperage (cold cathode and neon)
- Safety glass
- Vapor requirements
  - Damp labeled
  - Wet labeled
  - Standard UL label
  - Explosion-proof

Table 6–1. (Continued)

• Louvering	• HVAC functions
Acrylic	Supply air
Metal	Return air
White	Static
Alzak	• Architectural construction details
Other colors	Cove
Small-cell parabolic	Slot
Large-cell parabolic	Valence
Flush or regress	• UL label
Reveal-edge	• IBEW label

flectors, lenses, and/or light shields. If the luminaire is proprietary and contains patented elements (e.g., lens assembly), then consult with the manufacturer before writing the luminaire description in order to avoid releasing sensitive information in the specification.

The appearance of the luminous portion of the luminaire should be addressed, along with the optical characteristics. For example, simply specifying a "glass opal lens . . . to diffuse light" is not sufficient to avoid hot spots or streaks on the lens. These faults may be due to either poor–quality opal glass forming or lamp(s) being mounted too close to the glass lens. Therefore, the specification should be expanded to include a statement such as this: ". . . opal lens shall appear uniformly luminous when luminaire is electrified, with luminance uniformity of 4:1 (maximum to minimum)." The designer must establish such ratios by mocking up a luminaire that appears acceptable and then measuring the luminances.

Luminaire finish is an important detail if a project is to be a design–integrated entity. Although the lighting requirements of a particular space may establish the finish of the luminaires' visible optical assemblies, trim and mounting hardware finishes should be specified to avoid incompatibility with other architectural finishes. If the architectural hardware finishes are brass, then perhaps luminaire mounting brackets should be brass. The lighting designer should coordinate all such aesthetic finish decisions with the appropriate architectural design team member. If the lighting specifier cannot secure aesthetic finish decisions at the time of specification writing, then the specification should indicate that "luminaire finish is to be determined by architect." Remember that many finish descriptions do not result in the same appearance from manufacturer to manufacturer, and be as specific as possible. Instead of "luminaire finish shall be white," consider saying that "luminaire finish shall be white to match color chip supplied by architect." Although such a statement sounds straightforward, the color chip implies a "special white" to the manufacturer and is likely to result in an increased charge for running the "special white."

Specifications regarding finish should indicate that the "finish shall be homogeneous, with no streaks, cracks, or surface irregularities," unless, of course, a rough finish is desired (possible in restoration work when an "authentic" aged look is desired).

When long expanses of metal luminaires are used, particularly pendent units, the designer should beware of welded points and seams that could telegraph through the finish. Such long units also are subject to handling dinks, dents, scratches, sagging, and waviness. Heavier–gauge steel housings can minimize such faults, and extruded aluminum housings tend to eliminate the majority of such problems.

Where long runs of ceiling–recessed equipment are used, the potential exists for some mismatch between ceiling system module and luminaire runs. This is of special concern in using newly designed equipment, modified equipment, or custom equipment, or when manufacturing quality control is subpar. For example, a luminaire manufactured just 1/32nd inch over tolerance could lead to a row of 20 luminaires being more than 1//2 inch longer than a typical 2–foot by 2–foot or 2–foot by 4–foot modular ceiling run. To force–fit such a gross intolerance would lead to visibly misaligned ceiling grids. Modifying the luminaires in the field for proper fit may lead to UL violation and local code problems. To minimize the potential for such mismatch between the ceiling system and the luminaire, the specification should specifically state the ceiling system with which luminaires must be integrated (or refer the contractor to the architectural section of the specification), and should state something to the effect that "luminaires shall be of such size and tolerance to provide for a complete, neat fit with ceiling system without introducing ceiling system component misalignment." A "nominal" luminaire size should always be listed in the luminaire description. The specification should clearly state that the luminaire manufacturer is financially responsible for difficulties arising from poor luminaire quality control that could lead to field modification of luminaires or ceilings.

Luminaire mounting methods can be particularly problematic if not discussed in the luminaire description. It must be made clear how the luminaire shall be mounted to the architecture: ceiling–recessed, surface mount, wall mount, pendent mount, floor mount, or furniture mount. Within each category of mounting, there usually are several options for specific mounting techniques.

Mounting heights are critical to the contractor for proper installation. Sconces, pendants, and wall–mounted luminaires must be given specific mounting heights in the specification. For example, the specification for a sconce luminaire may include a statement that "luminaire shall be mounted 5'9" AFF to centerline of junction box." AFF is short for "above finished floor"; "Junction box" could be changed to "luminaire." Remember that the luminaire center point may be several inches or more different from the center point of the junction box. The junction box is that area usually consisting of a metal or plastic box 2 inches by 2 inches by 4 inches in which the main wiring from the electrical panel can be connected to the wiring of the luminaire (the junction of the two sets of wires—hence the term junction box).

Lamping is critical, of course, to the proper function and appearance of a luminaire, as Lamps must be specified for each luminaire type. Chapter 3 discusses lamps and their characteristics, as well as lamp designation. In the specification, the lamp designation should be listed, along with wattage and specific manufacturer trade names and ordering codes. For example, where high–color–rendering fluorescent lamps are desired, the specification should read: ". . . lamps shall be 32 watt fluorescent, high color rendering triphosphor type (GE F32T8/SP35/RS, Philips FO32/35, or Sylvania FO32/35K)."

In the general provisions section of the specification it should be clear that "the contractor shall not mix lamps from manufacturers or mix energy–saving lamps with standard lamps, as this can lead to color mismatch from lamp to lamp."

Ballasts and transformers should be clearly addressed in the lighting specifications. Chapter 3 discusses specifics of various ballasts and transformers. The appropriate characteristics for a given project should be included in the specification. Indicating the sound rating, amperage, and voltage for fluorescent ballasts along with the type of ballast (electromagnetic, electromagnetic dimming, electronic, electronic dimming) and the manufacturer is necessary. For transformers of incandescent lamps, primary (input) and secondary (output) voltages should be specified along with wattage requirements, electronic or electromagnetic type, and location (remote or in luminaire). Stepping functions (e.g., dual level transformers of 11 or 12 volts, 5.5 or 6 volts, and 6 or 12 volts are available), if necessary, must be noted in the specification.

Generally, to assure some operational quality and to meet codes and most insurance requirements, the specification must indicate the need for UL labeling (Underwriters' Laboratories) on luminaires. To provide for ease of installation and no misunderstanding with electrical contractors, all luminaires should have IBEW (International Brotherhood of Electrical Workers) labels. This should be indicated in the specification. Some jurisdictions require specific IBEW labels. In New York City, luminaires need the IBEW Local 3 label.

Table 6–2 indicates which characteristics typically apply to various luminaire types.

The following is one way of writing a luminaire/lamps/ballast schedule section:

5. *Luminaire/Lamp/Ballast Schedule*

Luminaires have been assigned type designations consisting of three letters followed by a number in order to facilitate communication between the lighting designer, the design/construction team, and the owner. The first three letters indicate the source type, lamp (bulb/enve-

Table 6–2.
Specification characteristics for luminaire types, categorized by sources.

Typical characteristics to consider	Standard voltage incandescent	Quartz	Low voltage incandescent	Cold cathode/neon	Compact fluorescent	T8/T10/T12 fluorescent	High intensity discharge
• Luminaire dimension	•	•	•	•	•	•	•
• Mounting method	•	•	•	•	•	•	•
• Ceiling type	•	•	•	•	•	•	•
• Thermal protection	•	•	•		•		
• Reflector	•	•	•		•	•	•
• Lensing/louvering	1	1	1		1	•	1
• Safety glass		2					2
• Orientation of lamp	•	•	•	•	•	•	•
• Lamping (quantity and type)	•	•	•	•	•	•	•
• Ballasts (amperage and type)					•	•	•
• Transformers			•	•			
• Vapor requirements	•	•	•	•	•	•	•
• HVAC function					3	•	
• Architectural details	4	4	•	•	•	•	4
• UL label	•	•	•		•	•	•
• IBEW label	•	•	•		•	•	•

1. Lensing/louvering may be used and therefore needs specifying, but for the most part these sources are used in open reflector luminaires.

2. Some sort of safety glass is required to prevent hot glass and/or UV radiation from escaping if lamp violently fails.

3. HVAC functions may be a consideration on the larger compact fluorescent lamp luminaires.

4. These lamps can be put into architectural construction details, but typically are not.

lope) type, and general photometric distribution, respectively; the number distinguishes luminaires of the same type that have only minor differences which are discussed under the specific description for each luminaire.

Example: ARA1 (also see Figure 6–3)

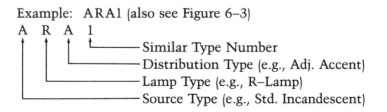

A R A 1
— Similar Type Number
— Distribution Type (e.g., Adj. Accent)
— Lamp Type (e.g., R–Lamp)
— Source Type (e.g., Std. Incandescent)

First Letter Designations—Source Type
    A = Standard Voltage Incandescent
    C = Cold Cathode
    F = Fluorescent
    H = Mercury
    L = Low Voltage Incandescent
    M = Metal Halide
    N = Neon
    Q = Quartz
    S = Sodium (High or Low Pressure)
    T = Track/Theatrical Hardware
    Z = Assignable (Blank)

Second Letter Designations—Lamp Type/Characteristics
    A = A–Lamp Envelope
    B = B–Lamp Envelope
    C = Compact Fluorescent
    E = E–Lamp Envelope
    G = G–Lamp Envelope
    M = Multi–reflector (e.g., MR–16)
    P = PAR Lamp Envelope (two–piece reflector)
    R = R–Lamp Envelope (one–piece reflector)

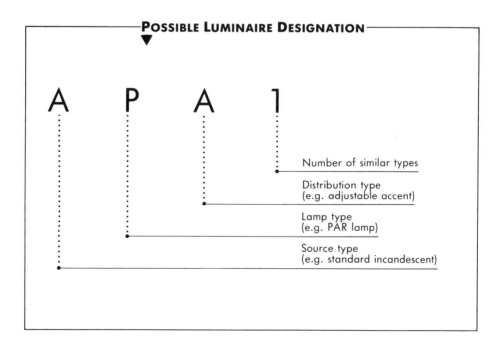

FIGURE 6–3.

S = S–Lamp Envelope
T = Tubular
U = Tube/Strip Lights (e.g., Tivoli)
Z = Assignable (Blank)

Third Letter Designations—General Photometric Distribution
For Incandescent Sources
A = Adjustable Accent
B = Bollard
C = Cove—Architectural (Indirect)
D = Open Downlight
E = Exposed (Bare Lamp)
F = Flood
G = Globe
J = "Junk"
K = Steplight
L = Lensed Downlight
M = Mirror Detail
O = Spot
P = Pendant
Q = Sconce
S = Slot
T = Track Head/Theatrical
U = Uplight
V = Valance
W = Wallwash
X = Exit/Emergency
Y = Torchiere
Z = Assignable (Blank)

Third Letter Designations—General Photometric Distribution
For Fluorescent Sources
A = Asymmetric Indirect
C = Cove—Architectural (Indirect)
D = Downlight
E = Exposed (Bare Lamp)
F = Furniture–integrated (Indirect)
G = General Direct
H = General Direct/Indirect
I = Industrial
J = "Junk"
K = Steplight
L = Luminous Element
M = Mirror Detail

P = Pendant (General Indirect)
Q = Sconce
R = Wraparound Lens
S = Slot—Architectural (Direct)
T = Task (Free–standing or Panel–hung)
U = Furniture–integrated Task (Under–cabinet/Bins)
V = Valance
W = Wallwash
X = Exit/Emergency
Y = Torchiere (Free–standing)
Z = Assignable (Blank)

Third Letter Designations—General Photometric Distribution
For High Intensity Discharge Sources
A = Area
B = Bollard
C = Furniture–integrated Indirect
D = Open Downlight
E = Exposed (Bare Lamp)
F = Floodlight
G = General Direct
H = General Direct/Indirect
I = Industrial
J = "Junk"
K = Steplight
L = Lensed Downlight
M = Hi–mast
P = Pendant
Q = Sconce
R = Decorative Low–level
S = Spotlight
T = Track
U = Uplight
W = Wallwash
Y = Torchiere
Z = Assignable (Blank)

FTA1   One–lamp T8 fluorescent asymmetric reflector luminaire
shall be mounted on vertical face of raised ceiling area provided
and oriented as indicated (see Detail B) [reader: see Figure 4–2
in this text] to wash ceiling. Luminaire housing shall have
overall nominal dimensions of 4¾″ high by 8″ wide by lengths
(and 90–degree corner pieces) as necessary to extend com-

pletely around perimeter of cavity recess soffit, and shall be single piece extruded aluminum construction, finished in standard white.

Luminaires shall mount to side of ceiling cavity soffit to form a single continuous length, without sagging, snaking, or twisting. Bottom of luminaire shall align with lower ceiling height (10′6″ AFF).

Luminaire shall use Lutron HI–LUME dimming ballast controlled by Lutron Versaplex 8 dimming control system, with two lamps sharing one 2–lamp ballast where possible, and shall operate at 120V. Luminaire shall use knife–edge sockets and shall use one [1] F32T8 or F25T8 fluorescent lamp in cross–section (see plan for location of 3″0″ and 4″0″ lamps), with a color temperature of 3500 degrees Kelvin by G.E. (TRIMLINE/SP35) or Sylvania (OCTRON/35K).

PEERLESS LST-10005-D/T8 w/LUTRON HI–LUME DIMMING BALLAST.

FTG1   Recessed fluorescent 1 x 4, one–lamp T8, 8–cell parabolic luminaire shall be suitable for mounting in acoustic tile ceiling TBD by architect. Parabolic louver shall be nominal 3″ deep and be finished in semi–specular, low iridescent clear aluminum. Luminaire shall be tandem–wired in master/slave configuration so that two luminaires operate from one 2–lamp ballast located in the master luminaire.

Luminaire shall have optics (reflector and louver) designed for use with T8 lamps, shall use one [1] F32T8 lamp by G.E. (SP35) or Sylvania (OCTRON) with color temperature of 3500 degrees Kelvin, and shall operate at voltage TBD by electrical engineer. Luminaire shall have air handling capabilities as specified by mechanical engineer.

COLUMBIA T8 P4–141X–43193

FTP1   One-lamp T–8 fluorescent widespread indirect luminaire shall be suspended, via aircraft cables, at 10′6″ AFF to bottom of luminaire and shall have white reflector component. Luminaire housing shall have overall nominal dimensions of 4¾″ high by 8″ wide by length of 12′0″, and shall be single piece extruded aluminum construction, finished in standard white. Power feed shall be straight white cord from one end of luminaire (all luminaires shall have feeds from the same end), attached to cable. Luminaire shall have three cable support locations, one at each end as determined by manufacturer and one centered along luminaire length.

Luminaire shall use Lutron HI–LUME dimming ballast controlled by Lutron Versaplex 8 dimming control system, with two lamps sharing one 2–lamp ballast where possible, and shall operate at 120V. Luminaire shall use knife–edge sockets and shall use one [1] F25T8 fluorescent lamp in cross–section (4 total lamps per luminaire), with a color temperature of 3500 degrees Kelvin by G.E. (TRIMLINE/SP35) or Sylvania (OC-TRON/35K).

PEERLESS LST–010001–O–12'/T8 w/LUTRON HI–LUME DIMMING BALLAST

LPD1   Recessed low voltage incandescent luminaire shall have square aperture nominal opening of 5½", and shall be suitable for mounting in acoustic tile ceiling TBD by interior architect. Luminaire shall have matte black extruded aluminum square ridged baffle with minimal overlap trim. Luminaire shall use one [1] 25PAR36/WFL (wide flood) 12 volt lamp by General Electric, and shall be circuited to handle up to 50W each.
KURT VERSEN 7824–MOD–12V/PAR36

LPD2   Similar to Type LPD1, except shall have transformers remote–located in an accessible, well–ventilated and sound–isolated area (e.g., in Mechanical Room) separate from room in which luminaires are to be installed, and connected to Lutron dimming panel/Versaplex 8 dimming control system.
KURT VERSEN H7824–MOD–12V/PAR36–REMOTE TRANS.

SWITCHING

Switching technically is the responsibility of the electrical engineer for the purpose of contract documents, but the lighting designer needs to indicate the suggested switching scheme. As Figure 6–2 illustrates, a reflected ceiling plan alone is not enough information for the contractor; and ultimately the owner should know how to operate the lighting system. Figure 6–4 shows a switching scheme for the office lighting plan introduced in Figure 6–2. Some luminaires are switched from wall switches, whereas others are switched by the building energy management system (hence "to Panel" designation is used). Typically, for energy management reasons and for code reasons, there must be override switching controls—all lights should not be switched from an electrical panel.

The set of three switches in Figure 6–4 is shown to be located 6 inches from the open door position. It is poor practice to hide switches behind opened doors. To add finality to the design documentation, a wall elevation should be made that indicates the switches' vertical locations above the floor and relative to other wall–mounted devices—thermostats, music, or sound controls.

When only one switch location is required for a switching circuit, the typical symbol is "S" as shown in Figure 6–4. If the switch is to be a dimmer control also, a subscript "d" is used (S_d). When two different switch locations are desired for the same switching circuit, then a subscript "3" is used (S_3).

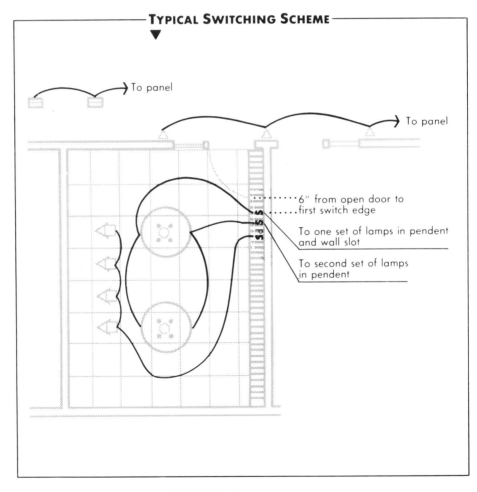

FIGURE 6–4.

CONTROL DEVICES

For simple switching or dimming functions, a couple of switches located near the door to a room usually are sufficient. At times, however, more sophisticated control is required, for (1) flexibility of room function, (2) subdivision of one large room into a series of smaller rooms, (3) a daylight/electric light interface, or (4) electric light energy management.

A host of electronic control devices are available to meet most any control need. For specification and documentation purposes, the lighting control circuits must be clearly identified, and a schedule of scenes must be developed. Scenes are the lighting effects achieved by pushing specific control buttons. For example, in a restaurant it may be desirable to have four scenes: lunch; dinner; dinner–after–sundown; cleanup. A control station consisting of five buttons (one for each scene and one for "off") must be located in a convenient location for the shift manager or maitre d' to use at appropriate times during the day.

Time machines and photocells can be used to automatically control the electric lighting, irrespective of or in conjunction with daylighting. These devices can be rather small and simple, or they can be more complex computer devices that not only control lighting but handle mechanical controls.

SHOP DRAWINGS

The shop drawing phase is the designer's opportunity to make certain that the specified equipment will be purchased for the project. It is also an opportunity to ensure that all of the specification information has been correctly interpreted by the contractor, distributor, and manufacturer. Finally, it is the designer's opportunity to be sure that the correct catalog information was reported in the specification (no typographical errors in catalog numbers or number of lamps, etc.).

Reputable contractors use the shop drawing phase to be certain that they have correctly interpreted the specification. The designer must review these drawings carefully and quickly to assure correct and timely installation.

Shop drawings are always to be supplied by the contractor prior to the purchase and installation of any lighting equipment. This can be a particularly tricky phase. At times, the contractor will "sit on the shop drawings," a tactic that obviously will put the designer behind the eight ball, having to approve them at once upon their release from the contractor. This is a ploy intended to force substitutions upon the project; once the contractor releases shop drawings to the designer, the designer is responsible for their disposition, and a slow response or a rejection by the designer may mean a delay in the project. With such a threat of delay, the contractor will seek to override the designer by taking the decision to the client (owner). To avoid such shenanigans, the designer needs to clarify the situation early in the project, in both oral and written form, making it clear that the contractor must allow sufficient time for approval of appropriate shop drawings and that the client (owner) understands the ramifications of substitutions (e.g., perhaps lower cost to owner, higher profits for the contractor, and poor performance for the end user).

To eliminate the unnecessary hassle of incompetently made substitutions, the designer should qualify the specification to indicate that the contractor shall incur the cost of fees required to review, calculate, and revise designs based on contractor–proposed substitutions. After all, the client hired professional designers for their professional expertise and opinions, and hired the contractor to execute those opinions.

The registered professional (architect or engineer) is responsible for final authority on shop drawing approval. The lighting designer should review the lighting shop drawings, however, and confirm that the proposed equipment will meet the lighting design intent. Typical disposition of shop drawings includes: (1) approved; (2) approved as noted; (3) approved as changed; (4) not approved for reasons noted; or (5) no substitutions accepted. Having indicated their disposition, the designer should then sign and date the shop drawings, and forward them to the engineer or architect.

INDEX

INDEX

(References to pages with related figures are in italics type. References to pages with related tables are in bold type. References to the Color Section include only the figure number, which begins with a "C".)